MISSION SUDARSHAN CHAKRA

India's Integrated Aerospace Command and Control System

MISSION SUDARSHAN CHAKRA

India's Integrated Aerospace Command and Control System

Editors

Sujan Chinoy

Sukhbir Kaur Minhas

MANOHAR PARRIKAR INSTITUTE FOR DEFENCE STUDIES AND ANALYSES
मनोहर पर्रिकर रक्षा अध्ययन एवं विश्लेषण संस्थान

PENTAGON PRESS LLP

First published in 2026 by
PENTAGON PRESS LLP
206, Peacock Lane, Shahpur Jat
New Delhi-110049, India
Contact: 011-26490600

Typeset in AGaramond, 11.5 Point
Printed by Aegean Offset Printers, Greater Noida

ISBN 978-81-997728-1-6

www.pentagonpress.in

Contents

SECTION III
SPACE BASED SYSTEMS

SECTION IV
TECHNOLOGY

Foreword

Imagine the battlefield of Mahabharata and the blazing Sudarshan Chakra wielded by Lord Krishna. It did not turn just one battle in favour of warrior Arjuna – it remains omnipresent and ever ready. Today, in a world characterised by contestation and conflict, India must be prepared to protect its sovereignty and territorial integrity against an array of threats, both conventional and non-conventional. In this era of multi-domain warfare, aero-space has particularly emerged as a domain of infinite proportion and limitless possibilities, technology being the only constraint.

Securing the nation and its 1.4 billion people is a key task, involving a continuous process of boosting India's military capabilities by enhancing defence budgets, promoting the adaptation of high-end technologies and transforming the military-industrial complex in favour of self-reliance (Atmanirbharta). As India progresses from being the world's fourth-largest economy to becoming the third-largest, it is bound to face numerous challenges, including military threats to its key decision-making nodes, economic assets, critical infrastructure and even places of worship. Burgeoning urban centres with dense populations will also have to be secured *en masse*. In an era of network centric warfare in which stand-off weapons, missiles, rockets and drones are increasingly being deployed, the task of securing the nation against threats from the aero-space domain has acquired urgency. Operation SINDOOR has highlighted these concerns. The solution lies in imagining and developing, with a long-term perspective, an invincible and impenetrable protective system, a "kavach" so to speak, albeit with both defensive and offensive capabilities.

It is in this context that Prime Minister Modi, in his 79th Independence Day address on August 15, 2025, announced "**Mission Sudarshan Chakra**" – an ambitious and indigenous defence initiative designed to create a multi-layered security shield for India. Achieving this national objective will require a national effort involving scientists, the armed forces, the para-militaries as well as the economic ecosystem across states. A herculean effort such as this will call for perfect integration between the armed forces as well as achieving the pinnacle of civil-military fusion. By 2035, it aims to adapt and outpace future threats through an Integrated Air and Missile Defence (IAMD) shield, fusing orbital, cyber and cognitive domains with the aero-space domain and futuristic technologies.

This national effort defined by convergence of technology and multi-domain warfare represents a significant juncture in the evolution of India's national security architecture – that of participatory civil defence, through informed public discourse. This edited volume aims to do just that, offering a scholarly analysis of an initiative that seeks to integrate missile systems, radars, space-based surveillance, cyber capabilities, and advanced defence technologies into a unified, operational and effective architecture.

This academic study is a parallel effort by strategic thinkers to provide an alternative perspective, complementing the endeavour underway by the concerned government departments. One hopes that it will add value by way of critical analysis, contextual comprehension, and the achievement of long-term strategic goals. It exemplifies the complementary aspects of practice and theory. As the contributors to this collection reflect on their long years of practical domain experiences, they write through the academic lens within the wider framework of geo-political imperatives, technological developments and India's strategic culture.

However, the most significant contribution of this volume is its effort to enhance public understanding of a complex system, enabling informed discourse within the limits of permissible security parameters. The role of citizens in a democracy is not limited to public discourse and transparency but also involves a better understanding of how important their contributions are to understanding and dealing with national security threats, particularly in the aero-space domain.

As readers engage with the writings of individual authors, they will benefit from a review of extant global systems and current status in India, besides acquainting themselves with the possible architecture, technological requirements and the overall roadmap for the mission. It is our hope as editors that this volume will support and enrich, rather than duplicate, the work of defence professionals, besides serving as a scholarly record documenting the conceptual evolution and rationale of such a major security initiative.

Sujan Chinoy

Sukhbir Kaur Minhas

List of abbreviations

AA	Anti-Aircraft
AAD	Advanced Air Defence
AAPs	Adaptable Aerial Platforms
ABM	Air Battle Management
AD	Air Defence
ADDCs	Air Defence Direction Centres
ADFCRs	Air Defence Fire Control Radars
ADGES	Air Defence Ground Environment System
ADHS/SADHS/FADHS	Automatic/Semi-Automatic/Futuristic Data Handling Systems
ADSO	Air Defence Systems Operator
AESA	Active Electronically Scanned Array
AFNET	Air Force Net Work
AI	Artificial Intelligence
Airborne ESA Radars	Airborne Electronically Scanned Array Radars
AIS	Automatic Identification System
AMES	Air Ministry Experimental Station
AMS	Akash Missile System
AMSL	Above Mean Sea Level
AOR	Area of Responsibility
APKWS	Advanced Precision Kill Weapon System
AR	Augmented Reality
ASAT	Anti-Satellite
ASM	Airspace Management
ASRAAM	Advanced Short Range Air to Air Missile

ASW	Anti-Submarine Warfare
ATE	Advanced Threat Evaluation
AEW&C System	Airborne Early Warning and Control System
AWACS	Airborne Warning and Control System
BADC	Base Air Defence Concept or Base Air Defence Centre
BDA	Battle Damage Assessment
BEL	Bharat Electronics Limited
BMAT	Ballistic Missile Analyst Technician
BMC4I	Battle Management, Command, Control, Communications, Computers, and Intelligence
BMD	Ballistic Missile Defence
BVR	Beyond Visual Range
C&R	Control and Reporting
C2BMC	Command, Control, Battle Management and Communication
C2C	Command and Control Centre
C4ISR	Command, Control, Communications, Computers, Intelligence, Surveillance, and Reconnaissance
CABS	Centre for Airborne Systems
CAMM	Common Anti-Air Modular Missile
CAP	Combat Air Patrol
CAPF	Central Armed Police Forces
Cartosat	Cartography Satellite
CASDIC	Combat Aircraft Systems Development and Integration Centre
CBDL	C-Band Data Link
CBMs	Confidence-Building Measures
CCU	Command and Control Unit
CERT-In	Indian Computer Emergency Response Team
CIS	Communications and Information Systems
CIWS	Close in Weapon System
CLIAD	Comprehensive Layered Integrated Air Defence
CO	Chain Home Overseas

CDMA	Code Division Multiple Access
COL	Chain Home Overseas Low
COMINT	Communication Intelligence
COP	Common Operational Picture
COTS	Commercial Off-the-Shelf
CRCs	Control and Reporting Centres
CSIO	Central Scientific Instruments Organisation
CSM	Communication Support Measures
DAC	Defence Acquisition Council
DADC	Divisional Air Defence Control
DCN	Defence Communication Network
DDoS	Distributed Denial-of-Service
DDoS attacks	Distributed denial-of-service attacks
DEW	Directed Energy Weapons
DRDO	Defence Research and Development Organisation
DRS	Data Relay Satellite
ECCM	Electronic Counter Counter Measures
ECM	Electronic Counter Measures
EIAD	Extended Integrated Air Defence
EMP	Electromagnetic pulse
EO	Electro-Optical
EOTS	Electro-Optical Tracking System
EP	Electric Propulsion
ESM/ELINT	Electronic Support Measures/Electronic Intelligence
ESSI	European Sky Shield Initiative
EW	Early Warning
EW	Electronic Warfare
FCs	Fighter Controllers
FDI	Foreign Direct Investment
FDIA	False Data Injection Attacks
FOL/FOS	Forward Operating Location/Forward Operating Site
FPV	First-Person-View
GBIs	Ground-Based Interceptors

GCI	Ground Control Interceptor
GEO	Geo Stationary Orbit
GHRC	Geoimaging High Resolution Camera
GISAT	Geo Imaging Satellite
GMD	Ground-Based Midcourse Defense
GOR	Gun Operations Rooms
GSAT	Geosynchronous Satellite
GSLV	Geosynchronous Satellite Launch Vehicle
GSO	Geo Stationary Orbit
GSSAP	Geosynchronous Space Situational Awareness Program
GUI	Graphical User Interface
HAPS	High-Altitude Pseudo- Satellite Systems
HBTSS	Hypersonic and Ballistic Tracking Space Sensor
HCMs	Hypersonic Cruise Missiles
HF R/T	High Frequency Radio Telephony
HGVs	Hypersonic Glide Vehicles
HMI	Human Machine Interface
HPM	High Power Microwave
HPR	High Powered Radar
IACCS	Integrated Air Command and Control System
IAD	Integrated Air Defence
IADWS	Integrated Air Defence Weapon System
IAF	Indian Air Force
IAI	Israel Aerospace Industries
IAMD	Integrated Air And Missile Defence
IASC2S	Integrated Aerospace Command and Control System
IC	Intercept Control
IC&BM	Intercept Control and Battle Management
ICBM	Intercontinental Ballistic Missile
IFC	Information Fusion Centre
IFF	Identification Friend or Foe
IGMDP	Integrated Guided Missile Development Programme
IMINT	Imagery Intelligence

INSAT	Indian National Satellite System
IoT	Internet of Things
IP	Internet Protocol
IRNSS	Indian Regional Navigation Satellite System
IRST	Infrared Search and Track
ISR	Intelligence, Surveillance and Reconnaissance
ISRO	Indian Space Research Organisation
ISTAR	Intelligence, Surveillance, Target Acquisition, and Reconnaissance
JADC	Joint Air Defence Centre
JADC2	Joint All-Domain Command and Control
JIAMD	Joint Integrated Air and Missile Defence
JLNs	Joint Logistic Nodes
KAI	Korea Aerospace Industries
KBDL	Ku-Band SATCOM Data Link
KKW	Kinetic-Kill Weapons
LADC	Limited Area Defence Control
LAWs	Lethal Autonomous Weapons
LEO	Low Earth Orbit
LFE	Large Force Engagement
LGCI	Limited Ground Control Interception
LL	Low Level
LL CUAS	Low-Level CUAS
LLLWR	Low Level Light Weight Radars
LLQRM	Low Level Quick Reaction Missile
LLTR	Low-Level Transportable Radar
LOS	Line of Sight
LRDE	Electronics and Radar Development Establishment
LRNG	The Low-Level Radar Networking Group
LRR	Long-Range Radar
LRSAM	Long Range SAM
LRTRs	Long-Range Tracking Radars
MAW	Missile Approach Warning
MCCC	Missile Combat Crew Commander

MDA	Missile Defense Agency
MDO	Multi-Domain Operations
MEO	Medium Earth Orbit
MFCR	Multifunction Fire Control Radar
MiG-29 UPG (Aircraft)	MiG-29 Upgrade
MITM	Man-in-the-Middle
ML	Machine Learning
MOC	Maritime Ops Centre
MoU	Memorandum of Understanding
Arudhra MPR	Arudhra Medium Powered Radar
MRUs	Mobile Radar Units
MUMT	Manned-Unmanned Teaming
NADCP	National Air Defence Command Post
NASAMS	National Advanced Surface-to-Air Missile System
NATINAMDS	NATO's Integrated Air and Missile Defence System
NAVIC	Navigation with Indian Constellation
NBC	Nuclear, Biological, Chemical
NCA	India's Nuclear Command Authority
NCP	National Command Centre/Post
NCR-IADS (US)	National Capital Region Integrated Air Defense System
NCW	Network-Centric Warfare
NEP	Nuclear Electric Propulsion
NMD	National Missile Defense
NTP	Nuclear Thermal Propulsion
NTRO	National Technical Research Organisation
OCA	Offensive Counter Air
OOAC	Out-of-Area Contingency
OODA	Observe-Orient-Direct-Act
Orbat	Order of Battle
OSINT	Open Source of Intelligence
OTH	Over the Horizon
P&T	Post and Telegraph
PAC-3	Patriot Advanced Capability-3

PAD	Prithvi Air Defence/Passive Air Defence
PLAAF	People's Liberation Army Air Force
PLARF	PLA Rocket Force
PNT	Positioning, Timing and Navigation
PSLV	Polar Satellite Launch Vehicle
PSS	Passive Surveillance Systems
PWSA	Proliferated Warfighter Space Architecture
QRSAM	Quick Reaction Surface-to-Air-Missile
R&D	Research and Development
RAF	Royal Air Force
RASP	Recognised Air Situation Picture
RCS	Radar Cross Section
RIAF	Royal Indian Air Force
RISAT	Radar Imaging Satellites
ROE	Rules of Engagement
RTOS	Real-Time Operating Systems
RWR	Radar Warning Receiver
SACEUR	Supreme Allied Commander Europe
SAGW	Surface to Air Guided Weapons
SAM	Surface-to-Air Missile
SAMAR	Surface to Air Missile for Assured Retaliation
SAR	Synthetic Aperture Radar
SATCOM	Satellite Communication
SBIRS	Space-Based Infrared System
SBS	Space-Based Surveillance
SDA	Space Domain Awareness
SDI	Strategic Defence Initiative
SDR	Software Defined Radio
SEAD/DEAD	Suppression of Enemy Air Defence/Destruction of Enemy Air Defence
SEP	Solar-Electric Propulsion
SHORAD	Short-Range Air Defence
SLOCs	Sea Lines of Communication

SM-3	Standard Missile-3
SM-6	Standard Missile-6
SOC	Sector Operations Centre
SOPs	Standard Operating Procedures
SP	Self-Propelled
SSA	Space Situational Awareness
SSKP	Single Shot Kill Probability
SSMs	Surface-to-Surface Missiles
SSO	Sun Synchronous Orbit
SPYDER ADS	Surface-to-Air Python and Derby Air Defence System
TBA	Tactical Battle Area
TDRS	Tracking and Data Relay Satellites
THAAD	Terminal High-Altitude Area Defense
TOC	Tactical Operations Centre
TWCZ	Terminal Weapon Control Zone
UAS	Unmanned Aircraft System
UAVs	Unmanned Aerial Vehicles
UCAVs	Unmanned Combat Aerial Vehicles
UGVs	Unmanned Ground Vehicles
USSTRATCOM	The US Strategic Command
V/UHF	Very/Ultra High Frequency
VA/VP	Vulnerable Area/Vulnerable Point
VHF-SR	VHF band Surveillance Radar
VLRTRs	Very Long-Range Tracking Radars
W/T	Wireless Telephony
WAN	Wide Area Network
WVR	Within Visual Range

List of Figures and Tables

FIGURES

TABLES

About the Editors and Contributors

Amb. Sujan Chinoy is the Director General of the Manohar Parrikar Institute for Defence Studies and Analyses (MP-IDSA), New Delhi. A career diplomat from 1981-2018, he was Ambassador to Japan and Mexico and the Consul General of India in Shanghai and Sydney. A specialist on China and politico-security-military issues, he headed the Expert Group of Diplomatic and Military Officials negotiating the confidence-building measures (CBMs) dialogue with China on the boundary dispute from 1996-2000. At the National Security Council Secretariat (NSCS) from 2008-2012, he handled external and internal security policy issues. During his public service spanning four and a half decades, he has dealt with political, security, defence, trade and economic issues. His Foreign Service career included postings at the UN in New York and Saudi Arabia. He was the Chair of the Think20 engagement group for India's G20 Presidency. He is a member of the Executive Council of the Society of the Prime Ministers Museum and Library (PMML) and Member, Governing Council, Indian Council of World Affairs. Amb. Chinoy has also chaired the Mid-Term evaluation of the Modernisation Plans for Central Armed Police Forces (CAPFs). He was a Member of the All-Party MPs Delegation to the UAE and West Africa in the context of Operation SINDOOR. He speaks fluent Mandarin and is conversant in Japanese, German, French and Spanish. He is the author of World Upside Down: India Recalibrates its Geopolitics (Harper Collins, 2023) and Global Tumult: India as a Pole Star (Rupa, 2024) and has edited several books on defence security, and IR issues.

Gp Capt Sukhbir Kaur Minhas, an Indian Air Force (IAF) officer, is a Research Fellow at Manohar Parrikar Institute for Defence Studies and Analyses (MP-IDSA), New Delhi. Her area of research includes Air Defence and Air Battle Management doctrines.

Mr Rahul Wankhede is a Research Analyst at the Manohar Parrikar Institute for Defence Studies and Analyses (MP-IDSA), New Delhi. His research areas are defence cooperation, defence modernisation and defence economics.

Lt Gen BS Nagal PVSM, AVSM, SM (Retd) has a distinguished service record with the Indian Army, besides being a former Director at Centre for Land Warfare Studies (CLAWS). He writes on Nuclear and Strategic Issues.

Air Marshal RGK Kapoor PVSM, AVSM, VM (Retd) was the Air Officer Commanding-in-Chief of Central Air Command, prior to superannuating from the IAF. He has been writing articles on air power, military aviation and geo-strategy, besides participating in podcasts on military issues.

Air Marshal Vijay Pal Singh Rana PVSM VSM retired as the Air Officer-in-Charge Administration (AOA) from the IAF. He is the author of 'Invisible Warriors', a book on the Air Defence of India, besides other published works on water security and environmental issues.

Wg Cdr M V N Sai (Retd) a veteran IAF officer, is a Network Centric warfare expert. He is the founder and Chairperson of Apogee C4I LLP, as well as Apogee Aerospace, a company involved with aircraft operations and manufacturing.

Prof S Chandrashekar has served at the Indian Space Research Organization (ISRO) for more than two decades. He is currently an Honorary Visiting Professor at National Institute of Advanced Studies (NIAS) and specialises in Space, Missiles and related technology areas.

Ms Sai Susmitha Guddanti is a Ph.D. Student in Aerospace Sciences, University of North Dakota, focusing on space propulsion projects, with core interests in nuclear, sustainable, and advanced propulsion systems.

Dr Y Sreenivas Rao is the former Director General (NS&M), DRDO. He is known for his work in Missile Systems and Missile defence systems, besides being the Project Director for the development and realization of the Interceptor Vehicle in Mission Shakti.

Mr Cherian Samuel is Research Fellow (SS) in the Strategic Technologies Centre at the Manohar Parrikar Institute for Defence Studies and Analyses (MP-IDSA), New Delhi. He has written on various cyber security issues, including critical infrastructure protection, cyber resilience, cybercrime, and Internet governance.

Mr Rohit Kumar Sharma is a Research Analyst at the Manohar Parrikar Institute for Defence Studies and Analyses (MP-IDSA), New Delhi. His areas of research include Internet governance, cybersecurity, cyber insurance and Israeli domestic politics.

Introduction

Over the years, the Red Fort (Lal Qila in Hindi) at Delhi has served as more than just a historic monument; it has become a powerful national platform from which Indian Prime Ministers have laid down the country's future course, primacies, and aspirations. Since Jawaharlal Nehru's iconic *Tryst with Destiny* speech and his first Independence Day Address in 1947, the Red Fort has symbolised continuity in leadership and the evolving narrative of a growing nation. Over time, the Red Fort has evolved as a living symbol of India's democratic dialogue and the growing ambitions of its people. In recent times, Prime Minister Atal Bihari Vajpayee had officially announced India's first Moon mission, Chandrayaan-1, during his Independence Day Address from the ramparts of the Red Fort on 15 August 2003, while Prime Minister Manmohan Singh had announced India's Mars mission, from the Red Fort during his Independence Day Address on 15 August 2012.

On 15 August 2025, Prime Minister Narendra Modi announced the launch of Mission Sudarshan Chakra, an envisaged National Security Shield that aims to enhance and strengthen India's defensive and offensive capabilities by 2035.

Presently, India's security environment is shaped by a complex mix of external threats, regional rivalries, and emerging technological challenges. The country faces the unique reality of sharing borders with two nuclear-armed neighbours who have invested heavily in cruise and ballistic missiles and speedily deployable assault capabilities. For years, the Indian State is facing tensions on borders and State-sponsored terrorist attacks have further complicated the security situation. On the other hand, the adversaries are investing in advanced weapon systems such as hypersonic missiles and lethal autonomous weapon systems, which in turn are adding new layers of vulnerability. All this demands that India remains prepared beyond conventional warfare fighting capabilities. Broadly, the country needs to safeguard its growing network of strategic infrastructure on ground, in and under water and also in outer space.

India also faces major challenges associated with its geography. India is a country with diverse geographical features, which include peninsula with long coastlines (more than 11,000 km) and tropical rainforests, vast deserts in the western part of the country and the northeast region with extensive forests. The Himalayas are situated in the northern part of the country. This youngest mountain system in Asia extends for more than 2,400 km across China, Nepal, Bhutan, India and Pakistan. The Himalayan range encompasses about 15,000 glaciers and includes the highest mountains. The Indian subcontinent experiences impact from both tropical and extra-tropical weather phenomena.

The varied terrains require specialised military capabilities like amphibious and air-transportable vehicles for coastal and riverine areas, and robust logistics networks for deserts, jungles and mountains and snow-covered areas. The Indian climate creates a wide range of environmental challenges that significantly shape military operations. Forces should be prepared to operate in different types of climatic conditions, with each demanding different strategies, equipment, and training.

Today, making a full-bodied missile-defence shield is a necessity for India. In this context, a multi-tiered missile shield capable of detecting, tracking, and neutralising incoming threats, becomes a strategic necessity. It strengthens deterrence, reduces the risk of catastrophic damage, and ensures that India can respond to crises from a position of strength.

Owing to the unpredictability of potential threats, India cannot rely solely on traditional deterrence or conventional defence measures. Hence, developing a robust, multi-layered missile defence architecture becomes important. The necessity of such a structure is two-fold: to protect major population centres, military bases, and critical infrastructure and to strengthen the county's nuclear deterrence-related preparedness. Overall,

India's missile defence shield must be a highly adaptable, multi-layered system capable of maintaining consistent performance despite extreme and rapidly changing environmental conditions. This demands rugged hardware, robust communication networks and platforms with all-weather sensors. The doctrines should project the need for redundancy in the system and flexible deployment strategies.

Nuclear tests were conducted by India in 1974 and 1998. The first test, codenamed 'Smiling Buddha/Pokhran-I' took place on 18 May 1974 while the second, a series of five tests under 'Operation Shakti'/Pokhran-II, were conducted on 11 and 13 May 1998. India began its major investment in missiles with the start of the Integrated Guided Missile Development Programme (IGMDP) in 1983. Subsequently, the Ballistic Missile Defence (BMD) programme was initiated in 1999–2000. By that time, India had fought three wars (the1962 war with China and the 1965 and 1971 wars with Pakistan) and a military operation (Operation Vijay) in Kargil with Pakistan in 1999.

For the Indian defence establishment there have been various military technology upgrades from the 1960s to the 1990s. India's military technology evolved significantly across the 1962, 1965, 1971, and Kargil (1999) conflicts, moving from using largely World War II-era equipment in 1962 to incorporating advanced systems like precision-guided munitions and flyby-wire fighter jets, in the Kargil conflict. The Kargil conflict was characterised by high-altitude combat with Infantry playing an important role. This conflict demonstrated the importance of surveillance and precision strikes. India's battlefield experience in all these wars, underscored the necessity for developing a robust defence strategy and adequate investment in military technologies.

During the 21st century, India's adversaries are found modernising their missiles, aircraft, and submarine capabilities at a fast pace. Presently, nuclear China and Pakistan are developing longer-range, highly accurate ballistic and cruise missiles, stealth aircraft, lethal drone platforms, and quiet, missile-armed (nuclear-capable) submarines that can launch precision strikes from land, air, or under water. China has the capacity to fight a war in and from space. Artificial Intelligence and stealth technologies are making modern platforms and weapon systems far more potent and significantly harder to detect. As missiles, aircraft, and drones become stealthier, faster, and guided by advanced algorithms, the time available for early warning is likely to shrink. This reduced detection window increases the difficulty of tracking hostile attacks and creates better opportunities for an adversary to achieve successful surprise attacks.

In the above backdrop, a credible missile defence shield is a necessity. It would not only reduce vulnerability to evolving threats, but would also strengthen the deterrence component of India's defence architecture. Since the region's war waging abilities are becoming more sophisticated, India's investment in missile defence becomes a strategic necessity.

The idea of a missile defence system has a long history. In the 1980s, the then US President Ronald Reagan had conceptualised a missile defence architecture to guard against nuclear attacks. On 23 March 1983, in a nationally televised address, he had announced the need for pioneering research in a national defence system that could render nuclear weapons obsolete. This proposal was popular as the Strategic Defence Initiative (SDI). At its core, the SDI programme aimed to develop a space-based missile defence system capable of protecting the US from a large-scale nuclear attack. While SDI spurred the development of various advanced technologies, the exact vision conceptualised by Reagan never fully materialised. However, technology has evolved much during the last five decades, and modern technologies have the capability to build a reasonably secure missile defence system.

For more than two-and-a-half decades now, India is investing in the development of an indigenous missile defence system and has achieved noteworthy growth along the way. At the same time, to address immediate operational requirements and strengthen its defences, India has complemented its indigenous efforts by importing advanced missile systems. This dual approach is serving India to shape long-term self-reliance while ensuring reliable protection against present and emerging threats.

India's pursuit of a robust missile defence capability has developed steadily over the past three decades in response to evolving threats from adversaries. India launched the Ballistic Missile Defence Programme in

1999–2000, directing India's Defence Research and Development Organisation (DRDO) to develop a two-tiered system consisting of the Prithvi Air Defence (PAD) interceptor for high-altitude threats and the Advanced Air Defence (AAD) interceptor for lower-altitude engagements. Successful tests of both systems in 2006 marked a major milestone, demonstrating India's ability to neutralise incoming ballistic missiles. From 2016 onwards, India strengthened its defences further through advanced foreign procurements like the Russian S-400 Triumf surface-to-air missile (SAM) system. It has also deepened technological collaboration with Israel on the Barak-8 surface-to-air missile (SAM) system. There are some reports mentioning that around 1995, India had procured Russian S-300 SAM batteries while some indicated that the purchase was associated with procurement of S-300 radars. However, there is no official confirmation in this regard. Broadly, all these investments reflect India's long-term strategy to build a layered, modern, and credible missile defence shield capable of countering a wide spectrum of regional threats.

In January 2025, US President Donald Trump announced that the US would develop an American Iron Dome. In this connection, on 28 January 2025 he signed an Executive Order directing the Pentagon to develop a comprehensive missile defence system. The Executive Order called the system 'Iron Dome for America'. It is likely that President Trump could have been impressed with the performance of this system in the Israel-Hamas war that began on 7 October 2023. The Iron Dome is an Israeli mobile all-weather air defence system to intercept and destroy short-range rockets and artillery shells fired from distances of 4 to 70 km. This system became operational in 2011 and has a success rate of more than 90 per cent.

However, within a month, the US Missile Defense Agency (MDA) labelled this project as the 'Golden Dome for America'. Possibly, this change in name could have been prompted since the name 'Iron Dome' is a registered trademark. More importantly, the Iron Dome was developed for a limited purpose, primarily to counter threats from non-State actors. In contrast, US requirements span many additional dimensions, which could explain why the system's name may have been adapted to the Golden Dome.

At present, investments in projects like the Golden Dome are becoming essential since there is a realisation that the current missile defence systems would be unable to address the existing and futuristic threats. With time, new missile technologies are being created and in future, these threats are expected to grow in scale and sophistication. Some major powers are actively designing missile systems to exploit gaps in the current setup. Beijing's success with hypersonic missile technology is known. They have also established a near-space command to deal with various aspects of hypersonic technology. Moscow is modernising its intercontinental-range missile systems and developing advanced precision strike missiles. Russian hypersonic weapons are now battle-tested systems since they have used hypersonic missiles on targets in Ukraine (2022 onwards). During October 2025, Russia had successfully tested the Burevestnik nuclear-powered cruise missile, and the Poseidon, a nuclear-powered underwater drone.

Future wars are likely to centre on Multi-Domain Operations (MDO), where conventional battles fought on land and in the air will be complemented by parallel engagements in the cyber and space domains. The arrival of AI and quantum technologies in the military sphere is likely to transform the character of warfare altogether. In such an environment, success depends on the seamless integration of sensors, shooters, data networks, and decision-making systems across all Services, enabling forces to detect, track, and neutralise threats faster than the adversary. In this complex environment, missile defence becomes an essential pillar of national security. The future threats are expected to originate from multiple platforms like aircraft, drones, cruise missiles, ballistic missiles, space-based systems and cyber-attacks.

Hence, there would be a need to develop a state-of-the-art missile defence system capable of handling emerging challenges. The basic tasks for any modern missile defence architecture would remain the same: detecting, tracking, and intercepting diverse threats. However, since the nature of threats is expected to become far more complex, the new missile defence architecture would have to cater for simultaneous, multi-vector attacks involving cruise, ballistic and hypersonic missiles, drones, lethal drones, swarms, and loitering munitions. It would also need to integrate advanced sensor networks, including space-based early-warning systems. There also would be AI-enabled data fusion, and resilient communication links to ensure real-time situational awareness. Agencies would be required to ensure that the system is highly interoperable, hack-resistant and capable of functioning within a broader MDO framework. It is expected that the next-generation missile defence architecture would be flexible, layered, and adaptive, safeguarding protection against fast-evolving threats.

Overall, there is a need to protect India against sophisticated future threats. India has imported a few required systems. However, India's focus has been to rely more on indigenous capabilities. There are some successes towards building a layered, multi-domain shield. But all these systems have some limitations. Various wars fought during the 21st century indicate that the nature of warfare is fast changing and MDO is a reality. Particularly, for India there is much to learn from Operation SINDOOR (7-10 May 2025) when India had launched missile strikes on Pakistan, to eradicate the terror network there. The attack lunched by India was a calibrated and precise strike, using modern, indigenous technology. This operation highlighted the success of India's indigenous air defence systems.

Operation SINDOOR demonstrated the need for stronger missile defence by exposing gaps in areas like electronic warfare and low-level radar technology even as it highlighted the success of India's indigenous air defence systems like the Akash missile system. The Operation revealed weaknesses in the Pakistani defence grid but also highlighted that in case of India, there are gaps in electronic warfare, counter-drone systems and low-level radar technology. Operation SINDOOR emphasised that while India has advanced capabilities, there is a need to strengthen and expand the missile defence architecture.

India's proposed missile defence project *Sudarshan Chakra* is a response to the rapidly evolving security environment marked by growing regional missile capabilities. The entire project has to emerge as an indigenous, multi-layered defence architecture with the integration of advanced sensors, space-based systems (catering for surveillance and other requirements), AI-enabled data fusion, and strong command-and-control structures. The project is expected to achieve strategic self-reliance towards building a future-ready defence posture capable of protecting critical infrastructure and population centres in an era of MDO.

It is important to note that the *Sudarshan Chakra* is not intended to be a direct upgrade of the existing missile defence system developed by DRDO. India's existing system is primarily a terrestrial missile defence structure, whereas the *Sudarshan Chakra* is intended as a broader and more comprehensive space-enabled system. Essentially, the *Sudarshan Chakra* draws upon various existing missile defence models around the world, but significantly expands its scope to include space-based surveillance and interception, making it a system with both defensive and offensive capabilities. The real challenge before India's technological and strategic community is to develop such a system within a limited timeframe of ten years. Financial challenges may also arise, necessitating meaningful engagement by the mission's developers with private industry. At the same time, policymakers will need to present India's case logically and convincingly at various international fora, including those involving the United Nations, to ensure that no country can claim that the *Sudarshan Chakra* project could trigger an arms race in space.

India's 'Mission Sudarshan Chakra', is a work in progress. Possibly, apart from the missile programme, this would be one of the largest military research, development, and innovation initiatives undertaken by the country's defence apparatus. It represents an ambition to strengthen national defence through indigenous development of advanced, multi-domain capabilities. Such crucial military ideas will require a deep convergence of strategic vision and technological innovation. It would be too early to identify the exact focus of this project from the strategy and technology point of view. Broadly, from the systems perspective, it may involve space-based sensors, radars, missile silos, network-centric warfare elements, integrated command-and-control systems, rapid-response mechanisms and some other systems.

This work brings together ideas and reflections from experts across diverse domains. The aim is to elucidate both the opportunities and the challenges embedded in 'Mission Sudarshan Chakra'. Given the Mission's complexity, informed perspectives from those who have worked with similar systems or large-scale defence initiatives, are essential. As these are still early days, a sustained multi-disciplinary dialogue is necessary, which could help enrich the Mission's conceptual foundation and help identify the specific details required to realise a project of such vast magnitude.

This edited volume has four sections and ten chapters, an Introduction and a Conclusion. Before delving into the specifics of 'Mission Sudarshan Chakra', this work provides a review of existing missile defence systems across the world, along with an overview of India's current investments in the field. Military professionals have contributed their insights on the force structure, operational feasibility, and real-world battlefield requirements, and explore how 'Mission Sudarshan Chakra' fits within India's broader national security architecture. Technology specialists discuss the need for developing and upgrading of critical systems, including advanced sensors, autonomous platforms, resilient communication networks, and the potential integration of AI/ML across platforms, weapon systems, and ground – or space-based infrastructure. Given the project's scale, a significant emphasis rests on space technologies, and several space-based systems relevant to the Mission have been identified. Cyber technologies, which can both be a boon and a vulnerability for any digitally intensive programme, are also examined in this context.

All the chapters draw on information available from open sources, and the authors have relied on their professional experience to debate and analyse various issues. A range of books, Reports and publicly accessible online material including AI-enabled tools, have been consulted in the development of these chapters. In the context of *Sudarshan Chakra*, the terms Mission and project are used interchangeably. In some chapters, there may be a repetition of similar ideas. This is intentional; removing such an overlap would disrupt the line of reasoning of the authors in those chapters. Hence, ideas of the individual authors are retained as is. The views expressed are those of the authors. It is hoped that this work will contribute to building a comprehensive understanding of the opportunities and challenges surrounding 'Mission Sudarshan Chakra'.

SECTION I

Global Scan and India's Current System

1

A Global Scan of Integrated Air and Missile Defence Systems

Rahul Wankhede

Introduction

The evolution of integrated air and missile defence (IAMD) systems reflects the interplay of technology, strategy, and geopolitics. Once conceived as tactical tools to protect cities and troops from aerial bombardment, today's air defence architectures have expanded into multi-domain networks. They are now instruments of deterrence, alliance management, and defence diplomacy.

The wars in Ukraine and West Asia have revived global interest in multi-layered, integrated air defence systems capable of countering threats ranging from unmanned aerial vehicles to intercontinental ballistic and hypersonic missiles. This article provides a global survey of contemporary air defence systems, focusing on five principal theatres: the United States, the United Kingdom, Israel, Australia, and Europe. Each represents a distinct model of how nations reconcile technological ambition with strategic necessity.

A Global Scan

Missile defence systems initially focused on defence from enemy aircraft and ballistic missiles. But today, defence from other airborne threats like cruise missiles, drones, loitering munitions etc. also forms a part of IAMD architectures. It is beyond the capabilities of underdeveloped and most of the developing countries to raise, operationalise and maintain these systems. Therefore, globally only a select few countries have been able to develop and deploy indigenous IAMD systems. The following sections examine the same.

1) United States

The United States operates the most extensive and technologically diverse air and missile defence network in the world, collectively referred to as the National Missile Defense (NMD) programme.[1] It aims not only to protect the American homeland from missile and aerial threats but also to defend overseas US bases, deployed forces, and allied territories. The American approach integrates kinetic interceptors, radar networks, command-and-control nodes, and space-based early-warning satellites,[2] that merges deterrence, collective security, and power projection.[3]

A. Operational Principles and Systems Used

At the core of this architecture lies the hit-to-kill principle. While officially defensive, US missile defence is dual-use that serves, both to deter attacks, and to preserve freedom of offensive action, by reducing vulnerability to retaliation. The US Missile Defense Agency (MDA) oversees all of the major air and missile defence programmes.[4] American planners have long concluded that intercepting missiles in their boost phase is impractical;[5] hence, the focus has shifted towards engagement during the midcourse and terminal phases. To put this into practice the following systems are utilised:

1. The Ground-Based Midcourse Defense (GMD) system represents the United States' principal line of defence against intercontinental ballistic missile (ICBM) threats.[6] It relies on 44 Ground-Based Interceptors (GBIs) deployed in California and Alaska, that carry exo-atmospheric kill vehicles.[7] Despite its pioneering design, the GMD has faced persistent criticism over high costs,[8] limited success rates, and questionable reliability.[9] Independent assessments

describe it as technologically ambitious but operationally uncertain. Complementing the GMD are three theatre-level systems designed to counter short- and medium-range airborne threats.

2. The main weapon system among these, is the Aegis Ballistic Missile Defense (BMD) system, which is a ship-based system integrating sensors, radar, interceptors, and command networks. The Aegis system has a maximum range of 2500 kms and employs two primary interceptors: the Standard Missile-3 (SM-3) for mid-course engagements and the Standard Missile-6 (SM-6) for terminal interception.[10] Its flexibility allows ships to operate both independently and as part of a larger integrated missile defence network. Deployed across the Indo-Pacific and European theatres, it underpins Washington's alliance commitments. The land-based Aegis Ashore installations in Romania, Poland, and Guam serve as fixed nodes of this network,[11] offering regional coverage against ballistic missile threats. Cooperative development with Japan, including the co-production of the SM-3 Block IIA interceptor,[12] underscores how missile defence collaboration doubles as a form of alliance management and defence diplomacy.
3. At the next layer lies the Terminal High-Altitude Area Defense (THAAD) system, operated by the US Army, which has a range of 200 km and an interception altitude of 150 kms.[13] Designed to intercept short- and medium-range ballistic missiles in their terminal phase, THAAD combines truck-mounted interceptors that provide rapid deployment and high-altitude interception capability.[14] The system occupies a middle tier between the GMD and the lower-altitude Patriot systems. THAAD's export to the United Arab Emirates and Saudi Arabia[15] and its deployment to Guam and South Korea,[16] signal the US' commitment to regional security.[17] Obviously, this has provoked China, which perceives that the THAAD's radar is being used to spy on Chinese military activities. But the US continues to extend its defensive umbrella, to bind allies into US-centric security frameworks while sustaining its defence industrial base.

4. The Patriot (MIM-104) system with its range of 160 km and interception altitude of over 24 km forms the final layer of short-range air and missile defence for the US and its allies. Initially developed as an anti-aircraft system, it has evolved into a multi-role interceptor, capable of engaging cruise missiles, aircraft, and ballistic threats.[18] The latest variant, the Patriot Advanced Capability-3 (PAC-3), employs highly agile hit-to-kill missiles launched from mobile units.[19] Its record of combat, including in the Iraq War, in Israel recently and in Ukraine since 2022, has cemented its reputation as a reliable lower-tier defence solution. The Patriot's extensive export footprint spanning 18 countries, including Japan, Israel, South Korea, and several Gulf countries,[20] highlights its dual role as a military asset and as a diplomatic instrument.

B. Space-Based Early Warning and Sensor Integration

Supporting the above-mentioned air defence systems is a sophisticated space-based and ground-based sensor network. The Space-Based Infrared System (SBIRS) provides early-warning operations, providing near-continuous detection of missile launches.[21] It integrates geosynchronous and highly elliptical orbit satellites to ensure global coverage. Complementing this are newer initiatives such as the Hypersonic and Ballistic Tracking Space Sensor (HBTSS) and the Proliferated Warfighter Space Architecture (PWSA).[22] This network is supported by numerous early warning systems that the US has positioned in Alaska, the UK and also in Greenland.

C. Future Development and Debates

US missile defence has long been intertwined with broader strategic debates about deterrence stability and arms control. The 2022 Missile Defense Review reaffirmed that the GMD is not intended to counter the full arsenals of Russia or China, acknowledging the enduring logic of mutual deterrence. Instead, missile defence is framed as a limited defence against rogue actors and emerging technologies such as unmanned aerial systems and hypersonic weapons. The same review introduced the concept of "integrated deterrence", linking missile defence, nuclear forces, and diplomacy as mutually reinforcing elements of national security.

Domestically, missile defence programmes have faced scrutiny over cost-effectiveness and technical feasibility. Several ambitious initiatives launched since the days of the Bush administration – particularly those emphasising space-based interceptors and boost-phase technologies – were cancelled or scaled down due to prohibitive costs and limited operational success.[23]

Despite early realisations that such projects are impractical, in May 2025, the United States announced the Golden Dome Project.[24] The initiative seeks to establish a multi-layered, space-based defence architecture capable of intercepting ballistic, hypersonic, and cruise missiles even before launch or during flight. Rather than protecting a limited territorial expanse, it envisions a planet-spanning web of thousands of orbital interceptors.

Critics have pointed out that the name is misleading, as the system would rely on rapidly orbiting weapons rather than a static barrier over US territory.[25] The feasibility and the strategic wisdom of this endeavour has been questioned, while technical experts[26] note that the system's vast geographic coverage, the need for rapid orbital coordination, and the energy requirements for boost-phase interception make it an engineering challenge. Moreover, the idea of weaponising orbits has reignited international legal and diplomatic debates since the Outer Space Treaty (1967) prohibits the placement of weapons of mass destruction in orbit and promotes the peaceful use of space.

Several UN members have expressed concern that Golden Dome's pre-emptive "left-of-launch" elements could violate this norm and destabilise global arms control regimes. Russia[27] and China[28] have called the plan as a violation of space neutrality and strategic stability. Canada despite receiving an invite to join in the project has rejected the proposal.[29] In practical terms, Golden Dome's realisation looks bleak.

2) United Kingdom

The United Kingdom's air defence strategy reflects a cross-governmental, multi-layered and multi-national approach. Rather than viewing air defence as a purely domestic task, the UK looks at air defence as part of a wider Euro-Atlantic security ecosystem that combines national capabilities with NATO's Integrated Air and Missile Defence System (NATINAMDS) and bilateral cooperation with the United States.[30] The foreign collaboration also seems to have taken shape from the UK's realisation of its limited capabilities to develop IAMD systems – that got neglected over the past few decades due to the UK's excessive focus on expeditionary operations.

A. Integration and Architecture

The UK is deeply embedded in NATO's air and missile defence structure, which operates under the command of the Supreme Allied Commander Europe (SACEUR). Two critical installations in Yorkshire: the RAF Fylingdales[31] and RAF Menwith Hill[32] underscore Britain's role as both, a host and a participant in the US-led global missile warning and intelligence network. Fylingdales, part of a global chain of five US early-warning radar sites, provides 24-hour ballistic missile tracking and early warning for both Washington and London. Its radar, with a range exceeding 480 kms also monitors objects in space. Menwith Hill Base, operated by the US National Security Agency, functions as a major signals intelligence and data relay station, linking US' and UK's intelligence architectures,[33] and supporting the Space-Based Infrared System (SBIRS).

Within the UK's armed forces, only the Royal Navy possesses a dedicated ballistic missile defence (BMD) capability, primarily through its Type 45 destroyers equipped with Aster-30 interceptors[34] and advanced radars. The Army and Air Force share responsibility for short- and medium-range ground-based systems, most notably the Sky Sabre that replaced the older Rapier system, in 2021.[35] Sky Sabre integrates the CAMM (Common Anti-Air Modular Missile), featuring a 10-kg warhead and a range of approximately 25 km, capable of engaging a wide array of targets, from drones and loitering munitions to fighter aircraft and helicopters. The system's modularity allows its components (launcher, radar, and command nodes) to be deployed flexibly for either area or point defence missions. The Royal Navy's ongoing Type 45 modernisation programme includes[36] upgrading the ships' air-defence radars and integrating new missile interceptors to enhance ballistic missile defence capabilities. The British Parliament in 2025 has confirmed plans to reduce dependence on NATO assets,[37] by improving self-sufficiency in air defence. Under this plan it has allocated £1 billion over the coming years, including an estimated $118 million for the acquisition of additional interceptor missiles.[38]

B. International IAMD Cooperation

The UK actively participates in collaborative European initiatives aimed at improving continental defence. Through the DIAMOND initiative, London seeks to achieve greater interoperability between its own systems and those of France, Germany, Poland, Sweden, Norway, and Latvia,[39] thereby enhancing collective situational awareness and joint responses.

In 2023, Britain also joined Germany's European Sky Shield Initiative (ESSI), a multinational framework of over 23 countries,[40] that is dedicated to building a layered, ground-based air and missile defence architecture through shared procurement, maintenance, and training. Interestingly, Turkiye which has imported the Russian S-400 air defence system is also a part of the ESSI. Further diversifying into the IAMD domain, in 2024, the UK signed the European Long-Range Strike Approach Programme, alongside France, Germany, Italy, and Poland.[41] The initiative aims to develop advanced long-range missiles by 2030, ensuring NATO's capacity to engage evolving aerial and ballistic threats more effectively.

Despite these commitments, British defence reviews have acknowledged persistent vulnerabilities in the nation's air defence posture. They have emphasised the need to "strengthen resilience and protect critical national infrastructure."[42] Criticism from NATO partners, as well as from within the UK Parliament, has highlighted the relatively modest scale of Britain's missile defence contributions that came from years of neglect and over-reliance on the US protective umbrella.

The absence of a strong air defence architecture has also led to criticism regarding the absence of a formal National Defence Plan in British parliamentary debates. Some former defence ministers[43] and think-tanks have advocated the development of an indigenous air defence network inspired by Israel's Iron Dome,[44] arguing that the UK faces growing risks from Russia and from non-State actors capable of launching rocket or missile attacks. Some military leaders and analysts in the UK though have questioned the suitability of such a model for Britain's context. Their Chief of Defence Staff has called the replication of Israel's short-range architecture "illogical,"[45] stressing that the UK's threat environment and geography demands a different approach. Critics have instead recommended integrating offensive counter-air operations as part of a broader defensive construct, prioritising protection against cruise missiles before addressing the more complex threats of ballistic and hypersonic weapons.[46] Britain's defence industry is also being drawn in for developing the offensive and counter-strike missile projects that will complement its defensive posture. But as on date, these projects remain aspirational.

3) Israel

Few countries have faced as sustained and diverse airborne threats as Israel. Israeli estimates suggest that more than 15,000 rockets and mortars[47] have been launched at its population centres since 2001. This threat environment has shaped Israel's entire air and missile defence doctrine. As a result, Israel developed a layered defence architecture that combines kinetic interception systems with directed-energy systems. These systems protect Israel's territory while giving it leverage to conduct offensive air operations without fear of effective retaliation.

A. Iron Dome: Backbone of Israel's Short-Range Defence

At the base of Israel's defensive structure lies the Iron Dome. Designed jointly by Rafael Advanced Defense Systems and Israel Aerospace Industries (IAI)[48] with substantial US financial and technological support, the system was conceived after the 2006 conflict with Hezbollah. Iron Dome is specifically engineered to intercept short-range rockets, artillery shells, and mortar shells with trajectories between 4 km and 70 km.[49] Each Iron Dome battery typically comprises three to four launchers, each holding 20 Tamir interceptor missiles. The system employs an advanced battle management algorithm to determine their projected impact point. Only those threats that are likely to strike populated or critical areas are engaged; others are allowed to fall in open ground. This selective engagement process significantly reduces operating costs. The Tamir interceptor, priced at around $50,000 per missile, detonates onto the other targets, mid-air, instead of directly hitting it.[50] Each launcher can cover a medium-sized city, with interceptors boasting a 15-year maintenance-free life cycle. The Iron Dome's performance in successive conflicts has enhanced its popularity, though drone swarms and loitering munitions have increasingly tested its saturation ability[51] to discriminate between different threat profiles.

B. Arrow, David Sling, THAAD and Iron Beam

Above Iron Dome in Israel's defensive hierarchy lies the David's Sling system, co-developed by Rafael and the US firm Raytheon. With a range between 40-300 kms, it is designed to intercept medium-range threats, including cruise missiles, drones, and rockets.[52] Like the Iron Dome, it selectively targets incoming projectiles that pose genuine danger to populated areas. Each Stunner interceptor used in this system costs about $1 million.[53] David's Sling provides the crucial mid-tier link between the Iron Dome and the longer-range Arrow interceptors.

Supporting the David Sling, at the top of Israel's air defence umbrella stands the Arrow programme, developed by Israel Aerospace Industries in collaboration with Boeing. Conceived in response to the Scud missile attacks during the 1991 Gulf War, the Arrow 2 system is designed to intercept short- to medium-range ballistic missiles at altitudes up to 50 km and ranges of around 100 km.[54] Each interceptor can travel at nine times the speed of sound and engage up to 14 targets simultaneously. Arrow 2 saw its first reported combat use in 2017, intercepting a Syrian surface-to-air missile.[55]

Building on this, the Arrow 3 system extends interception capability beyond the atmosphere, engaging long-range ballistic missiles at range of up to 2,400 km and an interception altitude of over 100 kms.[56] It has been used successfully against Houthi-launched ballistic missiles. Both Arrow variants are integrated into Israel's broader multi-layered national air defence command network, which also employs US-origin Patriot batteries and, more recently, a US-deployed THAAD unit with US Army troops,[57] for additional coverage.

C. Future Systems

Israel is now developing a new system to intercept incoming threats with laser technology. Named the Iron Beam, this system is expected to reduce the 'cost-per-kill'.[58] Although not yet operational, Iron Beam is expected to become a game-changer, providing continuous and low-cost protection against saturation attacks. The reported range of Iron Beam is around 10 kms[59] which means that it will help reduce the burden on the Iron Dome, in countering UAVs, paratroopers, balloons etc. But given the current status of laser-based air defence systems globally it would not be safe to assume that they are not prone to attacks. especially in case of saturation attacks. Thus, despite having a robust air defence architecture, Israel will have to rely on foreign support, notably the US, for funding, co-development, early warning and strategic planning.

4) Australia

Australia's air defence debate has entered an era of never-seen-before urgency. At a recent seminar in September 2025, an Australian professor delivered a stark warning on the evolving air threat environment,[60] calling for fundamental reorientation of Australia's air defence strategy. He drew on contemporary wars to highlight emerging lessons for Australia, given its relative lack of air defence capabilities to protect the nation from Russia's use of ballistic missiles and the Shahed drone. The academic also emphasised that Australia would not be able to defend itself across the threat spectrum on its own and hence international collaboration is necessary.

A. The Vulnerability

Australia's vast geography creates both opportunity and exposure. Any long-range, one-way strike system such as drones or cruise missiles must traverse extensive oceanic distances, offering valuable early warning and interception windows.[61] However, such advantages diminish against ballistic or hypersonic threats originating from the South China Sea, which could target their key airbases, naval ports, and command infrastructure. This compels Canberra to prioritise point defence of critical military targets rather than attempting comprehensive territorial defence.[62] Add to this the fact that the country does not have any sophisticated air defence system[63] like the other countries mentioned above. One reason behind this is that till date, Australia did not face any significant threats, in response to which an air defence architecture could have been made.

But today China's military modernisation represents Australia's most immediate strategic concern. The PL-15 air-to-air missile is said to have surpassed most NATO equivalents. Given this situation, Australia seems to be moving away towards self-reliance in air defence. This move is also motivated by unreliability of US support.

Another major challenge for Australia now is how to prioritise its defence budgets between the upcoming air defence plans and its long-term strategic procurements. It has already committed funds to the AUKUS leaving its Army and Air Force with a limited pie. Scholars like Justin Bronk have hence called for the country to develop other defensive capabilities like civilian awareness, increasing shelter networks and to augment runway repair and public alert systems.

B. Australia's Air Defence Status

One of the most promising technological developments in Australia currently is the Advanced Precision Kill Weapon System (APKWS).[64] It is a retrofit kit that converts standard 2.75-inch rockets into laser-guided interceptors. Costing $20,000–35,000 per unit, the APKWS provides a significant reduction in the cost-per-kill ratio plaguing traditional Western air defences.[65] For Australia, the APKWS is said to offer a practical pathway toward scalable and affordable air defence integration. Existing F/A-18F Super Hornets of the Australian Air Force could act as interceptor platforms, supported by Australian F-35s providing sensor coverage and target designation.[66] A single aircraft can carry 28-49 APKWS rounds, allowing sustained engagements against swarm attacks.[67]

C. Future Plans

Australia's principal ground-based air defence effort centres on Project LAND 19 Phase 7B, which will deliver the Short-Range Air Defence (SHORAD) system.[68] This will form the inner tier of Australia's emerging Joint Integrated Air and Missile Defence (JIAMD) network. Approved in 2019, the programme, led by Raytheon Australia in partnership with Kongsberg Defence & Aerospace, introduces the National Advanced Surface-to-Air Missile System (NASAMS) as the Army's key air defence weapon.[69]

NASAMS employs the AIM-120 AMRAAM interceptor, capable of engaging aircraft, UAVs, cruise missiles, and precision-guided weapons at ranges of 15–20 miles and altitudes up to 15 kms. The system integrates AESA radars with electro-optical sensors and the AN/AAS-52 Multispectral Targeting System. The result would be a networked, mobile, and modular architecture that will enable Australia to defend dispersed assets effectively. This $2.5 billion programme also anchors significant domestic industry participation.

Australia's broader Integrated Air and Missile Defence (IAMD) initiative aims to link sensors and shooters across domains of land, sea, and air into a unified command network[70] capable of defeating multiple, simultaneous threats. Complementing NASAMS, it has announced a $4.7 billion acquisition of US-made SM-2 and SM-6 interceptors.[71] The SM-6, in particular, will provide terminal ballistic missile defence and anti-ship strike capability, marking a major qualitative leap for the Royal Australian Navy. Australia also became the first country outside the US to successfully launch an SM-6 missile from a warship. This integration underlines the growing technological convergence between the two allies under the AUKUS framework as well as Australia's priority to give the highest attention to developing air defence[72] capabilities.

In this case the examples of the UK and Australia look similar in the context of lacking domestic air defence capabilities. Relying on the US, which was once considered successful diplomacy, has now become a hard-to-fill vulnerability for both countries.

5) Europe

For much of the post–Cold War period, Europe did not confront any major threat requiring comprehensive air and missile defence. The collapse of the Soviet Union in 1991 led to the gradual downgrading of air defence as a priority, as NATO shifted from territorial defence to expeditionary crisis management. The use of ballistic and cruise missiles, drones, and precision-guided munitions employed in the Russia-Ukraine conflict exposed Europe's vulnerability and catalysed a continent-wide reassessment of integrated air and missile defence (IAMD).

But what is often not stated in European media and scholarly works is that Europe's paranoia regarding such threats comes mainly from the lack of robust air defence systems in EU countries (without US support) and the large-scale use of drones and rockets in other conflict zones like West Asia and the Indian sub-continent.

Today, European Air Forces operate modern multi-role aircraft and a mix of US-made and indigenous air defence systems. Yet national level inventories remain thin, stockpiles of interceptors are low, and industrial capacity cannot easily surge to wartime production levels. This shortfall extends across all tiers, from short-range counter-drone systems to long-range ballistic missile interceptors. Add to this the fact that EU States have committed multiple weapons and systems for Ukraine, which has in turn impacted their own stockpiles and force deployments.

A. Current Status of European IAMD

Europe possesses a sophisticated technological base in guided weapons, radar sensors, and interceptor design, but its capabilities are fragmented across national lines.[73] The United States continues to provide most of Europe's terminal-phase and exo-atmospheric missile defence coverage, through Patriot systems and the Aegis Ashore sites in Romania and Poland. This dependence has spurred renewed debate within Europe about sovereignty in defence-industrial production and strategic autonomy in deterrence.[74] NATO's February 2025 Defence Ministerial has endorsed a new Integrated Air and Missile Defence Policy, acknowledging the need to expand both the volume and quality of available systems.[75] Secretary-General Mark Rutte underscored this by calling for a 400 per cent increase in IAMD capabilities, which is seen as an implicit admission of the long-standing neglect of air defence investments in Europe.[76] This defensive argument also has an undertone of concern regarding Russia's well-developed IAMD architecture that has shown decent performance against NATO attacks.

The Germany-led European Sky Shield Initiative (ESSI), launched in 2022,[77] represents the most ambitious attempt in Europe, to close these gaps through collective procurement and integration. By 2025, twenty-four countries had joined, including almost all NATO members and traditionally neutral States such as Austria and Switzerland.[78] The ESSI envisions a layered air defence network using off-the-shelf platforms: the Skyranger 30 for point defence, the IRIS-T SLM for medium range, the Patriot for long range, and Israel's Arrow 3 for exo-atmospheric interception.[79] Germany's planned procurement of the Arrow 4 system, now under development, is expected to provide an additional upper-tier layer.[80] While the initiative aims to strengthen NATO's collective shield, it has also ignited intra-European friction. France has criticised the ESSI for over-reliance on non-European equipment,[81] arguing instead for greater support to systems such as the Franco-Italian SAMP/T.

The Eurosam SAMP/T, jointly produced by France and Italy is a promising system.[82] It uses the Aster 30 missile with an engagement range exceeding 150 km.[83] It is fielded both on land and at sea (in the UK's Sea Viper configuration). Despite its proven combat performance, including successful intercepts of ballistic missiles in the Red Sea, the SAMP/T production has been slow, with individual missile manufacturing taking over three years, before the Ukraine War accelerated timelines.[84] Efforts are underway to halve the production time and develop the Aster 30 Block 1NT, capable of intercepting medium-range ballistic missiles up to 1,500 km.[85]

Building up on these efforts is Europe's medium-range segment. Germany's IRIS-T family, derived from the air-to-air missile of the same name is supporting this segment. The IRIS-T SLM (range 40 km+) is already in service in several European States and Ukraine, while the SLX variant under development is expected to extend range to 80 km.[86] Norway's NASAMS, developed with Raytheon, has proven effective in Ukraine and is deployed in Finland, Lithuania, the Netherlands, Norway, and Spain.[87] The system's modular architecture allows the integration of various interceptors, including AIM-120 AMRAAM-ER and AIM-9X Sidewinder II missiles. In the UK, MBDA's Common Anti-Air Modular Missile

(CAMM) forms the basis of the Land Ceptor system, offering a 25-km range.[88] The CAMM-ER extends this to 40 km, and the two are being jointly produced with Poland under the Narew programme.[89] A follow-on CAMM-MR project aims to provide a longer-range interceptor, reinforcing the model of multinational co-development that characterises Europe's current approach.

In terms of ballistic missile defence, Europe's architecture remains a patchwork of national initiatives underpinned by US technology. Patriot PAC-3 interceptors have till now provided terminal defence against short-range and tactical ballistic missiles. But the US' Patriot stockpile too is running low[90] on account of being diverted towards Israel and Ukraine. The US MIM-104 Patriot remains the backbone of continental missile defence, fielded by Germany, Greece, the Netherlands, Poland, Romania, Spain, Sweden, and Ukraine. Production bottlenecks, particularly in rocket motors, have led to shortages, prompting European co-production efforts in Poland, Spain, and Germany. To meet rising demand, the COMLOG, which is a Raytheon and MBDA Deutschland joint venture, has begun building a new production line for PAC-2 GEM-T interceptors in Germany.[91]

In this scenario, the Aster 30 is Europe's only indigenous missile with terminal ballistic capability. At exo-atmospheric level coverage, Europe has realised its vulnerability of totally depending on US support. Aegis Ashore installations in Romania and Poland have left other parts of Europe vulnerable. The Arrow 3 system, procured by Germany from Israel, marks Europe's first step towards sovereign high-altitude interception capability, with operational readiness expected by 2030.

B. Counter-Drone and Directed Energy Systems

Saturation attacks by loitering munitions and first-person-view (FPV) drones during the Ukraine War have driven Europe to integrate its short-range and counter-UAV defences within IAMD planning. Recognising that expensive interceptors are ill-suited for low-cost aerial threats, several countries are investing in directed-energy weapons and drone interceptors.

The UK's Dragon Fire laser system, rated at 50 kW, successfully intercepted aerial targets in 2024 tests.[92] Germany's Rheinmetall and MBDA Deutschland have demonstrated a 20 kW naval laser on the Sachsen-class Frigate,[93] while France's HELMA-P (2 kW) system was deployed operationally during the 2024 Paris Olympics.[94] The multilateral TALOS and TALOS-TWO projects, supported by the European Defence Fund, aim to field a 100 kW laser weapon by 2030.[95] Parallel efforts include low-cost missile and drone interceptors such as MBDA's DefendAir and indigenous initiatives by European start-ups in Poland, Germany, Latvia, and Estonia.[96] Together, these efforts represent a shift towards scalable, cost-effective point defence options that can complement high-end systems, reducing vulnerabilities and foreign dependency.

Conclusion

Integrated Air and Missile Defence has become a defining element of global military transformation. The proliferation of advanced missile systems, low-cost drones, innovative threats like balloons and parachute assisted munitions, hypersonic glide vehicles etc. has forced a rethink on boundaries between offence and defence. Across the world, countries are converging on a layered and networked model that integrates space-based sensors, ground radars, artificial intelligence, and modular interceptors.

Yet, this convergence conceals divergent strategic motives due to different geographies, the nature of threats faced and the realisation that most countries are not fully equipped with the necessary capabilities required to cover the entire national airspace. This has led to a rationalisation of ambitions to location-specific defence. Governments will find it challenging to allocate the requisite funds for their future air defence projects, some of which may take decades to materialise. Hence, countries have increasing sought foreign collaboration, mostly through joint ventures. In times of conflict involving multiple countries, such ventures may face a dilemma on which regions and threats to prioritise.

At the same time, the rapid expansion of air defence technologies has raised political and ethical questions. The weaponisation of outer space, the erosion of arms control norms, and the financial burden of sustaining these systems, all carry implications for global stability. Systems like the Golden Dome underscore both the promise and peril of over-reliance on technology as a substitute for strategic restraint.

Ultimately, air and missile defence do not exist in isolation. They function as part of a wider ecosystem. Their effectiveness depends not only on hardware and algorithms but also on diplomacy, arms control, and credible signalling. As the global environment becomes contested and the aerospace domain more crowded, nations will increasingly view air and missile defence as both a shield and as a statement, thus defining their place in an era of technological and geopolitical uncertainty.

NOTES

1 "National Missile Defence in the US", The Parliamentary Office of Science and Technology, London, 2000.

2 "US Ballistic Missile Defence", Report, Center for Arms Control and Non-Proliferation, 21 May 2025.

3 "2022 National Defense Strategy of the United States of America", Department of Defense, 27 October 2022.

4 "Missile Defense", Report, Center for Arms Control and Non-Proliferation, 2025. A US Government Factsheet mentioning the details is available at https://www.war.gov/Portals/1/Interactive/2018/11-2019-Missile-Defense-Review/MDR-BMDS-Factsheet-UPDATED.pdf.

5 "Making Sense of Ballistic Missile Defense", Report, National Academies, 2012.

6 "Ground Based Interceptors", Report, CSIS Missile Defense Project, 26 July 2021.

7 Ibid.

8 "Missile Defense: Observations on GMD Acquisition Challenges and Potential Contract Strategy Changes", Government Accountability Office, House of Representatives, USA, 21 October 2020.

9 CSIS Missile Defense Project, Ibid.

10 "Current U.S. Missile Defense Programs at a Glance", Factsheets and Briefs, Arms Control Association, January 2025.

11 "NATO Missile Defense Base in Poland Now Mission Ready", NATO, 10 July 2024.

12 "U.S., Japan Successfully Conduct First SM-3 Block IIA Intercept Test", Commander US 7th Fleet, 06 February 2017.

13 "THAAD Combat Proven Integrated Air and Missile Defense", Lockheed Martin, 2025.

14 Andrew Feickert, "The Terminal High Altitude Area Defense System", Library of Congress, US Government, 15 September 2025.

15 Doug Richardson, "Ground Based Air Defence in The Gulf Region", *European Security and Defence*, 08 March 2023.

16 Paula Hancocks and Joshua Berlinger, "Missile Defense System That China Opposes Arrives in South Korea", CNN World, 07 March 2017.

17 Ibid.

18 Andrew Feickert, "Patriot Air and Missile Defense System For Ukraine", Library of Congress, 17 July 2025.

19 "PAC-3", Lockheed Martin, 2025.

20 Anastassia Malenko et.al., "In Reversal Trump Arms Ukraine and Threatens Sanctions on Countries That Buy Russian Oil", Reuters, 15 July 2025.

21 "Space Based Infrared System", United States Space Force, March 2023.

22 "PWSA Tracking Layer", Space Development Agency, 2025.

23 Philip Coyle, "Rhetoric or Reality? Missile Defense Under Bush", Arms Control Association.

24 "US President Unveils 175 Billion Dollar Golden Dome Missile Defence Shield for the US", *All India Radio*, Government of India, 21 May 2025.

25 Ramin Skibba, "What's The Plan For Golden Dome? Even Experts Aren't Sure", *Scientific American*, 08 September 2025.

26 Stephen Clark, "Trump's Golden Dome Will Cost 10 to 100 Times More Than The Manhattan Project", *Ars Technica*, 18 September 2025.

27 "Russia Says Golden Dome Project Undermines Strategic Stability", Reuters, 27 May 2025.

28 David Brennan and Karson Yiu, "Trump's Golden Dome Risks Weaponisation of Space", ABC News, 21 May 2025.

29 Rob Gillies, "Senior Canadian Diplomat Compares Golden Dome To a Protection Racket", Associated Press, 28 May 2025.

30 Claire Mills, "UK Defence In 2025: Integrated Air and Missile Defence", Research Briefing, House of Commons Library, UK Parliament, 13 June 2025.

31 "The Station", RAF Fylingdales, 2025.

32 "Missile Defence CND Briefing", Campaign for Nuclear Disarmament, December 2019.

33 Claire Mills, no. 31.

34 Ibid.

35 "Guided Weapons Procurement Question for Ministry of Defence", UK Parliament, 23 October 2024.

36 John Birkler et.al., "The Royal Navy's New Generation Type 45 Destroyer", RAND Corporation, 2002.

37 "UK Defence: Hypersonic Missiles", Lords Chamber, Hansard, UK Parliament, 03 March 2025.

38 Ibid.

39 "Britain Bolsters NATO's Eastern Flank With New pact with Estonia and New Cooperation on Missile Defence", Press Release, UK Government, 17 October 2024.

40 "ESSI-European Sky Shield Initiative", Hensoldt.

41 Timothy Wright, "Europe's Missile Renaissance", IISS, 25 November 2024.

42 "Britain Vulnerable to Ballistic Missiles As Holes in Defence Revealed", Investigation Report, *The Times* UK, 4 January 2025.

43 Jane Merrick, "UK Missile Defences Inadequate Against Russian Attacks Ex Ministers Warn", *The I Paper*, 20 October 2024; George Allison, "Britain To Develop New Long Range Missile Capabilities", *UK Defence Journal*, 18 October 2024.

44 "UK-Israel Aerial Defence Collaboration", Report, Labour Friends of Israel, October 2024.

45 "Integrated Air and Missile Defence: Does the UK Need and Iron Dome?", Royal Aeronautical Society, 10 May 2024.

46 Sidharth Kaushal, "An Integrated Air and Missile Defence Architecture for the UK", RUSI, 28 August 2025.

47 Daniel Pomerantz, "Hamas: 30 Facts For 30 Years", *Honest Reporting*, 14 December 2017; "The Hamas Terror War Against Israel", Ministry of Foreign Affairs, Government of Israel, 01 March 2011.

48 Jim Garamone, "Iron Dome Missile System", US Department of Defense.

49 "Iron Dome Family", Rafael, 2025.

50 Sam Meredith, "What is Israel's Iron Dome?", CNBC, 13 June 2025.

51 Abhimanyu Kulkarni, "Israel's Iron Dome Failed To Defend Hamas Rocket Barrage: Here's Why", NDTV, 12 October 2023.

52 "David's Sling (Israel)", Missile Threat, CSIS, 13 July 2021.

53 "What are Israel's Iron Dome, David's Sling, Arrow and THAAD Missile Defences", BBC News, 16 October 2024.

54 Ibid.

55 "Israel's Arrow anti-missile system first hit", BBC News, 17 March 2017.

56 "Air Defense Systems", Israel Aerospace Industries, 2025.

57 Anushri Jonko, "US Used 20% of its THAAD Missiles To Defend Israel For 12 Days: Report", NDTV, 28 June 2025.

58 Srishti Kapoor, "Israel To Soon Deploy Game Changer Iron Beam", NDTV, 18 September 2025.

59 Sakshi Tiwari, "Iron Beam 450", *Eurasian Times*, 18 September 2025.

60 Robbin Laird, "The Air Defence Reality Check: Why Australia Has Less Time Than It Think", Sir Richard Williams Foundation, 19 September 2025.

61 Harrison Gray, "An Essay on Development of an DF Integrated Air and Missile Defence Capability To Combat Advanced Air and Missile Threats", Commonwealth Australia, 2020.

62 Ibid.

63 Mick Ryan, "A New Defense Review For Australia", Report, CSIS, 27 April 2023.

64 "Advanced Precision Kill Naval Systems", The Royal Australian Navy, 2025.

65 Ibid.

66 Robbin Laird, no. 61.

67 Ibid.

68 "Short Range Ground Based Air Defence", Defence Activities, Government of Australia.

69 Ibid.

70 "Integrated Air and Missile Defence System", Projects and Programs, Royal Australian Air Force.

71 "Safeguarding Australians with Boost to Air and Missile Defence", Media Releases, Government of Australia.

72 "2024 National Defence Strategy and 2024 Integrated Investment Program", Strategic Planning, Defence, Government of Australia.

73 "European Integrated Air and Missile Defence: Slow Progress", Chapter 3, *IISS Strategic Dossier*, IISS, 2 September 2025.

74 Ibid.

75 "NATO Defence Ministers Conclude Meeting, Focus On Defence Spending and Support For Ukraine", NATO, 13 February 2025.

76 Ibid., *IISS Strategic Dossier,* no. 74.

77 "European Countries Are Banding Together In Missile Defence", *The Economist*, 25 July 2024.

78 "European Sky Shield Initiative Gets Two More Participant", NATO, 15 February 2023.

79 *IISS Strategic Dossier*, no. 74.

80 Lars Hofmann, "Germany Wants Arrow 4 Amidst Air Defence Modernisation", *Calibre Defence*, 07 May 2025.

81 Gregoire Lory, "EU Plans To Boost Air and Missile Defence With 18 Member States, *Europe News*, 21 November 2024.

82 "SAMPT NG: The New European Long Range Ground Based Air Defense System", EUROSAM, 2025.

83 Ibid.

84 *IISS Strategic Dossier*, no. 74.

85 Ibid.

86 Ibid, p. 14.

87 "NASAMS vs Patriot : Complementary Pillars of NATO Air Defense", *Norskluftvem*, 06 July 2025.

88 "MBDA's Common Anti Modular Missile", *Air Force Technology*, 08 April 2020.

89 *IISS Strategic Dossier*, no. 74, p. 42.

90 Hugo Lowell, "US Has Only 25% of All Patriot Missile Interceptors Needed For Pentagon's Military Plans", *The Guardian*, 08 July 2025.

91 *IISS Strategic Dossier,* no.74, p. 41.

92 Doug Falkner, "Dragonfire Laser: MoD Tests Weapon As Low Cost Alternative To Missiles", BBC News, 19 January 2024.

93 John Hill, "German Navy Completes Laser Weapon Demonstrator Trials", *Naval Technology*, 25 September 2023.

94 "3 More HELMA-P For The French Armed Forces", Press Release, CILAS, 18 October 2024.

95 *IISS Strategic Dossier*, no. 74, p. 43.

96 Ibid.

2

Control and Reporting: The Indian Way

Gp Capt Sukhbir Kaur Minhas

Introduction

The ancient Indian tradition of the *Upanishads* uses an analogy from the act of a Spider weaving its web to underscore that the manifest world threads from the subtle *Brahman*, each strand binding the seen and unseen into an intricate, interwoven expression of one source.[1]

Now imagine an Integrated Air and Missile Defence (IAMD) system in India's context as an intricate spider's web, each silken thread weaved to create a robust, adaptable 'offence-defence' network with the current Integrated Air Command and Control System (IACCS) at the hub of the web, up scaled in the future to a National Command Post.

This chapter traces the doctrinal origin and evolution of the Air Battle Management (ABM) element of IAMD systems, also referred to as Control & Reporting (C&R) in the IAF, thereafter using the metaphor as above, to define its status and scope in Mission Sudarshan Chakra.

Navigating Complexities

Mission Sudarshan Chakra and IAMD Systems in general, is a highly complex subject with information in open domain limited to a broad overview of weapon systems and strategic effects.

Given the intricacies, a common pitfall observed in public discourse is a tendency of 'reductionism',[2] where air operations across the spectrum of conflict from Peace to War –are seen as distinct and non-related activities, resulting in a flawed understanding.[3] Hence, terms such as 'Air Defence (AD)', 'Offensive Air Defence', 'Aerospace Defence', 'Offensive Air', 'Air Space Management', 'Air Battle Management', 'Ballistic Missile Defence', etc. are inaccurately perceived as mutually exclusive functions. For an academic navigation of these complexities, the concept of 'holism', based on doctrinal perspectives on Air Power and its interdependence with other parts of the larger 'System', may be better suited.[4]

A second aspect is the debate on control of assets and functions; a subject best suited for internal and confidential deliberation. The issue gets further compounded as a practitioners' take on the subject– however discrete – invariably offers insights into core aspects of a nations' systems revealing vulnerabilities for adversaries to exploit. To cite an example, it can be suggested that publicity of the 'Command and Control System'[5] and "Comprehensive Layered Integrated Air Defence" (CLIAD) system of Pakistan's defence forces[6] through a large part of 2024 may have offered valuable pointers for the Indian planners to break its Air Defences during the 98 hours of Operation SINDOOR. It is for this reason amongst others, that information on global IAMD Systems is kept vague.

Keeping these aspects in mind, the chapter covers the subject from a doctrinal and analogy perspective to enhance understanding of India's C&R element in this vital national mission without it contributing to additional Open Source of Intelligence (OSINT).

Doctrinal Underpinnings

The Beginnings of Air Defence

A fascinating piece of history reveals that the world's first 'Air Defence hit' on a military aircraft flying a combat mission predated the first 'combat bombing sortie'. On 26 October 1911, as the Italo-Turkish War (1911-12) raged on, Captain Riccardo Moizo, an Italian military aviator on a reconnaissance mission over a Turkish encampment over Libya came under enemy fire, suffering three hits on the wing.[7] Merely five days later, on 01 November 1911, Lieutenant Giulio Gavotti, flying an Etrich Taube monoplane, dropped four "Cipelli" bombs over Turkish positions, ushering in the 'conjoined twin era of air offense and air defence'– using mere monoplanes and rifle fire.[8,9] A century later the offensive air warfare landscape has evolved from Gavotti's monoplane to fighters, strategic bombers and now includes loitering drones, advanced fighter jets, and hypersonic missiles. To meet this challenge, defensive air warfare has also transformed from improvised ground fire by the Turkish in Libya to a plethora of sensors, weapon systems (ground, sea and air-based) and the underlying Command, Control, Communications, Computers, Intelligence, Surveillance, and Reconnaissance (C4ISR)/IAMD framework that enable them to take effect. This reinforces that the development of air offensive and defensive capabilities is often an iterative and intertwined process. However, what one often misses is that the application of these capabilities also remains undivided and effective 'Command and Control of Air' flows from a singular source, architecture and strategy[10] and more often than not, a single operations room.

Two Sides of the Same Coin

Simply put, offensive and defensive air power are like two sides of a coin, inherently interconnected and manifested in strategy.[11] IAMD, exemplifies this paradox, a defensive shield in nomenclature, but inherently offensive as a concept. The understanding of this simple yet vital tenet of air power is echoed globally, foundations of which were cast during the First World War, and amplified through lessons in the Second World War.

One considers the Air Defence and IAMD concepts to augment this understanding. These stem from an existential crisis – to save populations from aerial bombardments and the need to destroy the adversary's aerial attack vectors as far away as possible from own territory. Traditionally, in the Within Visual Range (WVR) era, this was achieved by intercepting and destroying the attacker at the farthest possible range from the Vulnerable Area/Point (VA/VP) being defended. This informed intercept geometries and the concept of looking deep in enemy territory through Early Warning (EW) sensors placed along the borders, and later the airborne platforms.

The concept of 'layered defences' ensured continuous fire on the attackers ensuring 'defence in depth' to VA/VPs being protected. Space interceptors envisaged as part of the US' Project Golden Dome, employ the same philosophy, i.e. destruction of a missile in the boost phase itself, followed by continuous fire in attempts at destruction before impact.

World's First Integrated AD System

In 1917, the German Zeppelin, fighters and Gotha bombing raids, exposed Britain's vulnerabilities, highlighting the need for a more organized and unified air strategy. This led to an urgent creation of the Royal Air Force (RAF) the following year.[12] The inter-War years saw fierce doctrinal debates on the offensive and defensive uses of air power, with the latter philosophy manifesting as the world's first IAMD system,[13] the 'Dowding System' (named after its creator, Air Chief Marshal Hugh Dowding), developed for the RAF's Fighter Command.

The 'Secret under the Hill', a poetic description by Sinclair McKay in his book on the subject, refers to the underground location of the Command in the London suburbs, at 'Bentley Priory, a former eighteenth century house that once hosted poets and princes'.[14] From July to October 1940, the system comprising Chain Home radars and the Observer Corps as sensors, defended Britain through fighter interceptors, Anti-Aircraft (AA) arty guns, balloon barrages and search lights, coordinated through the 'filter' and 'control rooms' of Bentley Priory and respective control HQs (Group Operations Centre, Sector Operations Centre (SOC) and later Ground Control Interceptor (GCI) Units. The system held up against German raids during the Battle of Britain, as RAF chose to preserve its fighters for defence rather than peter them out in support of allied offensive operations. This integration of sensors, interceptors and ground-based artillery through the Fighter Command's operations rooms enabled a common operating picture, centralised decision-making and decentralised execution – mirrored by all modern IAMD concepts.

In contrast, the Germans, who possessed radars, formidable fighters, missiles and AA artillery guns along with production capacity, failed to organise a central system coordinating its air strategy.

Evolution of IAMD

The V-1 Challenge

Later, during the War, this system adapted to rise to the challenge of the German V-1, a winged and pilotless bomb, in 1944-45. Tactics used the concept of layered defences (fighters along the coast, and AA arty guns and Balloon barrage units as Point defence), besides re-enforcing the 'left of launch' strategy by fighter attacks on launch sites, supply dumps, production facilities and transportation networks forcing dispersal of launch sites and complicating logistics.[15]

Offence with Defence

With the threat of a land/sea offensive on Britain thwarted, the Fighter Command initially conceived as a defensive shield, evolved into an aggressive force. Despite heavy losses of fighters in its offensive campaign in 1941, by 1944 it had experimented with and introduced tactics of fighter sweeps (intruder operations over France), fighter escorts (over Germany), ground attack and air interdiction (airfields, coastal shipping and railways), close air support to the land and naval forces as a Tactical Air Force, "a long way from the desperate scrambles of the 'Spitfire summer' of 1940."[16]

This concept evolved into the modern Offensive Counter Air (OCA) operations "aimed at destroying, disrupting, or limiting the enemy airpower (both before and after launch) including targets such as enemy aircraft, Surface to Air Guided Weapons (SAGW) systems, AD radars, other sensors, communications, C2, Integrated Air Defence System nodes, weapon storage, fuel storage, airfields and operating surfaces, and aircraft servicing facilities, etc."[17]

The defensive elements of modern IAMD systems complement this philosophy partially through Offensive AD and anti-access/area denial (A2/AD) strategies in gaining the desired control of the air for enabling strategic objectives alongside enabling/supporting operations of ground/sea forces.

However, the fundamental point to note is that OCA and Air Defence operations are nation agnostic and globally all Air Forces plan and execute them as part of a singular strategy and a wider offensive effort against enemy targets. This integration is essential as there are 'no pure OCA missions' or 'pure AD missions' and hence modern IAMD systems operate "alongside offensive air power through shared battlespace awareness and coordinated operations."[18]

The Indian Context

The "Seers" – 24x7, 365 days

Just before the turn of the 21st century, the basic training for Fighter Controllers (FCs), Air Defence Systems Operators' (ADSOs) and technicians of the Indian Air Force (IAF) – the nucleus of India's Air Defence C&R organisation– centered around two paradoxical dictums. The first was about one being invisible yet ubiquitous through an unyielding 24x7x365 days rhythm. The second was to achieve singularity through dualism– a killer instinct balanced with cautious prudence– to bring down each 'hostile' and recover each 'friendly'.

The import of these statements unraveled through training curated to develop a conceptual understanding of air operations and the nuances of its control from ground –from 'Air Space control' to 'Command and Control of Air', and from 'Air Defence' to enable 'offensive parallel air operations'. The grounding stood steady, and saw the entire country's skies shrink to one 'Latitude and Longitude' with the advent of the Air Force Net Work (AFNET) and the IACCS. Now, a single set of skilled operators had the capability to orchestrate complex air battles miles away from their secure nodes, coordinated with own deployed sensors and weapons, in addition to those of sister services and civil networks.

When one was not practicing for war, the first dictum was reinforced in preparation for constantly evolving threats. It was then, as is now, a challenge to describe the nature of one's work profile. One could, hypothetically and literally speaking, in a span of 24 hours, move from controlling a practice Large Force Engagement (LFE) in an IACCS operations room, to a field location moving a radar for enhancing coverage or be deployed to augment the Joint Air Defence Centre (JADC) crew. Within an operations room, there is no distinction– a FC controlling an offensive sweep mission could, with just a swap of a console, move to controlling a defensive Combat Air Patrol (CAP); or movement and identification roles, or assist the Air Battle Manager in evaluation of threats and allocation of weapons. From planning, deployment, execution of missions, to post-mission analysis, these operators are trained to do it all. This underscores the fundamental approach of the IAF to Air battle Management – both doctrinally and operationally – which is the synergising of 'Air Defence' and OCA operations through the crew at an IACCS node.

This grounding and transformation has its roots not just in the trials and tribulations of a divided nation in 1947, but in the 'Indian' AD experience of the Second World War.

Indian AD in the Second World War

During the Second World War, the 'India Command' or the 'China Burma India' theatre of war gained the attention of the Allied forces only by mid-1942, as the pre-War threat assessment focused on the subcontinent's northwest coupled with a perception of India's defence requirements as 'slight'. The resultant low priority along with financial constraints, nascent radar technology and equipment shortages led to a near absence of any Air Defence Plan for India. Hence when the Japanese attacks commenced in 1941, there were neither radars nor any integrating organisation like Britain's Dowding System.[19]

By mid-1942, Japanese advances and the fall of Burma pressed inductions of radars, wireless units (for visual reporting) and manpower, and a C&R system with filter rooms came up across the Eastern coast of India and Ceylon (then under India Command). Records indicate that radar stations such as Chain Home Overseas (CO), Chain Home Overseas Low (COL) and Mobile Radar Units (MRUs) were rapidly deployed under RAF Group HQs, some under the nomenclature of Air Ministry Experimental Station (AMES) units such as AMES No 570, set up in April 1943 at *Kailasagiri*, Visakhapatnam. AMES No 566 was formed in June 1943 under the control of RAF 225 as a Chain Overseas Low (COL) Station. There are similar records of No 544 AMES sited at Diamond Harbour Calcutta in 1942 and No 590 AMES at Balasore. By 1943, "the

Bay of Bengal coastline was dotted with scores of radar stations operated by RAF technicians who were sworn to secrecy with a penalty of death."[20]

This C&R system eventually expanded to 52 operational radar sets along the coastline and port cities such as Calcutta, Vishakhapatnam, Balasore and Ceylon with seven filter rooms (Calcutta, Imphal, Comilla, Bombay, Madras, Colombo and Trincomalee*)*. Supplementing the radars were units for visual reporting of threats. Anti-Aircraft (AA) guns of the newly raised Indian Anti-Aircraft Regiments and Brigades linked up to these filter rooms for obtaining fire control orders through 17 Gun Operations Rooms (GOR).[21,22]

As the Allied Forces moved on the offensive into Burma, the early warning system, along with some of its radars moved on barges, jeeps, riverine crafts/amphibious vehicles and relocated to protect the temporary airfields, landing grounds and coasts in the Far East.[23]

It can be deduced that protection of the port facilities and airfields in India's major cities along its eastern coastline through Point and Limited Area Defence, was the guiding AD philosophy behind the C&R organisation of India during the Second World War. In India, the system faced challenges of vast geographies, climate, terrain, lack of trained manpower and unsuitable fighters but nevertheless, played an important role in achieving Allied air superiority.

The Journey after Independence

Records of Royal Indian Air Force (RIAF) retaining this C&R system post-1945 are unclear, however, on independence, the erstwhile radar branch personnel were recalled, setting up a system from this wartime institutional knowledge and repairing radar sets found dismantled at former RIAF airbases.[24,25]

The decade of 1950s saw the training of Technical/Signals Branch officers at Jalahalli[26] and the UK, who created a fledgling C&R system from 15 radars procured from Britain, set up along five 05 SOCs and associated GCI and EW units. In parallel, the first batch of FCs was trained in the UK in 1952, followed by the establishment of a C&R school in Jodhpur in 1958. The shooter resources were limited to a few squadrons of tempest/spitfires[27] and only two air defence artillery units of the Indian Army (IA).[28]

The resultant AD cover was scanty and limited to radar cover for Delhi, Bombay and Calcutta and along the Western borders with SOCs at Ambala and Jodhpur.[29] The system was mostly manual with communication, limited to Post & Telegraph (P&T) landlines, Wireless Telephony (W/T) and High Frequency Radio Telephony (HF R/T) as standby.

The decades of the 1960s and 1970s saw the AD landscape evolve through three wars and the resultant C&R system adapted to incorporate a layered sensor chain with static high-powered radars (Star Sapphires followed by THD-1955) at Air Defence Direction Centres (ADDCs equivalent to SOCs). The IAF engineers sowed the seeds of indigenisation in C&R as early as the 1965 War, when on abrupt cessation of US support they stepped in to operationalise the newly acquired American Star Sapphire radars.[30] This experience proved valuable as further inductions of high- and medium-powered radars under co-production at Bharat Electronics Limited (BEL) and the indigenous Tropospheric Scatter network was enabled by the Air Defence Ground Environment System (ADGES) plan set up in 1970.

Alongside the ADDCs, medium-powered radars such as PSM-33 and TRS-2215 were inducted as GCIs. Mobile radars such as the P-30/P-40 series, along with the ST-68/INDRA series inducted in the 1980s, formed the bulk of EW radars along the borders, also used in GCI/LGCI role when deployed. During the 80s as the low-level mobile radar capability enhanced, the IAF formed Control and Reporting Centres (CRCs) which fused pictures of all Low Level (LL) deployed radars under their Area of Responsibility (AOR), providing Limited Ground Control Interception (LGCI) or Limited Area Defence Control (LADC) capabilities. The CRCs undertook low-altitude identification and interceptions, integrating with both ADDCs, relevant BADC and Divisional Air Defence Control (DADC) centres. The vulnerability of air bases revealed in 1971 was addressed through point defence of each base through the adoption of the Base Air Defence Control (BADC) Concept/Terminal Weapon Control Zone (TWCZ), which was the innermost tier within the layered defence concept. Automation efforts in networking such as Automatic/Semi-Automatic/Futuristic Data Handling Systems (ADHS/SADHS/FADHS) processed data in-radar providing radar tracks, threat evaluation, weapon allocation and interception solutions as early as the 1980s. The Low-Level Radar Networking Group (LRNG) also known as the Automated CRC for the CRC network, eventually formed the backbone on which the IACCS philosophy was built and implemented.[31]

This system interfaced with the Command for directions through the Air Defence Control Centre (ADCC) and Command Operations Room and further with Air Headquarters through parallel verticals. Control of Offensive/Strike formations in this entire period was limited to radar and associated radio ranges of forward deployed LGCI units. The operationalisation of Airborne Warning and Control/Airborne Early Warning and Control Systems (AWACS/AEW&C) and IACCS enhanced not just the radio/radar ranges but also the ability of the IACCS nodes to control and manage the offensive air operations, through a shared situational awareness, hitherto possible only for 'Air Defence Operations'.

Analogy of a Spider's Web: Control and Reporting Network

Picking up the threads of the analogy from the *Upanishads* referred to in the introduction of this chapter, the current C&R network and its capabilities is described below.

IACCS Nodes

Through all the evolutionary changes in IAFs Air Defence philosophy– from SOC to ADDC and net-centric IACCS – the underlying philosophy of India's AD C&R System has retained its original character – a common picture disseminated to three levels – Strategic (Air HQ upwards), Operational (Commands), and Tactical (field). It is pertinent to reiterate that these Nodes, as also the ADDCs before them, coordinate the execution of OCA missions, apart from AD operations, as part of a common air war strategy – the IACCS enabling the same, through enhanced situational awareness.[32]

Just as the Spider picks up activities across its own web and does not need to be at every strand, the IACCS nodes integrate sensors (military and civil), and shooters [(Aircraft, SAMs, AD Arty, **Man-Portable Air-Defence Systems** (MANPADS)] into a chain of command linked to respective Command and Air Headquarters through Operations rooms.[33] Each IACCS node serves as a nerve centre for receiving tracks, creating a Recognised Air Situational Picture (RASP), identification, threat evaluation and designation of targets to appropriate shooters for interceptions/kills. The IACCS also facilitates real-time transport of images, data and voice, amongst satellites, aircraft and ground stations. This network-centric design fuses offensive and defensive operations into interdependent, synergistic air battles under centralised control and decentralised execution. Nodes enable shared situational awareness across the Services through networks of Akashteer and Trigun. During Operation SINDOOR, this integration created an effective air defence shield while enabling calibrated offensive actions and responses.[34]

Conceived as a two-phase programme, Phase I of the IACCS reportedly involved establishment of five IACCS nodes by 2015, with additional nodes and major enhancements underway since then. The IACCS provides net-centric capability pan-India including its Island territories, and coordinates the early warning and response aspects of the Indian BMD network.[35] Scalable and modular in its core architecture, the IACCS allows expansion of capabilities and interface with futuristic nodes envisaged under Mission Sudarshan Chakra.

The Radial Network (AFNET)

The Web's underlying framework in the form of radial threads originating from the centre till the edges, is the secure communication network riding on AFNET (a high-bandwidth 500-Mbps digitised encrypted communication network) and secure radio/data links. Launched in 2010, AFNET forms the backbone of IACCS and is integral to the net-centric strategy of the IAF, as it enables both communication and data transfer by integrating Satellite Communications (SATCOMs), Wide Area Network (WAN), and Internet Protocol (IP). The system allows integration with a state-of-the-art Human Machine Interface (HMI), and access to live visuals from Unmanned Aerial Vehicles (UAVs) and Imagery Intelligence (IMINT).[36]

Catering to demands of modern warfare, an upgrade of AFNET envisages a future-ready architecture bolstering the grid with features such as superior cybersecurity, Software-defined, converged network, big data analytics, forensic analysis tools etc.[37] Systems under the Software Defined Radio (SDR) framework are expected to further enhance the communication network.[38,39]

Sensor-shooter Network

The overlapping concentric spiral layers represent a 'defence in depth/layered defence' philosophy with sensors and shooters arranged along anchor points to create overlapping engagement zones ensuring continuous fire from first pick up till its destruction. Just as a spider's web can detect and trap any prey touching any strand, the sensor-shooter network detects and traps threats at varying altitude or ranges. The mobile sensors and shooters can be moved to any layer to complement Early Warning and either create covert ground traps for enemy aircraft, desired areas of A2/AD, or defeat enemy OCA effects, as the rapid mobility of the S-400 indicated, during operation SINDOOR.[40]

Outer Spiral: The Indian BMD Programme

The Indian BMD programme is double-tiered with Long-Range Tracking Radars (LRTRs) and Very Long-Range Tracking Radars (VLRTRs) as sensors, which cue land- and sea-based interceptor missiles, catering for both high-altitude and lower-altitude interceptions as part of a two-phased plan.

BMD Sensors: LRTR/VLRTR Series

Based on the design of Israeli Green Pine Radar deployed in 2002 and 2005, DRDO developed the Swordfish LRTR in 2009 with ranges in excess of 600 km. LRTR-2, an upgraded version, extends the coverage to 1,500 km. The first VLRTR, a successor of the LRTR series was made operational in 2017 with ranges of more than 3,000 km. The system detects space-borne threats, and the formation of two new units is approved under a Memorandum of Understanding (MoU) between the National Technical Research Organisation (NTRO) and the IAF.[41] DRDO's ongoing projects on Over the Horizon (OTH) radars and BEL's Long-Range Radar (LRR), SASTRA will complement this layer at expected ranges of about 2000 km.[42]

Maritime and Pseudo Space/Space Segments

The Indian Naval Ship *INS Dhruv*, commissioned in September 2021, adds a maritime component to the detection capability in this segment, besides the land- based radars.[43] Equipped with multi-band radars, the ship reportedly incorporates C3 systems and ELINT capabilities.[44] Development of High-Altitude Pseudo-Satellite Systems (HAPS) for surveillance in the Stratosphere region is also likely to enhance BMD surveillance capabilities[45] Space-based capabilities are to be enhanced under the framework of the Defence Space Agency in the coming years.[46]

Interceptor Missiles

First tested in 2006, the Prithvi Air Defence (PAD) Missile also called *Pradyumna*, undertakes exo-atmospheric interceptions at a maximum altitude of 80 km. The two-stage missile was designed to engage the 300 to 2,000-km class of ballistic missiles at speeds of 5 mach.[47,48] This is likely to be replaced by an upgrade under the nomenclature, Prithvi Defence Vehicle (PDV) interceptor, with altitudes of upto 150 km. In a test undertaken in 2017, the PDV was able to destroy a ballistic missile target launched from over 2000 km, at an altitude of 100 km.[49]

The Advanced Air Defence (AAD) Missile is designed to tackle threats leaking past the PAD, achieving a maximum speed of mach 4.5, at altitudes of 30 km and below, and ranges between 150 and 200 km. This two-tiered defence system intercepts threats launched from ranges of up to 5,000 km away. India's naval BMD capability was demonstrated on 21 April 2023 through a successful interception by an endo-atmospheric interceptor missile launched from a ship-based platform.[50] Phase 2 of the BMD programme is envisaged around the AD-1 and AD-2 hypersonic interceptor missiles capable of intercepting targets launched from beyond 5,000 km.[51]

Middle Spirals: The High/Medium Powered Radars and Ground-Based Area Defence Weapons

Behind the BMD layer, the Airborne Warning/Early Warning and Control Systems (AWACS/AEW&C) and fighter aircraft along with ground-based systems such as the S-400 create a twin-sensor shooter layer, depending on system specifics and dynamic deployment. This creates an offensive AD effect and desired areas of A2/AD strategy implementation.[52]

AWACS/AEW&C

The biggest advantage of the airborne sensors is their flexibility and reach, allowing dynamic surveillance and distributed control of C2 centres, both on land and in the air. The IAF operates the EL/2090 Phalcon AWACS, developed by DRDO in collaboration with Israel. The system features an active electronically scanned array (AESA) radar, Identification Friend or Foe (IFF), ESM/ELINT, and CSM/Communication Intelligence (COMINT) and uses a produces a fused awareness through continuous cross-correlated of sensor data.[53]

IAF also operates the DRDO-Embraer "Netra" AEW&C, featuring an AESA radar since 2017. The system features an on-board 'Intercept Control and Battle Management' (IC&BM) system with functionalities of Advanced Threat Evaluation (ATE), Battle Management, Weapon Assignment, Intercept Control (IC), Guidance and Recovery, allowing options for distributed control of air battle through FCs in the air and the nodes. The system achieves net centricity through fusion of voice and data through multiple lines of communication, including Line of Sight (LOS) and satellite, C-Band Data Link (CBDL), the Ku-Band SATCOM data link (KBDL), and the Very/Ultra High Frequency (V/UHF) bands.[54]

The IAF is planning to induct six new platforms of the next variant, the Netra MK-1A, developed by the Centre for Airborne Systems (CABS) under the aegis of DRDO that includes an AESA-based Primary Radar, ELINT and SIGINT capabilities along with enhanced ranges and other Advanced Mission System Avionics. At the same time, six pre-owned Airbus A321 aircraft have been transferred from Air India to the IAF for the Netra Mk-II programme. The system is likely to feature DRDO's Uttam AESA radar, with detection capabilities of more than 500 km alongside Next-Generation Sensors, Advanced Electronic Warfare Suites, and extended endurance. Both the Phalcon and AWACS are integrated into the IACCS network.

Additionally, the IAF hasplans to induct state-of-the-art Intelligence, Surveillance, Target Acquisition, and Reconnaissance (ISTAR) aircraft, with indigenous technology, enhancing battlefield situational awareness and effect of joint operations.[55]

Sensors-Ground Based Radars

High Powered Radars: The high-powered radar of THD-1955 with a range in excess of 450 km has been in service since the 1980s and has been upgraded by BEL to THD 2.0, including digitised modifications to the transmitter and receiver sections.[56] It is likely to be replaced in the near future by the High Powered Radar (HPR) under development in the Electronics and Radar Development Establishment (LRDE).[57] An active aperture-phased array radar based on solid-state trans-receive modules, the HPR is stated to have four large fixed radar panels and one rotating Identification Friendly or Foe (IFF) antenna, essentially a non-rotating design with planar arrays for 360-degree coverage. The HPR is planned for operations up to an altitude of 3,000 Above Mean Sea Level (AMSL), with a detection range of 2 sq. metre targets at more than 450km.[58]

Medium Powered Radars: The erstwhile PSM33 and TRS-2215 series in this category have now been replaced by Arudhra Medium Powered Radar (MPR) series and Rohini radars. The Arudhra is a 4-D multi-function phased array radar with electronic steering in both azimuth and elevation for surveillance, detection and tracking of aerial targets.[59] Assessed to be capable of tracking 2 sq. metre targets at 300 km between 100 metres to 30 km altitude, Arudhra incorporates an ability to operate under 'intense Electronic Counter Measures (ECM) environment and possible electromagnetic interference'.[60] Reports indicate further development and acquisition by the IAF, of its 'mountain adapted version' for bolstering surveillance capabilities.[61]

The 3D Surveillance Rohini Radar is configured as three mobile units mounted on three vehicles and boasts of high altitude and fast deployability. It operates in S-band, has a surveillance range of more than 200 km covering an elevation of 18 km in height, and incorporates Electronic Counter Counter Measures (ECCM) features of side-lobe blanking, frequency agility and jammer analysis.[62] The radar is designed by LRDE, and is produced through a joint venture between BEL, Larsen & Toubro, Astra Microwave and Entec.[63.64]

Shooters

Rafale: The Rafale features an AESA AI radar (RBE2-AA) with detection ranges upto 200 km. Its air-to-air missiles include MICA in both active/ infrared radar seeker modes, reportedly using a thrust-vectoring motor for improved agility (range around 37 miles), and MBDA Meteor (likely range around 130 miles).[65] AEROS, its all-weather, night-and-day-capable reconnaissance system, adds to sensor capabilities through information such as images in real-time to ground stations. The SPECTRA electronic survival system combines a radar warning receiver (RWR), a laser warning receiver, a Missile Approach Warning (MAW) system which cue a phased-array radar jammer and a decoy dispenser.[66]

Su-30MKI: The Su-30MKI is equipped with N011M AI radar with a detection range of about 150 km in air-to-air mode. An Infrared Search and Track (***IRST***) sensor and optical laser range finder (OLS-30) along with Tarang RWR, and EL/M-8222 EW pod for jamming, combine the effects for surveillance and self-protection. Upgrades to the indigenous Virupaksha AESA radar are planned, for enhanced performance. Air-to-air missiles include R-77 (NATO reporting name AA-12 Adder) with a maximum range of upto 50 miles, indigenous Astra Mk-1 (capable of engaging supersonic targets at a ranges up to 61 miles), R-27 Radar (R)/ Thermal (T) and its extended versions the ER/ET (ranges of upto 37/31/ 59/56 miles respectively), and R-73 for short-range all-aspect infrared homing (maximum range of up to 18.6 miles head-on, 8.7 miles tail-on engagement).[67] The mainstay of the AD fleet, the platform is undergoing the "Super Sukhoi" upgrade.[68,69]

MiG-29 (UPG): Equipped with ZHUK-ME AESA multi-mode AI radar, detection ranges for this aircraft are estimated at about 120 km for a 5 m^2 RCS target. Avionics upgrades include the indigenous dedicated EW Suite D-29, OLS-UEM with detection ranges of 15-55 km, enhanced cockpit with multifunction displays and in-flight refuelling probe for prolonged missions. It integrates R-77 RVVAE BVR missiles (80-100KM range) for active-radar homing, alongside Astra (indigenous BVR), R-27 variants (semi-active radar/infrared ranges from 40-130 km), and R-73 (infrared guided missiles).[70,71]

Tejas: The indigenous LCA MK1 used the Israeli origin Elta EL/M-2032 radar (150 km range), while the Central Scientific Instruments Organisation (CSIO) is upgrading Mk-1A to DRDO's Uttam AESA AI radar.[72] Avionics include a head-up display and Radar Warning Receiver from the Combat Aircraft Systems Development and Integration Centre (CASDIC). Missiles comprise the Astra Mk-1 (100 plus km, tested 2023-2025),[73] the Derby ER with 'full-sphere launch envelope' (61 miles), and short-range options like Python-5, or heat-seeking Advanced Short Range Air to Air Missile (ASRAAM) (31 miles).[74]

Ground Based Weapons

S–400: Inducted in the IAF in 2021, this Long-Range Area Defence weapon system integrates into the IACCS and is capable of engaging aerial targets ranging from ballistic and cruise missiles to UAVs. It can strike at ranges up to 400 km and an altitude of up to 30 km, integrating a mix of radars and a multi-missile system [9M96E (40 km), 9M96E2 (120 km), 48N6DM (250 km), and 40N6 (400 km)]—thus targeting a broad spectrum of threats at various ranges.[75] The IAF contracted for five such systems from Russia, and inductions started in 2021. The system was battle-tested during Operation SINDOOR in May 2025, with the IAF referring to its performance as a "game changer".[76] DRDO's Project Kusha (also referred to as the 'Desi-400') will further enhance this capability.[77]

MRSAM: MRSAM was inducted in the Indian AD network in 2021. Jointly developed by the Defence Research and Development Organisation (DRDO) and Israel Aerospace Industries (IAI), its collaboration included

Indian private and public sectors and MSMEs.[78] Its stated range is 70 km with dual guidance of Command and Active Radar Seeker (RF).[79] While there are unconfirmed reports of extension of this range to 100 km,[80] an enhanced range of 150 km is planned under an Extended Range programme.[81]

Mobile/Inner Spirals: Short-Range and Tactical Sensor Shooters

Low Level Transportable Radars: Highly mobile, these radars are configured for rapid deployments, and include the ST-68, the French LLTR, the LRDE developed Ashwini, 3D tactical control radars and Reporter besides the first indigenously developed erstwhile INDRA series, first built in the 1980s. The IAF operates 19 French LLTRs, 13 of them built in India by BEL. The Ashwini is stated to be a 4-D active array, based on state-of-the-art solid-state technology, is capable of tracking targets ranging from fighters to UAVs and helicopters.[82] The system has a maximum range of up to 200 km, and picks up 0.2 sq. metres Radar Cross Section (RCS) targets up to a range of 50 km, with an altitude coverage from 30 metres to 15 km. It operates in two Revolutions per minute (RPM's) and covers 360-degree azimuth with an elevation coverage of 40 degrees. Its staring mode allows 120 degrees of azimuthal coverage with 40 degrees in elevation.[83]

Low Level Light Weight Radars (LLLWR): The mountainous, valley and urban region radar gaps along with tactical scenario requirements have been addressed through the induction of a series of LLLWRs, named Ashlesha and Bharani. Bharani is a 2-D radar developed for the AD weapon system of the IA. The Ashlesha series is a 3-D surveillance radar, which is quadpod-mounted and detects and tracks fighter aircraft, UAVs and helicopters.[84]

Air Defence Fire Control Radars (ADFCRs): These radars in conjunction with anti-aircraft guns ensure point defence against aerial targets at short and very short ranges. Developed by the LRDE, they incorporate X-band and Ka-band radars, and electro-optical sensors, linked to a gun control unit for directing fire.[85]

Akash Missile System (AMS): Developed by DRDO and produced by Bharat Dynamics limited, AMS is a mobile SAM with an approximate range of 45 km. Its acquisition radar is known as 'Rajendra' and it has four launchers with three missiles each. Akash NG, the future variant, features an active phased array multi-function radar, with a maximum range of 120 km and fire control of up to 80 km, along with an Electro-Optical Tracking System (EOTS) with a range of 45 km.[86]

SAM-3 and SAM-8: The Pechora, also known as SAM-3 in the IAF,[87] has been its mainstay for limited area defence since the 1970s. The system consists of a radar-guided missile launcher and a fire control unit, has an operational firing range of up to 30–35.4 km, with some upgraded versions reaching 35.4 km. It can engage targets flying at altitudes from 20 metres up to 20–25 km with a kill probability of around 92 per cent.[88] The Indian Air Force refers to the OSA-AK SAM as the SAM-8. Equipped with a target acquisition and a target tracking radar, this system can detect targets at a range of up to 45 km and track them at distances of up to 30 km. Its upgrades include modifications to the alignment system from the ground up for the vehicle, mast, antennas, tracker, software, and improved communication. The system has radio command guidance, targeting aerial threats at an altitude ranging from 25 metres to 12,000 metres and at distances up to 15 km.[89]

SPYDER (Surface-to-Air Python and Derby Air Defence System): The SPYDER system is capable of engaging aircraft, helicopters, UAVs and precision-guided munitions.[90] Python 5 and Derby are in service in the IAF, as part of the Spyder Low Level Quick Reaction Missile (LLQRM) programme with a maximum range of 15 km and as air-to-air missiles on the LCA. The system features a truck-mounted Command and Control Unit (CCU) with a surveillance radar and ECCM capabilities, and is capable of 'search-on-the-move fire' within a short halt.[91] The system has been slated for an upgrade vide recent **Defence Acquisition Council** (DAC) clearances.[92]

L-70 Guns: The 40 mm anti-aircraft system was inducted in the IA post the 1962 War. With a maximum range of 4 km, the gun is designed to counter low-flying aircraft through high speeds of elevation and traverse, combined with a high rate of fire. It has undergone upgrades over time to include an electric power lay, laser range finder and thermal imagers for an improved sighting system, on-board computer and a matching generator, making it both mobile and capable of autonomous operations as single gun. Recent upgrades include integration to Akashteer and a drone guard system effectively used in Operation SINDOOR.[93]

The ZU-23-2: This Russian-made 23 mm anti-aircraft system was inducted in the 1960s and is characterised by light-weight and highly mobile configuration along with a high rate of fire. The upgraded version, ZU-23-2B, is fitted with day and night camera, laser range finder and digital fire control computer.[94]

Self-Propelled (SP) Schilka System: Inducted in the early 1970s for mechanised forces, this highly mobile system came on a tracked chassis, generating a high cyclic rate of fire of 3400 rounds per minute with its four barrels, on-board fire control radar and power supply. Upgrades by BEL include a new fire control radar, computer, sighting system, engine and cabin modifications.

Tunguska: Shilka's successor, the 2K22 Tunguska, is of Russian origin designed for AD protection to infantry and tank regiments against low-flying aircraft, helicopters, and cruise missiles in all weather conditions.[95]

Quick Reaction Surface-to-air-Missile (QRSAM): Developed for the IA, this truck-mounted system has a range of 25-30 km and a Single Shot Kill Probability (SSKP) of 80 per cent.[96] The IAF also plans to induct these for point defence.

Surface to Air Missile for Assured Retaliation (SAMAR): Developed by IAF's Maintenance Command in collaboration with Indian private sector companies, SAMAR has a range of 12 km. It essentially refurbishes the air-to-air missiles – R-73E and R-27 – for surface-to-air roles.[97]

Very Short-Range Air Defence (VSHORADS): The DRDO-developed VSHORADS is a Man Portable Air Defence system (MANPAD) tackling aerial targets at a maximum range of 8 kilometres and at altitudes of 4.5

km. This is likely to augment the IGLA series, which operates at similar ranges.[98]

Counter Unmanned Aircraft System (CUAS): Hard-Kill options including Directed Energy Weapons (DEW) along with soft kill, are being explored actively for CUAS roles for both mobile forces of the IA and point defence of VA/VPs.

Mobile Tactical Forces: The deployed forces of the IA integrated under *Akashteer* system, can be envisaged as dynamic networks, which maintain anchor to the web through JADCs on the northern and western borders and associated communication protocols, as they deploy and redeploy in their offensive campaigns. A similar arrangement exists with the Indian naval forces at sea, through the *Trigun* across both coasts. This maintains the web's core strength-distributed sensing and synergistic application of ground fire while adding mobility. A similar arrangement can be created for 'out-of-area contingency' operations in future.[99]

Specialty strands: DRDO's planned developments such as the photonic radars, infrared sensors, space radars, space-based assets, very-high-frequency (VHF)-band surveillance radar (VHF-SR), integrating systems such as the 'Raksha Kavach – Multi-layer Protection against Multi-domain Threats',[100] add additional detection layers. In addition, systems such as the Passive Surveillance Systems (PSS),[101] under various stages of development will develop the sensor grid for the CUAS category.

Sensor-to-Shooter Efficiency: This is where the analogy packs a punch. When a prey enters one strand of the web, the spider does not need to move to catch it – it addresses the threat from an optimum solution. Similarly, in IACCS/future versions, all sensors can cue all shooters. As a space-based asset detects an enemy missile launch, the optimal shooter – airborne, land-based or shipborne – can engage without using its own radar for detection. Built-in redundancies allow overlapping coverage areas alongside communication and backup command and control in the form of standby nodes.

The Future Battle Management Scenario

India's Air Defence transformation – from the Second World War to 2025 – rides on the twin pillars of doctrinal synergy in employment of Air Power (air defence enabling air offence and air offence reinforcing air defence) and a steady path to strategic autonomy. Today, the heart of India's Air Battle Management System, including the IACCS and radars (Arudhra, Ashwini, Ashlesha, HPR, Mountain radars) – are home-grown. AD weapons such as the Akash NG, co-developed MRSAM, commitment to Tejas/LCA series fighters, A-A missiles such as Astra, project Kusha, Close in Weapon System (CIWS)/VSHORADS/QRM, etc. also point to an increased indigenous future.

As the blueprint for Mission Sudarshan Chakra takes shape, these systems will further enhance integration, which will manifest in several ways. Expansion of IACCS with these sensors and shooters creates enhanced A2/AD environments, enabling sustained offensive operations. Suppression and Destruction of Enemy Air Defence (SEAD and DEAD) missions neutralise the adversary's air defence capabilities, allowing follow-on strikes. Meanwhile, FCs at IACCS cue offensive platforms towards targets of opportunity. Networks with the Akashteer and Trigun enable seamless communication, allowing dynamic re-tasking of offensive vectors based on emerging threats or opportunities, while keeping one's own platforms safe. The future system will exemplify this evolution, coordinating with stealth fighters, manned-unmanned teaming, and hypersonic missiles, to achieve air superiority while maintaining defensive coverage and denying use of airspace through A2/AD weapons. This seamless offensive-defensive integration represents the maturation of Air Power employment: a 'system of systems' approach where defensive capabilities enable offensive operations, and offensive actions enhance defensive posture –synergising effects through a non-dual approach to air warfare.

The Way Ahead

Modern IAMD systems have evolved exponentially in scale and intricacy while retaining Dowding's 'cat's cradle network of intelligence'. As a starting point, imagine the current set up expanding to form a National Command

Post at the strategic level and additional nodes such as a low-level node (for drone-counter drone operations) adding up at the tactical level in the immediate future, with a phased addition of capabilities and layers.

The whole web, at whichever stage of development, responds as one being – radars/sensors detecting, threads communicating, command deciding, and shooters engaging – all within seconds. The enemy's air borne vectors, and the supporting C2 structure guiding it, do not see individual systems but a single cohesive 'offence-defence' system that is greater than the sum of its parts and most importantly, is an elaborate expression of one source – the singularity approach.

NOTES

1 Indian Metaphysics Study Material, MA Philosophy, University of Calicut, School of Distance Education, https://sde.uoc.ac.in/sites/default/files/sde_videos/indian%20metaphysic%20%283%29.pdf

2 "The Theory and Practice of Air Power", 18 October 1999, Course 2, Syllabus - Topic 12,United States National War College

3 Air Marshal Diptendu Choudhury, Live on "India's Biggest Forces First Conclave", Republic World, 18 October 2025.

4 Christina Goulter and Harsh Pant, "Realignment and Indian Airpower Doctrine: Challenges in an Evolving Strategic Context", *Journal of Indo-Pacific Affairs,* Fall 2018, Air University, pp. 21-44 at https://www.airuniversity.af.edu/Portals/10/JIPA/journals/Volume-01_Issue-1/04-F-Goulter-Pant.pdf

5 Muhammad Khan, "PAF's Central Nervous System", *Second to None* 17 May 2024 at https://secondtonone.com.pk/2024/05/17/pafs-central-nervous-system/

6 "The Pakistan Army's Air Defence Systems", *Quwa,* 03 February 2024 at https://quwa.org/daily-news/analysis-the-pakistan-armys-air-defence-systems-2/

7 Walter J. Boyne, *The Influence of Air Power Upon History*, Pen & Sword Books Limited, 2005, p.37.

8 MSW, "First Military Uses of the Airplane", Air Warfare, 09 May2017; "How Carlo Piazza's Flight Changed Warfare Forever", History Hit, 23 October 2016.

9 Diptendu Choudhury, "Balakot Plus Plus: Positioning Offensive Air Power at the Centre of Indian Deterrence", Expert Speak, Raisina Debates, 21May 2025.

10 Quote by Field Marshal B. L. Montgomery, in Colonel Charles M. Westenhoff, *Military Air Power: The CADRE Digest of Air Power Opinions and Thoughts,* Airpower Research Institute, Air University Press, October 1990, p. 13.
Sanu Kainikara, *Essays on Air Power*, Air Power Development Centre, Australia, 2012.

11 Diptendu Choudhury, *Strategic Premises for the Future of India's Air Power*, Special Reports, Observer Research Foundation, 24 February 2025.

12 Sinclair McKay, *The Secret Life of Fighter Command*, Aurum Press Ltd., 2015.

13 Sophy Antrobus, "The Next Battle of Britain: Rebuilding the UK's Air and Missile Defence Posture", Kings College London, 13 May 2025 at https://www.kcl.ac.uk/the-next-battle-of-britain-rebuilding-the-uks-air-and-missile-defence-posture

14 Sinclair McKay, no. 12.

15 *The Evolution of Homeland Missile Defense*, CSIS Missile Defence Project 7 April 2017.

16 "What Did Fighter Command do after the Battle of Britain?" at https://www.iwm.org.uk/history/what-did-fighter-command-do-after-the-battle-of-britain

17 *Doctrine of the Indian Air Force 2000-22* at https://cms.spacesecurityportal.org/uploads/IND_Doctrine_Air_Force_832d5b6c62.pdf

18 *Counterair Operations*, US Air Force Doctrine Publication 3-01, US Air Force, 15 June 2023 at https://www.doctrine.af.mil/Portals/61/documents/AFDP_3-01/3-01-AFDP-COUNTERAIR.pdf

19 Preston-Hough and Peter Norman, "A Critical Analysis of the Royal Air Force Air Superiority Campaign in India, Burma and Malaya, 1941-1945", PhD Thesis, University of Wolverhampton, April2013 at http://hdl.handle.net/2436/299634

20 "Secret Radar at Rendugullapalem during World War II", Team Yo! Vishakhapatnam, April 2025 at https://www.yovizag.com/world-war-2-diaries-when-the-british-set-up-a-secret-radar-in-visakhapatnam/

21 *The Campaigns in the Far East, Vol III, India Command, September 1939- November 1943*, Air Historical Branch, Air Ministry.

22 Mandeep Singh, "The Answer Lies Within", *Force*, September 2020.

23 "WWII: People's War" at https://www.iwm.org.uk/collections/item/object/80012718

24 Anchit Gupta, "Eyes in the Skies: Air Defence that Shaped Wars", 07 April 2022 at https://iafhistory.in/2022/04/07/eyes-in-the-skies-how-indian-air-defence-shaped-war-outcomes/

25 Anchit Gupta, "Radars: Tales of the Scanners on the Radcliffe Line", 3 September 2023 at https://iafhistory.in/2023/09/03/radar-resilience-tales-of-the-scanners-on-the-radcliffe-line/

26 "Warbirds of India", Air Force Technical College, 25 November 2008 at https://www.warbirds.in/in/karnataka/bangalore/aftc-jalahalli/

27 https://indianairforce.nic.in/history-timeline

28 Amrita Nayak Dutta, "Corps of Army Air Defence Raising Day to Change to 15 September to Recognise World War II Origin", *The Print*, 31 August 2020.

29 "Eyes in the Sky: How IAF Secured India's Air Dominance", *The Times of India*, 25 May 2023.

30 Anchit Gupta, "IAF's Atmanirbhar Spirit: How Ingenious Engineers Surmounted Sanctions", 26 May 2024 at https://iafhistory.in/2024/05/26/iafs-atmanirbhar-spirit-how-ingenious-engineers-surmounted-sanctions/

31 V.P.S. Rana, *Invisible Warriors-Scientific Art of Fighter Controlling*, KW Publishers Pvt. Ltd., New Delhi, 2025, pp. 185-205.

32 "IACCS: Proves Mettle of IAF's Network Centric Operations", Expert View, Group Captain (Dr) Dinesh Kumar Pandey (Retd), CAPSS, 23 May 2025.

33 Ibid.

34 "Operation SINDOOR: Indigenous Systems Gave India the Edge – More Needs to be Done" at https://airpowerasia.com/2025/08/10

35 "India Versus China Military Balance – Air Defence- Part 4, Indian Radar Systems, Full Afterburner, 15 April 2021 at https://fullafterburner.weebly.com/next-gen-weapons/india-vs-china-military-balance-air-defense-part-4-indian-radar-systems

36 Harsh V. Pant and Kartik Bommakanti, "Towards the Integration of Emerging Technologies in India's Armed Forces", ORF Occasional Paper, 24 February 2023.

37 Gairika Mitra, "How is Technology Acting as the Game Changer in the Defence Sector?"20 July 2020 at https://www.crn.in/big-data-analytics/how-is-technology-acting-as-the-game-changer-in-the-defence-sector/

38 "IAF Develops Indigenous 'Vayulink' Platform for Jammer-proof Communication with Base Station", PTI, 17 February 2023.

39 "IAF Inks Contract with BEL to Procure Software-Defined Radios, Boosting its Communication Network", *India Strategic*, 11 February 2024.

40 With Superior Tactics, How India's Mobile S-400 Proved a "Game-Changer" in Op Sindoor, While Pak's Chinese HQ-9B Was a Sitting Duck, RonitBisht , Sep 24, 2025, Defence.IN News & Discussion

41 V.P.S. Rana, *Invisible Warriors-Scientific Art of Fighter Controlling*, KW Publishers Pvt. Ltd., New Delhi, 2025, p.164.

42 "DRDO's LRDE Developing Over-the-Horizon Radar (OTHR)", Indian Defence News, 30 March 2024; Jaydeep Gupta, "How BEL's Upcoming 2000km+ Range 'SASTRA' Radar Will Detect Stealth Aircraft and UAVs, Thread Starter", Defence.in, 6 September 2024 at https://defence.in/threads/how-bels-upcoming-2000km-range-sastra-radar-will-detect-stealth-aircraft-and-uavs.9741/

43 Daljit Singh, "C4ISR Architecture for an Integrated Air Defence and BMD: Necessity and Feasibility, *Synergy*, 1 (1), October 2022, p. 116.

44 Sebastien Roblin, "India Quietly Deploys Huge Spy Ship Designed to Track Nuclear Missiles", *Forbes,* 17 March 2021.

45 https://www.drishtiias.com/daily-updates/daily-news-analysis/high-altitude-pseudo-satellite-haps

46 Daljit Singh, no. 41, p.117.

47 https://www.jagranjosh.com/general-knowledge/complete-list-of-indian-air-defence-system-1746352839-1

48 https://cenjows.in/wp-content/uploads/2022/03/Operationalisation-of-India.pdf

49 "Prithvi Defence Vehicle (PDV) Successfully Tested", Team Salute, 14 March 2017.

50 "DRDO and Indian Navy Conduct Successful Trial of BMD Interceptor from Naval Platform", PIB Delhi, 22 April 2023.

51 Rajeev Bhutani, *Operationalisation of India's Ballistic Missile Defence,* Centre for Joint Warfare Studies, 2017 at https://cenjows.in/wp-content/uploads/2022/03/Operationalisation-of-India.pdf

52 Shaza Arif, "India's Acquisition of the S-400 Air Defence System: Implications and Options for Pakistan", *Journal of Indo-Pacific Affairs*, FALL 2021, 25 August 2021.

53 Swaim Prakash Singh, "Prioritisation of AWACS for the IAF", Centre for Air Power Studies,31 August 2022.

54 D.K. Pandey, "Netra – Eyes in the Sky –Indian AEW&C Platforms to Bolster Network-Centric Air Operations" at https://www.magzter.com/ja/stories/business/SPs-Aviation/

NETRA-EYES-IN-THE-SKY?srsltid=AfmBOooc_T7vA0QR1uhWY JwmpPIlBjL7iZf6mUd7Ql2OWMYdserXrBSM2, 2024.

55 "Hypersonic Weapons Represent a New Dimension of Strategic Deterrence", Interview: Air Chief Marshal Amar Preet Singh, Chief of Air Staff, *The Chanakya Aerospace Defence and Maritime Review* Indian Air Force Day Special Issue October 2025.

56 Raghav Patel, "BEL Modernizes IAF's THD-1955 Radar System, Boosting Surveillance Capabilities and Self-Reliance", 28 July 2024, Defence.in at https://defence.in/threads/bel-modernizes-iafs-thd-1955-radar-system-boosting-surveillance-capabilities-and-self-reliance.8708/

57 https://indiandefenseanalysis.wordpress.com/2024/02/24/rising-radar-power-of-indian-air-force-against-china-pakistan/

58 V.P.S. Rana, no. 39, pp. 171-172.

59 "Aatmanirbhar Bharat: MoD Inks Rs 3,700 Crore Contracts with BEL for Medium Power Radars 'Arudhra' and 129 DR-118 Radar Warning Receivers", PIB Delhi, 23 March 2023.

60 "ARUDHRA : India's 4D Medium Power Radar", DRDO/BEL at https://defenceupdate.in/drdo-bel-arudhra-indias-4d-medium-power-radar/

61 Dalip Singh, "DRDO's Arudhra Mountain Radars to Boost IAF Surveillance in J&K, Northeast", *The Hindu Business Line* 25 August 2025 at https://www.thehindubusinessline.com/economy/logistics/drdos-arudhra-mountain-radars-to-boost-iaf-surveillance-in-jk-northeast/article69974519.ece

62 https://bel-india.in/product/3d-surveillance-radar-rohini/

63 https://ssbcrackexams.com/iafs-first-indigenously-developed-3d-mobile-surveillance-radar-rohini-radar/

64 https://www.vrka.in/product/rohini-radar-forged-by-mobility-pvc-patch/

65 Thomas Newdick, "The Air-to-Air Missiles that Equip India And Pakistan's Fighters", TWZ, 8 May 2025.

66 Anil Chopra, "Make In India Rafale", *Indian Aerospace & Defence Bulletin*, 15 June 2025, https://www.iadb.in/2025/06/15/make-in-india-rafale/.

67 Thomas Newdick, no. 63.

68 Abhinav Yadav, "How the Su-30MKI Fighter Jets can Lock onto Targets without Even Facing Them, WION, 15 September 2025.

69 Athul, "Forget Rafale & Tejas: We Need Super Sukhoi Now!", DriveSpark, 2 September 2025 at https://www.drivespark.com/off-beat/why-upgrading-sukhoi-su-30mki-to-super-sukhoi-is-crucial-for-india-075549.html

70 Vishal Thapar, "Upgraded IAF MiG-29s SPAR with Omani F-16s", *SP's Aviation*, (11), 2019 at https://www.sps-aviation.com/story/?id=2670&h=Upgraded-IAF-MiG-29s-SPAR-with-Omani-F-16s

71 Pratisht Chaudhry, "The BAAZigars: All you need to know about the MiG-29 UPG", Air Power Asia, 06November2021.

72 "Uttam AESA Radar for Tejas Mk1A Confirmed by HAL" 23 September 2025 at http://ddefencenewsindia.in

73 "Tejas Fighter Jet Successfully Test Fires Air-to-Air Astra Missile", DD News, 13 March 2025 at https://ddnews.gov.in/en/tejas-fighter-jet-successfully-test-fires-air-to-air-astra-missile/

74 Thomas Newdick, no. 63.
75 https://www.studyiq.com/articles/s-400-missile-defence-system/
76 https://www.aninews.in/news/national/general-news/iaf-chief-says-s-400-missile-system-a-game-changer-did-not-let-enemy-operate-in-its-own-territory-during-op-sindoor20250919211852/
77 "Surveil and Defend", *Jane's Defence and Intelligence Review*, July 2025.
78 https://www.sps-aviation.com/story/?id=3002&h=Induction-of-the-MRSAM-Missile-System
79 https://bdl-india.in/MRSAM1
80 https://idrw.org/mrsams-extended-reach-iaf-quietly-inducts-upgraded-variant/
81 P.C. Katoch, "New MR SAM – Beefing Air Defence", *SP's MAI*, at https://www.spsmai.com/experts-speak/?id=231&q=New-MR-SAM-beefing-air-defence
82 "Aatmanirbhar Bharat: Rs 2,906 Crore Contract Signed with BEL for Low-level Transportable Radar (Ashwini) for IAF", PIB Delhi, 12 March 2025.
83 V.P.S. Rana, no 39, pp. 173-175.
84 https://bel-india.in/product/low-level-light-weight-radar-aslesha/
85 V.P.S. Rana, no 39.
86 https://bel-india.in/product/akash-new-generation-mfr-ccu/
87 https://www.facebook.com/IndianAirForce/videos/iaf-pechora-sam-3/399207807132503/
88 "Pechora Unleashed: Inside the Indian Stealth Killer that Hunted Pakistani Drones", Science Desk, *India Today*, 9 May 2025; Raghav Patel, "IAF's Upgraded Soviet-Era S-125 Pechora Proves Potent against Advanced Turkish-made Pak Drones, Validating Extensive Modernization Efforts", 16 May 2025 at http://defence.in/threads/iafs-upgraded-soviet-era-s-125-pechora-proves-potent-against-advanced-turkish-made-pak-drones-validating-extensive-modernization-efforts.14135/
89 https://www.zetwerk.com/blog/pinaka-indigenizes-the-osa-akms-missile-alignment-system-bolstering-indias-air-defense-capabilities/
90 Tulika Tandon, "Indian Air Force (IAF) SPYDER: All You Need To Know", *Jagran Josh*, 23 May 2022 at https://www.jagranjosh.com/general-knowledge/indian-air-force-iaf-spyder-all-you-need-to-know-1653309599-1
91 "Rafael's SPYDER ADS Family", *Vayu Aerospace and Defence Review*, 31 January 2020.
92 "IAF to Procure New Mountain Radars and Upgrade Weapons, *Air Force Technology*, 6 August 2025.
93 Sheershoo Deb, "Full List Of India's Air Defence Systems", Defence XP, 23 August 2020.
94 Naresh Chand, "Air Defence Guns – Current and Future Relevance", *SP's Land Forces*, 6, 2018 at https://www.spslandforces.com/story/?id=571&h=Air-Defence-Guns-andmdash;-Current-and-Future-Relevance
95 "India to Upgrade Soviet-Era Anti-Aircraft Guns to Counter Drone Threats Along Borders", Defence News Army, 7 January 2025 at https://www.armyrecognition.com/news/army-news/2025/india-to-upgrade-soviet-era-anti-aircraft-guns-to-counter-drone-threats-along-borders
96 https://bel-india.in/product/quick-reaction-sam-qrsam/

97 https://www.sps-aviation.com/experts-speak/?id=797&h=SAMAR-and-Akash-AD-Systems

98 https://vajiramandravi.com/current-affairs/vshorad/

99 *Net Security Provider: India's Out-Of-Area Contingency Operations,* Task Force Report, Military Affairs Centre, IDSA, 3 December 2012 at https://www.idsa.in/idsa-event/net-security-provider-indias-out-of-area-contingency-operations

100 "With the theme 'Raksha Kavach - Multilayer Protection against Multi-domain Threats', DRDO to Showcase Path-breaking Innovations during Republic Day Parade 2025", PIB Delhi, 23 January 2025.

101 "Indian Air Force to Acquire Twenty Passive Surveillance Systems for 'sharpening' its Air Defence Operations", *Organiser,* 25 January 2024 at https://organiser.org/2024/01/25/218170/bharat/indian-air-force-to-acquire-twenty-passive-surveillance-systems-for-sharpening-its-air-defence-operations/

SECTION II

Conceivable System Architecture

3

Sudarshan Chakra for India

Lt Gen Balraj Singh Nagal (Retd)

Introduction

Prime Minister's Statement, 15 August 2025

"When I remember Lord Shri Krishna, we are seeing that the methods of warfare are changing all over the world today. We have seen that India is capable of handling every new method of warfare. We have shown in Operation SINDOOR, whatever expertise we had in technology. Pakistan has attacked our military bases, our airbases, our sensitive places, our places of worship, our citizens with missiles and drones in countless numbers.... They could not cause even the slightest damage and hence, when technology is expanding in the battlefield, technology is becoming dominant, then for the protection of the nation, for the safety of the citizens of the country, we also need to further expand the expertise that we have gained today.

And that is why I am saying today from the ramparts of the Red Fort that in the coming 10 years, by 2035, all the important places of the nation, which include strategic as well as civilian areas, like hospitals, railways, any centre of faith, will be given complete security cover through new platforms of technology. This security shield should keep expanding, every citizen of the country should feel safe, Whatever technology comes to attack us, our technology should prove to be better than that and hence, in the coming 10 years, till 2035, I want to expand this national security shield, strengthen it, modernise it and hence.... Now the country will launch "Sudarshan Chakra Mission". This "Mission Sudarshan Chakra", a powerful weapon system, will not only neutralise the enemy's attack but will also hit back at the enemy many times more.

We have also decided some basic points for this Sudarshan Chakra Mission of India; we want to take it forward with great intensity in the coming 10 years. Firstly, this entire modern system, its research, development, its manufacturing should be done in our country itself, it should be done with the talent of the youth of our country, it should be made by the people of our country. Secondly, there will be a system which will calculate the possibilities of the future in terms of warfare and work out the strategy of Plus One. And the third thing was the power of the Sudarshan Chakra, it was very precise, it went wherever it had to go and came back to Shri Krishna. We will move forward towards developing a system for targeted precise action through this Sudarshan Chakra and therefore, I pledge to take this work forward with great commitment for the security of the nation and the safety of citizens in the changing ways of warfare." Prime Minister Narendra Modi said on 15 August 2025 in his the Independence Day Address.[1]

Concept of Sudarshan Chakra

The Prime Minister focused on, the dominance of technology in war and the need to remain ahead of the enemy, and stressed on developing a system which prepares for new methods of warfare and future possibilities in terms of strategy of plus one, looks at existing threats and those from emerging technologies, protection of important civil and strategic targets, the need to expand the protective cover, the research, development and manufacturing of future technology within the country by the youth, the creation of offensive and defensive capabilities – all in a span of 10 years, to achieve the goal of national protection and offensive capabilities.

An analysis of the mission statement reveals four features. First, a defining future strategy and warfare characteristics, second, the development of new and niche technologies, third, a roadmap for protection architecture and fourth, a self-reliant talent pool for research, development and manufacturing of the entire system.

The protection is from the northern and western adversary on land and in the air, jointly or separate from the maritime domain. Whilst the threat from these adversaries exists and may increase, there is a necessity to factor-in other countries in the neighbourhood, whose territory or maritime spaces can be used by these two or other inimical States, who may support them. The challenge of the terrain in the north and northwest is peculiar to India and will require special answers.

The Indian Chief of Defence Staff on 26 August 2025 speaking at a military eeminar unveiled the vision for "Mission Sudarshan Chakra", calling it a project that will act both as a protective shield and a striking sword against enemy air threats. "The Sudarshan Chakra is not just a defensive idea but a comprehensive national air defence grid".[2]

The CDS cited the Defence Research and Development Organisation's (DRDO) successful maiden tests of the Integrated Air Defence Weapon System (IADWS) as a major leap forward. The system integrated Quick Reaction Surface-to-Air Missiles (QRSAMs), advanced Very Short-Range Air Defence Missiles (VSHORADS), and a 5-kilowatt laser weapon, into one operational package.

International Systems

Currently, many air defence protection and offensive systems are being fielded by various countries. Some have been tested in war, some others are yet to demonstrate their claimed capability, whilst some systems are under development. India can benefit by adopting and coopting systems and technologies proven in recent wars. The Israel-Hamas and Russia-Ukraine conflicts and the recent Israel-Iran conflict, are valuable lessons to understand the weapons, radar networks and technologies in use. Operation SINDOOR, the Indo-Pak 100-hour standoff in May 2025, has provided lessons for future air defence needs. China held a Military Parade to commemorate the 80th anniversary of the end of the Second World War, displaying missiles and weapons systems that could be intercepted/ neutralised by India in the future.

The Israel-Iran War demonstrated Israel's dominance in the air interception technology. It successfully intercepted most missiles and rockets fired from Iran, Yemen, Gaza and South Lebanon. Israel developed the Iron Dome in 2006 in response to persistent rocket attacks from Hamas in Gaza and Hezbollah in Southern Lebanon, with an interception range from 4 to 70 km. Later, Israel developed the David Sling for missile and rocket interception for a range of up to 300 km and Arrow 2&3 systems for missile interception for ranges up to 2000 km. The Iron Beam, a laser-based interception system for ranges up to 2.5 km, is now ready for deployment. In all the interception systems, the integration of Radars and networks ensure that only those targets are destroyed which strike value targets while those landing in open areas are allowed to continue. This ensures conservation of interceptor missiles. India has very valuable lessons to draw from Israel's air defence systems.

The US air defence has the Short-Range Air Defense (SHORAD), the medium-range air Defence and the long-range missile defence system. The SHORAD is based on the Stinger and Hellfire Missile with a 30 mm chain gun in a close support role. Medium-Range Air Defence consists of the short- to medium-range ground-based system that uses the AIM-120 AMRAAM Missile in a surface-to-air role, for air and cruise missile interception. Long-range air and missile defence comprises Patriot (Phased Array Tracking Radar for Intercept on Target) System, designed to counter aircraft, cruise missiles, and tactical ballistic missiles, utilising interceptors like the PAC-3 or the SkyCeptor. The THAAD intercepts ballistic missiles in their terminal phase. With a long-range capability, it is capable of intercepting ballistic missiles at ranges of 150 to 200 kilometres and with a near-perfect success rate in testing. Some of the systems were deployed to aid of Israel during the war against Hamas and Iran, where the performance was excellent. These systems consist of Multifunction Fire Control Radar (MFCR), UHF Surveillance Radar, Battle Management, Command, Control, Communications, Computers, and Intelligence (BMC4I) Tactical Operations Center; Certified Missile Round (PAC-3 MSE and canister); Launcher, and Reloader. The Integrated Air and Missile Defense Battle Command System, is a unified command and control network designed to integrate data from various sensors and weapon systems to provide a single, integrated air picture and coordinate the defence effort.

The US systems are standalone, for deployment overseas or on naval ships. Now, President Trump has announced the concept of Golden Dome to protect the Homeland from air and missile attacks. The concept is still developing and is likely to be fielded by 2029.

China has deployed an integrated multi-layered air defence system based a number of weapons from short-range to long-range, for example, the HQ 9 TO HQ 29, but what is of great interest is the A2AD system, developed to counter the maritime threat on the east coast and the two island chains. The Chinese system employs satellites, Over-The-Horizon (OTH) Radars, Radars, communication networks, integration centres to coordinate the surveillance, detection, tracking, and manoeuvring ballistic missiles targeting aircraft carriers and ships.It also coordinates the air defence of the east coast of China. It will be valuable to study the Chinese system, to draw important lessons on concepts, technologies and integrated multi-layered systems.

The Russian air and missile defence systems around Moscow such as the S400 and the S500 are state-of-the-art. The war with Ukraine has brought to the fore the role and the threat from UAV, Unmanned Combat Aerial Vehicles (UCAVs) and drones. Both countries have deployed counter systems, which now address the closest and lowest layer of attack profile. Drones in an offensive role have been important in some attacks on Russian forces deep inside Russia and value targets in Ukraine. It will be useful to study the new weapons and systems introduced in the Russia-Ukraine War. Some of these systems are from NATO. The Russian produced new systems indigenously and coopted Chinese wherewithal, as also from other nations supporting Russia. The technology and weapons offer great scope for incorporation in India.

The Indian Context

The Russian S400 is already operational with India, therefore its technology is known, and now a similar system is under development in India under Project Kusha. During Operation SINDOOR, India fielded the Integrated Air Command and Control System (IACCS)[3] and the Akashteer,[4] and these were a barrier Pakistan's missiles failed to penetrate for nearly 100 hours. Essentially, the IACCS co-ordinates, integrates, and controls air defence systems like radars, surveillance systems like AWACS (Airborne Warning and Control Systems), and fighter jets. The IACCS increases the military's situational awareness, allowing it to deploy soldiers, equipment, or other assets, based on the type of threat. Akashteer is India's fully indigenous, automated air defence control and reporting system used by the Army. Akashteer is the core of the Indian Army's Air Defence (AAD) system. It connects smoothly with IACCS (Indian Air Force) and TRIGUN (Indian Navy), creating a clear and real-time picture of the battlefield. This enables the quick and effective use of both offensive and defensive weapons. The technology and systems for IACCS and Akashteer are a mix of imported and Indian systems,; therefore the basic knowhow is available to build and develop the Sudarshan Chakra. The Indian ballistic missile defence system, now under final stages of development, too will be integrated with the Sudarshan Chakra.

Future Characteristics and Trends in Warfare

Future strategy and warfare characteristics will be debated and crystallised continuously by the military and academia, and most will remain in the confidential domain. However, open source debates and predictions will provide the likely trends in the future. Currently the character of future wars is anticipated to be more intense, lethal, dispersed, would be fought simultaneously in all domains, would include economic infrastructure and will use autonomous weapons in all domains. Space and cyberspace will play very crucial roles in the outcomes. Technological improvements in warfare will focus on connectivity and data dominance; future wars will rely heavily on robust information networks and real-time situational awareness. Speed of collection, processing, and dissemination of information will determine effectiveness and success. The reliance on connectivity will make military systems vulnerable to disruption and manipulation by multiple means. Increased lethality and precision will increase the vulnerability of strategic and vital systems. Hypersonics and highly manoeuvrable weapons with greater speed, accuracy, and destructive potential will pose new challenges for the defence systems. Autonomous systems and robotics are poised to revolutionise combat by allowing platforms to operate with decreasing levels of human interaction. These already include unmanned vehicles such as drones (UAVs), Unmanned Combat Aerial Vehicles (UCAVs), unmanned ground vehicles (UGVs), and unmanned maritime systems for reconnaissance, supply, and combat. Lethal Autonomous Weapons (LAWs) could one day make their own targeting decisions. "Swarming" technology, where large numbers of interconnected, autonomous systems overwhelm an opponent, will pose the greatest problems for the interception systems. Future conflicts will feature cyberattacks to disrupt or destroy systems and infrastructure. Information warfare will be used to shape public opinion and build false narratives to cause confusion, disrupt governance and build influence campaigns. Employment of proxies or deniable forces is likely to increase in a "gray zone" between war and peace. Large-scale concentration of forces would be avoided because of the increased lethality of the long-range precision weapons and greater capabilities of combat forces. Forces may need to operate in smaller, more dispersed units with rapid concentration capability and mobility, to increase survivability. This will require resilient communication networks to conduct operations.

New and Niche Technologies for the Future

In the field of new technology development India will have to find solutions for stealth, surveillance, detection, interception and destruction technologies. In an ideal scenario, the aim should be to maintain stealth, and track and monitor every move of the adversary. This is the challenge for our scientists and academia. The most important change must occur in the role of our national technological institutions and universities, to join the government's and public sector undertakings' R&D efforts in determining new and niche technologies to be developed and pursued.

Architecture of Sudarshan Chakra

General

The Sudarshan Chakra will be an integrated multi-layered system. Functionally, it is described under the following features:-

a. Surveillance-cum-detection and tracking systems.
b. Interception and defensive systems.
c. Offensive systems.
d. Weapons systems.
e. Command and Control structures.
f. Communication networks.
g. Nodal Centres.
h. Airborne assets.
i. Non-Kinetics systems.
j. Cyber systems.

For the present, military systems for C4ISR (command, control, communications, computers, intelligence, surveillance, and reconnaissance), BMD, IACCS and Akashteer, will be the foundation for Sudarshan Chakra.

To address threats and attacks from multiple sources and land, sea and air, the Sudarshan Chakra will have architecture and structures comprising space-based surveillance and non-kinetic systems, Anti Satellite (ASAT) Weapons, AWACS, OTH Radars, fixed and mobile radars, UAVs, UCAVs, interception missiles, guns, directed energy weapons, microwave and millimetre wave weapons, particle beam weapons and sound weapons, computer networks, fail safe communication networks, protected command and control centres, airborne control centres, offensive missile systems, aircraft, cyber capabilities, electronic warfare, information and cognitive offensive systems, and artificial intelligence systems. India has adversaries whose missiles have ranges of 180 km, 290 km, 450 km, 600 km, 750 km, 1100 km, 2000-2150 km, 3000 km, 5500 km, 7000 km and 10,000 km. The systems being developed will be designed to cover an area having a radius of 7000 km, covering the entire China and the Indian Ocean.

Surveillance, Reconnaissance, Detection, Tracking, Interception Means

The non-kinetic means for surveillance, detection, tracking and interception will be configured as under:

a. The first or the top layer will be for ballistic missile defence.
b. The second layer will address the threats and attacks from aircraft and subsonic missiles, including cruise missiles.

c. The third layer will be for short-range missiles/rockets and long-range artillery, UAVs or UCAVs. It may be more focused on point/area defence or mobile forces air defence.
d. The fourth and lowest layer will be designed to counter drones, including loitering munitions or very low flying UAVs/UCAVs.
e. In the offensive role, systems and weapons which can attack enemy aerial assets in hostile enemy territory will be part of the top and second layer. The assets for this role at times may be common. The S400/S500 can offensively destroy enemy aerial assets 300-400 km from the launch base. New weapons will be developed to increase the ability to strike deeper into enemy air space.

There will be overlaps from one layer to the other as these functions are not performed in separate compartments.

The specific roles and tasks are elaborated below.

Space: The space domain will see the greatest contest and development in the future. India's surveillance needs will necessitate build-up of satellite capability of continuous monitoring of enemy assets, i.e., weapons, aircraft and missile platforms. The broad capabilities required would be:

a. Any hostile missile must be detected and its trajectory predicted on launch.
b. Tracking the enemy systems and feeding the data into the network grid.
c. Coordinating the destruction of enemy weapons and platforms by air, land or sea-based interceptors.
d. Neutralising the enemy's space assets by non-kinetic means.
e. The role of space will be confined to supporting the other systems, till it remains a weapons-free frontier.
f. Detection of heat signatures is a niche space-based technology that needs attention. While technology to detect ballistic missile launches exists, heat detection technology is needed to pick up signatures from missiles in flight, aircraft, aircraft fired missiles, UAVs, UCAVs, and long-range land fired munitions.

Surveillance and Detection – Land, Sea and Air: Surveillance and detection systems are also needed for air, land and sea sensors.

a. AWACS and OTH Radars for long-range surveillance and detection in air and sea will form the second layer of intelligence and information. These will be formed by fielding different range radars for surveillance, detection, and for tracking enemy targets.
b. Some of the above will be part of the central grid whilst a majority will be mobile systems handled by the Army, the Navy, the Air Force and the Tri-Services Integrated Commands.

Tracking and Interception – Land, Sea and Air at Strategic and Operational Level: During the final stages of tracking and interception a large number of radars will be part of the organisations/units/ships with interception weapons, deployed to intercept the incoming missiles, aircraft, UAVs, UCAVs, and drones/swarms. New types of radars and extremely sensitive movement/heat detection systems are required for a very small cross section of airborne UAVs, UCAVs and drones. Ground sensors to detect UAVs, UCAVs and drones will be deployed to form the closest line of defence.

Tracking, Interception and Destruction Weapons: The integrated networks will link and coordinate the work of organisations and structures with weapons for interception at operational and tactical levels. For each vulnerable area or point, organisations with tracking-cum-interception radars and weapons will be merged with the integrated networks. These are mostly mobile in nature or part of manoeuvrable forces.

Command, Control, Computers and Communication Systems

Integrated Networks for Analysis, Dissemination and Engagement: The information and intelligence from space and long-range surveillance and detection systems, and battle area systems, will need AI-driven networks to produce and disseminate the intelligence to vectors and systems in real-time to initiate action to track and destroy ingressing enemy missiles, aircraft, UAVs, UCAVs and other airborne weapons platforms. A large amount of data will need to be analysed in real-time. That means artificial intelligence, advanced computation, big data analytics, large language models, and even quantum technologies will become essential tools. At the same time, systems will also monitor aerial activity in enemy air space, to launch offensive weapons to destroy aerial systems over enemy territory. Some important targets will be AWACS, AEW aircraft, command & control aircraft and logistic supply chain aircraft of the enemy's Air Force, and strategic assets deep inside enemy territory. These will be in addition to surface-to-surface missiles of the Army.

Command and Control: Command and control organisations and structures evolve with experience and strategic need. Therefore they will evolve further from the current systems.

Weapons and Interception Forces

The weapons to destroy all threats and incoming weapons will correlate to the above layers. The top layer interception system will be based on exo-atmospheric and endo-atmospheric missiles forming part of the BMD.

The second layer interception systems will be based on long-range surface-to-air missiles such as S400/500, aircraft with long- and short-range air-to-air missiles. In the future, even energy weapons may be fitted on both manned and unmanned fighter aircraft.

The third layer will comprise surface-to-air missiles, guns and energy weapons.

The fourth layer will depend on short-range surface-to-air missiles, guns, energy weapons and ground systems to disrupt low-flying aerial craft.

For ships and aircraft carrier groups, all the layer of weapons and radars are fielded on the same platform as a composite system, to intercept at all levels from the same ship.

Israel and other countries are now fielding Directed Energy Weapons (DEW). India too will deploy these weapons in the near future. These will be on land, sea and air.

Cyber

Cyber forces will be established to address threats to communication systems, computer networks, command and control systems, and to offensivelydisable or destroy enemy C4ISR and air defence networks.

Joint Development of Defence

The fourth requirement will witness the joint and synergetic emergence of the military defence base in India. For 70 years the defence sector has depended on the Defence Research & Development Organisation (DRDO) for developing new weapon systems and supporting structures. Similarly, only Government organisations are authorised to produce weapons and supporting systems. Now, with the participation of Indian private sector companies in defence ventures, time is ripe to allow the Indian defence companies to research and develop systems and weapons for the Sudarshan Chakra. All Indian Defence companies working on crucial defence projects should be allowed access to the DRDO and Government Research Centres to optimise the synergy for Sudarshan Chakra. The Official Secrets Act should be applicable to all Indian defence companies working on sensitive projects of national importance. This joint development is crucial to meet the timeline of a decade. The Indian Diaspora has contributed immensely to the US defence and space industry; it is time to replicate the brilliance in India to meet the Prime Minister's deadline and make the nation secure.

Conclusion

The architecture of the Sudarshan Chakra will develop on the existing infrastructure and technology. Lessons drawn from international systems should be used to advance research and development. New warfare requirements will form the basis of future strategy and technology for the new architecture and structures needed. India has embarked on a very ambitious and challenging mission for itself for the protection of the nation from aerial attacks. The Government's defence organisations and the private sector defence industry have an opportunity to deliver the requisite hardware and software in the tight time schedule. The Government has to overcome the bias and apprehension against allowing access to the Indian civil industry to crucial and sensitive military technology. The synergy between the Government organisations and civil industry should also result in the increase of the export potential for the country, and economic development of the country.

NOTES

1 https://www.pib.gov.in/PressReleasePage.aspx?PRID=2156749
2 https://www.timesnownews.com/india/sudarshan-chakra-mission-india-answer-to-iron-dome-to-shield-nation-skies-article-152527136
3 https://www.pib.gov.in/PressReleaseIframePage.aspx?PRID=1855242
4 https://www.pib.gov.in/PressReleasePage.aspx?PRID=2129132

4

Mission Sudarshan Chakra

Air Mshl RGK Kapoor (Retd)

Prime Minister Narendra Modi made a far-reaching announcement from the ramparts of the Red Fort during his Independence Day speech on 15 August 2025. He launched "Mission Sudarshan Chakra", a shield that would protect strategic installations, civilian population centres and places of national and religious importance against enemy attacks. This announcement has deep strategic connotations, especially as we navigate an uncertain geo-strategic and geo-political landscape in a dynamic global environment. Operation SINDOOR brought out the importance of an integrated multi-layered air defence architecture against a variety of threats like drones, short-range missiles and aircraft. This was perhaps the motivation for the Prime Minister to announce "Mission Sudarshan Chakra" during his address to the nation on 15 August 2025.[1]

The Prime Minister christened it as "Mission Sudarshan Chakra", emphasising its importance and virtually equating it to the time-bound execution of "Mission Shakti", the ASAT test India conducted in 2019. He said that the Mission will integrate advanced surveillance, interception, and counter-attack capabilities to enable swift neutralisation of threats across air, land, and sea domains. He went on to say that "the entire modern system should be researched, developed, and manufactured in India, harnessing the talent of our youth. This powerful system will not only counter terrorist attacks but also strike back at the terrorists."

This announcement could not have come at a more opportune time, as Pakistan announced the creation of the Army Rocket Force Command. China also fields a large inventory of conventionally armed Surface-to-Surface Missiles (SSMs), cruise missiles and hypersonic weapons. As a result, India will face a significant long-range precision weapon threat from both fronts. Lessons learnt during Operation SINDOOR and various conflicts around the world are likely to have prompted this decision. The importance of defence against diverse threats has grown in recent years as nations develop multiple vectors to strike an array of targets at all depths in a contested environment. The announcement also signals the nation's strategic autonomy and clear understanding of the changing character of war. It recognises the need to start the defence of our nation not at our borders, but well outside them.

The Shield and the Sword, as CDS Gen Anil Chauhan called "Mission Sudarshan Chakra", will be a whole-of-nation system involving numerous agencies, those dealing with internal security and the armed forces. The fundamental question about the Sudarshan Chakra is what it is going to defend, from whom or what, and how much?

Nations with Missile Shield

The US is a leader in missile defence technology. It has spent more than US$ 400 billion on its missile defence system which comprises Patriot missiles against aircraft and missiles at short range, Ground-Based Mid-Course Defense against Intercontinental Ballistic Missiles (ICBMs), while they are still in space, the AEGIS Ballistic Missile Defense (BMD) system, primarily deployed on naval ships against ballistic missiles from short range to ICBMs, and the Terminal High-Altitude Area Defense (THAAD), which protects against short and intermediate range ballistic missiles. The US has initiated the development of the Golden Dome system at a cost of about US$ 175 billion, with the total cost likely to rise to US$ 831 billion over the next two decades. Golden Dome will have global coverage and will be a combination of offensive and defensive systems. It will be a 'system of systems' combining a robust space-based layer, which will not only undertake surveillance, detection and tracking of hypersonic and ballistic missiles, but also undertake the destruction of missiles in space. The system will be able to neutralise a threat prior to its launch. This is a futuristic autonomous system, which will integrate all five domains and work on the "AI-Enabled Fire Control Concept", to detect, identify, track and neutralise a variety of threats originating from different parts of the world, simultaneously. The system is likely to integrate presently available air defence equipment with those that are developed in the future, across domains.[2]

Russia's Advanced Layered Defences are highly sophisticated, designed to protect major strategic centres like Moscow. Moscow is defended by the A-135/A-235 Ballistic Missile Defence (BMD) system. The S-400 and S-500 systems provide added protection and could be deployed at other vital areas/vital points for their defence against ballistic missile attacks. Russia has optimised its defence against missile and air attacks in consonance with the strategic importance of the defended sites, rather than covering the entire nation with a large landmass, which would be extremely expensive to deploy and maintain. Russia has developed versatile counter-UAS systems during its war with Ukraine.[3]

Not much is in the public domain about China's defence shield. Recent writings indicate that China's air defence system includes HQ-29, HQ-22, HQ-20, HQ-11, HQ-9C and FK-3000, with advanced missile interception and multi-layered protection against aircraft, drones, missiles and hypersonic weapons. The system is integrated with modern radars, AI and drones. The HQ-19 and HQ-29 are designed to protect ground and space-based assets. China is also developing a hypersonic defence weapon designed to detect, track and engage weapons travelling at high Mach numbers. The integrated air defence network is the backbone of this system, which links all weapon systems for coordinated defence. The system can be broadly divided into the sensor layer comprising networked phased array radars in L, S, C and VHF bands, AESA radars, AWACS and AEW&C using AI and ML, to analyse sensor data, improve decision making and enable rapid response to multi-directional and multi-dimensional threats. The system also encompasses both offensive and defensive electronic warfare capabilities, in consonance with the Chinese Anti-Access/Area Denial strategy. Counter drone systems are rapidly moving towards DEW systems (Lasers and high-powered microwave), with kinetic kill being provided by FK-3000 and Type-625-gun systems. The entire system is supported by a space-based layer involving multiple constellations for ISR, communications and PNT. The satellites also complement ground-based radars for early warning and long-range target detection.[4]

The Iron Dome is a well-known defensive system against a wide range of UAVs, rockets and ballistic missiles. The system has matured from the initial Iron Dome, which was optimised for short-range rockets from the Hamas or the Hezbollah. However, as the threat expanded to longer-range missiles from Syria, Lebanon, Yemen and Iran, the shield was expanded to cater to missiles up to a range of 2400 Km. The shield proved to be effective during the 12-day war between Israel and Iran, intercepting almost 90 per cent of the incoming threats. The system comprises the Iron Dome, David's Sling, Arrow 2 and Arrow 3 systems. These were augmented with the Patriot and THAAD systems from the US during *Operation Rising Lion*. The system is highly automated to reject threats that are not likely to cause damage. Israel is considering technological improvements in the system through higher penetration of AI/ML to enhance accuracy, reduce processing time, improve decision making and provide improved situational awareness for a higher probability of interception.[5]

Turkey is developing its own integrated nation-wide air defence system christened "Steel Dome". This project was launched in August 2024. Many of the envisaged systems in the project are in service or are under development. The system is designed to defend against a variety of threats, including drones, aircraft and ballistic missiles. It is a 'system of systems' connecting radars, sensors, and shooters with a robust C2, utilising AI/ML to minimise detection and engagement time. It is segregated into four layers, with interception below 5 km (Short-range), up to 20 km (Medium-range) and beyond 20 km (Long-range).[6]

At least two dozen nations, including Iran and Taiwan, have or are in the process of acquiring missile defence and integrating it with counter-UAS systems to make a counter-air and missile system.

Why Does India Need Sudarshan Chakra

The character of warfare has transformed with advancements in technology. Proliferation of unmanned systems in the form of loitering munitions, kamikaze drones, First Person View (FPV) drones, UCAVs, ballistic and quasi-ballistic missiles and now hypersonic weapons, has become the weapon of choice for nations, since they can strike far with accuracy and lethality across the entire spectrum of conflict.

In the Indian context, Pakistan has announced the formation of the Army Rocket Force Command. Pakistan has developed a large variety of ballistic/cruise missiles and drones. It is also importing a wide variety of drones from China and Turkey. China has perhaps the largest array of conventionally armed missiles and drones in the world. The present air defence systems are inadequate to protect all strategic, civilian and select religious installations from a multi-directional saturation strike, deploying diverse weapons.

In view of the developing threat in our neighbourhood, especially with respect to first strike capability as well as response using drones and missiles, "Mission Sudarshan Chakra" will provide a two-fold effect. First, deterrence by denial, and second, a credible multilayered defence against a range of weapons coupled with a counterattack capability. Sudarshan Chakra will also complement the defence against any potential nuclear attack, thus raising both conventional and nuclear deterrence capabilities.

Sudarshan Chakra will deny any coercive intent our adversaries may have against us, by virtue of expanding drone and missile threats. This will allow a higher degree of safety for our population and allow a stronger response to any misadventure, by enhancing the survivability of our counterattack capability, even though the system may not promise 100 per cent interception of all threats.

What is "Mission Sudarshan Chakra"

"Mission Sudarshan Chakra" will be a nationwide shield to protect strategic, civilian and selected religious sites from enemy attacks, both conventional and terrorist.

Its goals are threefold: to ensure the entire system is researched, developed, and manufactured in India. It will help to anticipate future warfare scenarios through predictive technologies, and create precise, targeted systems for counter-action. By 2035, the aim is to provide a comprehensive national security shield for both strategic and civilian assets.

The networked system will incorporate diverse weapons developed and produced indigenously.

It will counter diverse threats like terrorist infiltrations and attacks, missiles, hypersonic weapons, aircraft-launched weapons, drones, etc.

It will be an integrated system encompassing diverse sensors from all domains and agencies and both kinetic and non-kinetic weapons.

It will incorporate counter-attack capabilities to neutralise threats proactively or dynamically based on real-time ISR.

"Mission Sudarshan Chakra" would fulfil Indian requirements and cater to threats faced from all directions. It should be a scalable and modular system with a building block approach, integrating legacy and modern systems under one architecture.

It must be able to integrate all legacy systems currently in use through digital interfaces. All imported systems must also be integrated into the network. The system must complement, connect and enhance systems in use presently.

A study of systems developed or under development across the world should be undertaken, to identify best practices and challenges.

The system must have full coverage to meet all possible threats to the nation in any medium/domain.

Some Questions on Sudarshan Chakra

- What do we need to protect?
- What are the threats?
- How do we detect the threats?
- How do we identify threats?
- How do we engage threats?

- How do we counterattack potential threats?
- What components are needed for the system?
- What components do we already have?
- How do we network the system?
- How will it be interfaced with other networks for counterattack?
- What would be the counterattack protocols and decision loop?
- How do we ensure decision support and decision-making protocols?
- How do we develop the unified multi-domain C2?
- Where would human-in-loop and human-on-loop be placed?
- How do we segregate the information on a need-to-know basis for decision-making?
- How do we use AI/ML for a decision support system?
- Is Indian industry capable of producing cutting-edge technologies in the designated time-frame?
- What would be the budget needed for such an ambitious system?
- Will the system be 100 per cent reliable to intercept incoming weapons? What is the acceptable level of reliability? What are the requirements for the stated reliability?
- Which agencies would be connected to the system, contributing to the system or drawing data from the system and what would be the prioritisation of the same?
- What would be the Wartime, Peacetime and No-War-No Peace protocols and RoE?
- What would be the manpower needed for the enterprise, and what would be the degree of automation?
- What would be the cyber security protocols?
- Should it be a single-phase or multiple-phase project following a building block approach?
- Very importantly, what would be the policy on how we manage civil traffic and connect commercial aviation agencies into the system, especially to communicate with them? Who takes the policy decisions?
- Will some major civil entities like Reliance Refinery defend themselves with CUAS systems, or will their defence be taken over by the armed forces?

Proposed Broad Structure of the System

The system should provide uninterrupted detection across the entire nation, including island territories, 24/7, 365 days a year. The detection should cater for surveying at least 2000-2500 kilometres beyond the Indian border/ LoC/LAC or the area of responsibility designated by the Government for the armed forces. This would cater for early detection of long-range weapons like cruise missiles, conventional missiles and hypersonic missiles held by our adversaries. It should have the capability to provide point, area and strategic air defence.

The system should be capable of performing both defensive and offensive functions. It must be decided whether the offensive functions would remain limited to the ground, maritime and airborne targets, or must they extend into space, targeting the adversary's space-based assets.

Identify Vital Areas (VAs) and Vital Points (VPs) to be protected by the system across India and island territories. Subsequently, identify the weapons that could threaten these VAs/VPs, to organise the defensive systems needed for protection. All VAs and VPs need not be protected by all the defensive systems. This identification would lead to efficient system positioning and economy of effort. The VAs and VPs could be categorised in order of priority and threat.

All military bases and installations would be protected by multiple systems to provide multilayered protection. Incidental protection offered by area defence systems like the S-400 and MR SAM should be factored into the overall protection matrix.

Provisioning could be worked out once the VAs/VPs are identified and prioritised.

The system should be capable of detecting and engaging all possible threats. This could be a building block approach from a lower level of threat to a higher level, like hypersonic weapons, which need complex defensive systems.

All systems should be agnostic of conflict status to deal with peacetime, No-War-No-Peace, hybrid, sub-conventional, conventional and full-spectrum conflict. Border defence organisations and intelligence organisations must also be connected to the network with access protocols for different situations. Drone incursions are slowly becoming a norm in border areas, and some organisations, including the police, are progressively procuring counter-drone equipment; these should be integrated with a separate data layer for CAPF organisations.

The network would be complex and should integrate all services and organisations involved in national security, since the drone and missile threats are not limited to the military installations alone. Each domain would have its own data layer, which would be fused to form a single picture where the data is drawn as required from a particular layer.

DRDO and PSUs have developed robust networks for the Services. IACCS is a pan-India network that has been connected with the Indian Army's Akash Teer system. The Indian Navy's Trigun is also under integration. This could form the backbone, and the NFS may be used.

There are more than 6000-7000 radars across India, and this number is increasing to fill any remaining voids. This could be the starting point. Additionally, reporting systems of border defence agencies need to be integrated into the network.

Space-based capability is currently negligible and needs rapid expansion for persistent ISR, redundant communication and reliable PNT.

Diverse weapon systems would be required to tackle multiple threats from all directions. Weapon systems should be optimised to ensure economy of effort while providing a high probability of destruction.

A layered system would ensure redundancy and the capability to tackle a saturation attack. Either Ballistic Missile Defence or long-range SAMs like S-400, with MR SAM forming the intermediate layer, would provide the outer long-range layer. The Akash Teer missile system, along with QR SAM and SPYDER, would form the short-range layer and VSHORADS, AD Guns, CIWS, and counter UAS systems would form the innermost layer.

BMD would be for strategic, politically important areas or financial capitals like Mumbai or any strategic installation/city as chosen in the target analysis. The S-400 would protect multiple VAs/VPs in proximity, covering all major air bases and strategic targets. A large number of such systems will be needed to provide overlapping cover.

All these sensors and shooters will have to be networked in a manner that the central joint operations room gets a common operating picture, which is processed using AI to provide decision support to the commander.

The system would be software and technology-intensive, running across all domains and through terrestrial, aerial and space networks. Redundant and secure communications would be an imperative. This will need cyber resilience and hardening with a zero-trust protocol.

The entire system should have centralised control and decentralised execution, where the centralised control provides guidance related to RoE and decentralised execution ensures speedy neutralisation of the threat.

The system would comprise detection, identification and tracking sensors, followed by interception and destruction of the threat and also proactively counterattack enemy targets and potential threats.

Sudarshan Chakra would be a scalable system that will protect in consonance with the envisaged threat. This would imply that while the sensor layer would cover the entire nation, including island territories extending at least up to 2500 kilometres beyond our border, the defensive layer would be structured in consonance with the envisaged threat. Therefore, strategic targets of highest value, like the national capital, would be defended by every component, from CUAS to BMD, while lower threat sites would be defended perhaps only by CUAS and SHORADS. The system should be able to filter out threats that are not likely to cause unacceptable damage. This would ensure that precious resources are conserved and the cost of defending is manageable, an approach similar to the Iron Dome.

Threats

The threats include tactical drones, Medium Altitude Long Endurance (MALE) UCAV, High-Altitude Long Endurance (HALE) UCAV, Stealth UAVs/UCAVs, cruise missiles, Collaborative Combat Aircraft (CCA)/Loyal wingmen integrated with 4.5 and fifth-generation fighters, supersonic cruise missiles fired from sub-surface/surface or air, ballistic and quasi-ballistic missiles of intermediate range, Intercontinental Ballistic Missiles (ICBM), and hypersonic glide vehicles and cruise missiles.

The threats would manifest multi-directionally in multiple dimensions and domains simultaneously, to saturate the sensors and defences.

Typical Sensor-to-Shooter Cycle

One or multiple sensors detect the threat ; thereafter it is identified, tracked by multiple sensors for redundancy, followed by assignment of the threat to a weapon system most suitable to engage. This is followed by an assessment of the success of engagement. All these steps must be automatically controlled, and algorithms must process data emanating from multiple directions in near real time for decision-making. Every step must incorporate adequate redundancy to cater for unserviceability, failure or non-availability due to enemy action.

An AI-enabled system will provide decision support to shorten the cycle time using the optimal resource.

Sensor Layer

A sensor in a single dimension or domain cannot detect wide spectrum of threats. A multi-dimensional and multi-domain sensor layer will be necessary to detect threats, using all mediums from sub-surface to space. Space has become the most dominant and utilised domain for ISR applications. Each domain will have its data layer, which will have to be fused for the formulation of a comprehensive picture

Threats like ballistic missiles, hypersonic weapons and stealth aircraft would have high chances of detection by space-based sensors. Full spectrum, including acoustic, infrared-, radar, electro-optical and passive sensors, are needed for timely detection and tracking. All these sensors need to be integrated into a single network with redundancy, and connected through terrestrial, aerial and satellite links.

Space-based sensors can only detect ballistic missile and hypersonic weapon launches due to line-of-sight issues with ground-based and airborne radars. A space-based layer supports and facilitates MDO; therefore, the space-based assets have to be protected against kinetic and non-kinetic attacks to ensure the integrity of the sensor system.

The radars must cover all bands – VHF, L, S, C and millimetre wave. AWACS, AEW&C and UAVs would be the aerial contributors to the sensor grid. Space-based radar, EO/IR, and ELINT payloads would also contribute to the detection of threats. Multiple systems would pick up the threat simultaneously; much of this data would be processed at the sensor level, while the inter-sensor inputs would be processed by an AI-enabled system at the ground station.

The AI-enabled decision-making will allow the commander at all levels to choose the most efficient, cost-effective and successful defensive weapon from a plethora of weapons in the area. For example, the AI solution would inform the commander that a DEW counter UAS system would be most suitable against a small UAS rather than a SAM, since it would match threats to available system capabilities.

For the offensive segment, the ISR part of the sensor layer would also process the ELINT and radar inputs, to detect a potential threat across the border, which would be confirmed using EO/IR satellites or aerial platforms. Once the target is detected, it is identified using AI image correlation to confirm the type of target. An AI-enabled system allows quick detection, identification and geo-location. The commander is then presented with the available vectors in the operational area along with time to target and the best option by an AI-assisted decision support system. This substantially shortens the sensor-to-shooter loop and enables near real-time dynamic targeting.

Defensive Segment

The first requirement of any defensive system is to detect the threat early to provide maximum warning. Thereafter, identify the threat, track it and then destroy it using the most effective weapon in the system.

Improvements in the accuracy and lethality of weapons necessitate a robust sensor layer. Both ground and air-based sensors have major limitations in picking up ballistic missiles, hypersonic weapons and stealth aircraft/UAVs. This limitation can be overcome by placing sensors aboard satellites in space. A combination of electro-optical, infrared, synthetic aperture radar and hyperspectral sensors is needed to cover the entire spectrum of threats and provide round-the-clock and all-weather capability.

India has adequate ground-based radars of the three Services and civilian agencies. These need to be networked for a seamless, redundant and Recognised Air Situation Picture (RASP). Airborne sensors in the form of AWACS/AEW&C need to be augmented to provide round-the-clock coverage across our borders. Other sensors include those deployed on P-8I/other airborne platforms and UAVs, which are likely to be augmented with more such systems in the future, including Sea/Sky Guardian UCAVs. All ground and airborne sensors would have to be integrated. Consequently, all these sensors would be integrated with space-based sensors for a single RASP at the central level (National Command and Control Centre) and limited geographic RASP at the operational level.

The command centre would be the nodal agency dealing with all the threats at the national level, with decentralised execution at the operational and tactical levels. After one or more sensors pick up a threat, it will be identified and then tracked by the most appropriate system for destruction. Since many threats are likely to appear simultaneously, including swarms of drones and salvoes of missiles, the information must be processed by an AI-enabled system. This is important after the experience of the Israel-Iran war, when more advanced Iranian missiles were able to evade defences.

The tracking and destruction of incoming threats would be undertaken by systems most suited to tackle the threat. The systems would be arranged in a multi-layered format. With CUAS and VSHORADS forming the innermost layer, followed by SHORADS (Spyder and OSA-AK, Pechora, Akash NG, QR SAM), medium-range SAM, S-400/Kusha long-range SAMs and the outermost layer of BMD to take care of ballistic and quasi-ballistic missile threat. The objective would be to choose the most appropriate weapon for the incoming threat. For example, even if a drone is detected at farther ranges, it would be allowed to come into the lethal envelope of the Counter UAS system rather than being engaged by a SAM at farther ranges.

The defensive layer would present a range of options from tackling the threat using interceptors in space against hypersonic or ballistic missiles, or using exo- or endo-atmospheric interception from ballistic missile defence systems, or using long-range SAM for intercepting short-range ballistic or cruise missiles to counter UAS systems or short-range SAM against diverse types of drones. It could also include a counter-missile or drone mission by an interceptor drone or fighter aircraft. Aircraft-to-aircraft engagement will also be a choice available in the defensive segment of the system. It is in this context that the right choice must be made and the right weapon/platform must be chosen. An AI-enabled fire control system would provide decision support under such circumstances.

The weapons available are space-based interceptors, BMD, S-400 or long-range SAM, MR SAM, AKASH, QRSAM, VSHORADS, CIWS, AD Guns, DEW systems, Counter UAS systems, fighter aircraft and interceptor drones. Their deployment would be guided by the classification of VA/VP.

Indigenous systems like Kusha, QRSAM, VSHORADS and CIWS would greatly enhance the capability and lethality of the defensive layer. With drones becoming less dependent on GPS and RF guidance, DEW (Laser and high-powered microwave) would become a weapon system of choice in engaging drones and swarms of drones. Counter-hypersonic weapons should be developed over the next ten years, during which the system is developed and deployed.

Considering the present status of space-based capability and plans for the near future, it would be prudent to leave the space interceptor capability for the future.

Offensive Segment

The offensive component of the system would ensure a quick counterattack against present or potential threats. The targets would include terrorist camps, UAS launch and storage bases, missile sites and launchers, leadership command and control centres, etc. Loitering munitions, kamikaze drones, sub-surface or surface, ground and air-launched cruise missiles, surface-to-surface missiles and air strikes, could undertake the task.

There is a need to formulate offensive protocols and RoE separately to ensure the response aligns with higher directions. The flow of information to the correct agency undertaking the strike is extremely important. Redundancy and Battle Damage Assessment of the mission must be factored into the mission profile, which would involve the inclusion of Space Command and Cyber Command in mission orders in future.

Command and Control Segment

Command and Control will be the most important function of this system and the nerve centre for decision-making. Key functions of the C2 system would be sensor and data integration to create a high level of situational awareness. Decision-making and coordination is necessary to respond rapidly to evolving threats by coordinating and synchronising actions in all domains and among all assets.

A unified command centre should be established to link all agencies at the central level. Representatives of all agencies for deconfliction and agency-related inputs, should man this. The system must present a coherent and user-friendly common operating picture at this level. The Graphical User Interface must be user-friendly, and the dashboard must have drop-down menus for quick action. Since the IAF is responsible for the air defence of the country, a senior IAF officer should be heading the control centre. The second layer of C2 would be at the respective commands or agency headquarters for undertaking interception.

The regional commands/theatre commands and field formations should have control over their assets and take decisions based on the directions of the higher formation. The system would be highly automated to process and analyse huge data to enhance situational awareness and assist the decision maker at all levels, to make a decision; consequently, action will be initiated at the unit or section level through precise fire orders.

For the counterattack, the decision must be taken at the command level, where the commander would be provided the optimal system to undertake the counterattack from amongst the available options. This would necessitate an updated own force disposition. This is where the rights must be distributed to the requisite commander to ensure that their own force disposition is available on a need-to-access basis.

Communication redundancy must be ensured by terrestrial, line of sight, Tropo and SATCOM with minimum latency. Dedicated CDMA links upgraded to 5/6G with services should also be leveraged. Communication satellites in Low Earth Orbit (LEO) will greatly reduce latency in communications.

Zero-trust protocol must be implemented at all network centres and operation rooms for the security of data.

This will be the most complex and challenging part of the system since the Services and agencies still operate in their own silos with their own protocols. Getting all the stakeholders into a single architecture will require a whole-of-government approach; otherwise, the system would be confined to the armed forces.

Network-Centric System

The entire system should be network-centric with main and standby data centres to ensure redundancy. The network must have redundancy through terrestrial OFC with alternate lines, Line of Sight links, SDRs, implement edge computing at the sensor nodes for real-time data processing, encryption of all data must be ensured, and as Quantum computing and cryptography are implemented, the network must also upgrade.

Network security must be ensured through biometric systems, access control, and cybersecurity, to upgrade to futuristic biometric technologies. The system must be resilient to attacks and should be able to monitor any anomalies automatically.

The network architecture must ensure that it is not susceptible to single-point failure. This calls for a distributed system architecture and a scalable and modular network. The data centre and sensor nodes must be well protected against terrorist, cyber or kinetic attacks. A mesh architecture would be preferable.

Role of AI/ML and Quantum Computing

AI/ML and later quantum computing and cryptography will be at the heart of the system. They will be integrated into every function, layers and decision-making cycle.

At the bottom of the pyramid, AI will be integrated at the sensor level. Consequently, it will integrate radars, EO/IR, SIGINT and EW feeds from all sensors. ML algorithms will perform real-time target correlation and deconfliction to identify and classify targets. Through their databases, they should be able to recognise low observable and high-speed manoeuvring targets and anticipate jamming conditions in congested environments. They would be able to clearly classify between friend and foe to avoid fratricide.

After target identification and classification, the algorithms would prioritise the most suitable weapon system.

AI/ML would help fuse data first between sensors of a Service, organisation and civilian sensors and then fuse all of them to form a common operating picture with minimal latency. Data would be flowing from the Military, DRDO, Indian Space Research Organisation (ISRO), National Technical Research Organisation (NTRO), Central Armed Police Forces (CAPF) and civil aviation. It would also help in trajectory identification and resource allocation to tackle incoming threats.

The system should leverage the advantages of quantum computing, quantum radars and sensors, Quantum Key Distribution (QKD) for un-hackable datalinks and real-time multi-threat engagement. This would be improving on the gains made by using AI/ML. Threat simulation models should first be developed using AI and then upgraded to quantum computing. Research & Development (R&D) organisations could also be tasked to develop quantum communication systems for secure/fail-safe communications.

Once quantum computing evolves to an operational level, AI-quantum integration could be studied. While AI/ML will provide the sensor-level and functional-level data processing and analysis, quantum computing will help in decision-making against a saturation strike. Quantum-enhanced ML will also offer solutions against technologically evolving threat scenarios like pattern recognition, likely radar frequency hopping, and adversary behaviour prediction.

Typical Scenario

A typical operational scenario would involve a base or city being attacked by multiple weapons like drones, cruise missiles and ballistic missiles. The defensive system would detect these threats, process information like the type of weapon, point of launch, trajectory, estimated point of impact and time available. This data would be compared with the defensive measures available in the area and at the base. The system would then choose the most optimal set of interceptors and designate the drones to the CUAS system and cruise missiles to a SAM system or even to a fighter class of aircraft and SSMs, to either long-range AD system/BMD for terminal/ Endo-atmospheric or Exo-atmospheric engagement. This will ensure that multiple weapons are not tackling the same threat. If the sensor grid establishes that some of the incoming weapons are likely to fall harmlessly, then they will not be engaged.

The system would also identify the place of launch and establish the presence of missile launchers and weapon storage nearby to undertake a counter strike using the most optimal weapon system from among the available loitering munitions, artillery, ship-launched missiles, land attack cruise missiles, surface-to-surface ballistic missiles or an air strike. Also, the command-and-control centre involved in the attack would be identified by space and cyber systems for a strike by the most suitable weapon system.

Possible Architectures and Phases of the Project

In view of the complexity and diversity of assets coupled with huge budgetary requirements, it is suggested that the project be phased out. Operation SINDOOR demonstrated basic multi-layered integrated AD capability. IACCS is a pan-India operational system. Akash Teer has been integrated, and so, the backbone to commence "Mission Sudarshan Chakra" exists.

In Phase One, the present architecture will provide defence against drones, missiles and aircraft in limited areas and to a limited extent, since both the network and weapons are limited in capability and capacity. However, this will lay the foundation for further expansion of the system and provide vital inputs for the likely challenges in the future. This phase should aim to integrate the three data layers of land, maritime and air domains. The C2 architecture needs to be established in this phase with clear directives for the way forward, as more technologies are added in subsequent phases.

The second phase could be spread over the next three years (2027-2030) by expanding the space-based layer, further expanding the network, inducting new weapons like the long-range indigenous SAM Kusha, CIWS, SHORADs and DEW. This will expand the counter-drone and missile umbrella, especially against short-range missiles. The specific space-based capability must be in the form of missile launch warning. Integration of the cyber and space domain data layers should be achieved in this phase, thus completing integration of all data layers and AI/ML assistance in the cognitive domain.

The third phase could be spread over the next five years (2030-2035), leading to completion of the system against all drone, aircraft, cruise missile and ballistic missile threats. However, the system would still not be fully functional against hypersonic weapons. This would call for expanding long-range DEW and BMD capability and further enhancing the space-based sensor layer to cover every assigned installation in India. By the end of the second phase, the capability will be ready in terms of networks, complete integration of all agencies, an AI/ML-based decision support system and integration of all data layers.

The fourth phase (starting 2035) could be developed in consonance with the technological developments over the next ten years. In this phase, the system could be expanded further in terms of its envelope, sensors, platforms, equipment and weapons. This phase would cater for sixth-generation fighters, next-generation drones and missiles, and hypersonic and space-based orbital weapons. Weaponisation of space is likely to have progressed in this timeframe by the US, Russia and China. The space layer during this phase should be completed to detect, track and engage other space-based systems, ballistic and hypersonic weapons. It is believed that quantum computing, cryptography and sensing would have reached some kind of maturity for operationalisation and therefore, these technologies could be inducted in the last phase. Consequently, the system could be upgraded based on the scalable, modular and open architecture philosophy.

Some Thoughts[7]

The first step should be to formulate a blueprint of the system in consonance with the scale of the system. A building block approach would provide immunity from unforeseen risks and technology disruptions. Drawing realistic qualitative requirements and phasing out of the programme will be key to implementation.

The budget requirement would depend on the architecture and technological requirements.

Multiple drones and missiles tend to overwhelm the defensive umbrella, where the decision cycle needs to be reduced to a few minutes. Modern missiles are highly accurate, and the current systems tend to get overwhelmed, as was observed during Iran's missile attack on Israel in the latter part of the conflict. The system needs to be developed with technological improvements in missiles and autonomous airborne, land and maritime systems.

With ground and airborne sensors in place, the space-based network would be inescapable for persistent surveillance. This would involve much more than what is envisaged in phase-III of Space-Based Surveillance (SBS). The space-based layer would involve satellites in Low Earth Orbit (LEO), Medium Earth Orbit (MEO) and Geo Stationary Orbit (GEO), for both surveillance and communication.

Intelligence Surveillance Target Acquisition and Reconnaissance (ISTAR) aircraft are also necessary in the sensor and control grid for rapid response to any threats by dynamic targeting.

Large number of CUAS systems will be needed to protect all the designated installations at all depths. Both hard and soft kill systems must make up this grid. The requirement of Directed Energy Weapon capability (Laser and high-powered microwave systems) to cover all sites will be high to counter autonomous drones. Air defence weapon systems will also be needed in large numbers. There is a need to develop longer-range DEW systems to intercept missiles. This will be more cost-effective in the long-run.

The system needs to be highly reliable with a high probability of engagement. No system can ensure 100 per cent interception of incoming threats.

Defining effectiveness in terms of the percentage of interception and destruction would guide the complexity of the system and technological requirements. This would guide the expectations from the R&D organisations and industry. A realistic assessment is therefore necessary.

The system must be able to handle threats across the entire spectrum from low and slow UAVs to hypersonic missiles.

The sensor layer must be highly accurate to identify the type, profile and likely point of impact of the incoming threat/weapon. This will help the system ignore weapons that are not likely to cause damage.

The cost needs to be reasonable for implementation. This can be achieved by adopting a building block approach, a scalable and modular system based on an open architecture philosophy, to absorb future technologies. The first step should be to network, deploy all available systems, and test their viability through an exercise. Each layer of sensor, defensive and offensive segments could be expanded as technology and assets improve.

A red team should be formed to regularly assess the system readiness and its operational capability. War gaming and simulation must become an integral part of the system.

Assessment of technology requirements and their availability or timeline for development and integration needs to be clearly defined.

Peer review of the project at every stage of development by an independent team of experts would ensure adherence to the technology and capability roadmap of the project.

It is a high-risk project and needs to be supported by all agencies. Risks in integration and inter-agency issues need to be factored-in, in terms of cost and time.

The project must be jointly executed in a public-private partnership leveraging the capabilities of private industry and start-ups, especially in space, drones, communication, EW and AI/ML.

Challenges in developing anti-ballistic missile solutions include a long gestation period.

The number of satellites needed for the space-based sensor layer, especially for the hypersonic threat, needs to be identified, and a project initiated in a time-bound manner.

Development and operationalisation of different components of the system, including sensors and weapons, need to be developed and integrated in designated timeframes.

Proliferation of unmanned systems and stealth platforms demands a large number of sensors to detect them. Conventional radars and sensors need to be replaced by a large number of counter-stealth or low-observable sensors.

Sudarshan Chakra should effectively cover all the island territories, which would involve extended surveillance and deployment of defensive equipment across a large number of islands. The sensors must be designed for unmanned extended operations through remote access and monitoring.

A pan-India system with thousands of constituents and an expansive space layer would be an expensive proposition. This would necessitate earmarking a substantial budget. This budgetary allocation must be finalised at the earliest, to meet designated timelines. The mission would involve R&D agencies, the academia and private industry since the Prime Minister has categorically directed that Sudarshan Chakra be a completely indigenous system.

The entire project could be phased out in a building block approach by integrating the existing assets and networks to establish a multi-layered pan-India defensive and counterattack system in selected areas with available weapons. Subsequent phases could be plug-and-play, with scaling up of the preceding phase by integrating more sensors and weapons to expand the capability of detecting more complex threats and assets capable of engaging them. This will ensure that the technologies are integrated as they evolve, and any delays in design and development can be absorbed without major compromise on deterrence.

NOTES

1 Air Marshal RGK Kapoor, 'India's "Golden Dome"! From Drones To Hypersonic Missiles, Here's How Sudarshan Chakra Will Defend India', *The Eurasian Times*, August 26, 2025,

2 'Strategic ballistic missile defense, Challenges to defending the U.S.', March 3, 2025, https://www.aps.org/publications/reports/strategic-ballistic-missile-defense

3 Jacob Mezey, 'Russian and Chinese strategic missile defense: Doctrine, capabilities, and development', Atlantic Council, September 10, 2024,

4 Zhao Lei, 'Ground-based air-defense and anti-ballistic missile systems shine at V-Day parade', chinadaily.com.cn, updated: 2025-09-03

Priyanka Dahima, 'China Latest Air Defence System: A Deep Dive into Advancement', 14 Sept, 2025, https://www.pw.live/defence/exams/china-latest-air-defence-system

5 Gerry Doyle, Mariano Zafra, Adolfo Arranz and Jitesh Chowdhury, 'Israel's Iron Dome, How layers of air defences protected the country against the biggest onslaught of missiles and drones in its history', *Reuters*, April 18, 2024.

6 'Erdogan unveils Turkey's new 'Steel Dome' integrated air defense system', *PBS News*, Aug 27, 2025.

7 Air Marshal R.G.K. Kapoor (Retd), 'Indian Air Force – Post Operation Sindoor', SP's Aviation, Issue 09, 2025.

5

New Age Concept: Sudarshan Chakra (Network of Networks)

Air Mshl VPS Rana (Retd)

Introduction

Though India's air defence demonstrated its capabilities during Operation SINDOOR, the Operation it also served as a reality check for future challenges in extending the air defence authority across the entire country, considering that our civilian populace, religious sites and cities were targeted. In his Independence Day Address, the Prime Minister gave a clarion call to our young scientists, researchers, and military professionals to develop and operationalise 'Sudarshan Chakra' by 2035. The timeline itself indicates the complexities involved in creating an impregnable Aerospace shield over Indian skies due to the evolving nature of threats in new-age warfare. Therefore, an integrated, multi-layered Aerospace Defence Shield needs to be developed for protection against hypersonic missiles, stealth aircraft, drone swarms, cruise missiles, and space-enabled threats. India is on the right track to develop capabilities to counter these threats from both air and space. However, extending this capability across every corner of the country is a formidable task considering the geographic spread of our country.

President Trump also made a similar announcement to field the 'Golden Dome' for the protection of the US which is envisioned to include ground and space-based capabilities that can detect and stop missiles at all four major stages of a potential attack: detecting and destroying them before a launch, intercepting them in their earliest stage of flight, stopping them midcourse in the air, or halting them in the final minutes as they descend toward a target. This is envisioned to put US weapons in space. The system would supposedly have the capability of intercepting missiles even if they are launched from space.[1]

Space and cyber security have thus become integral to air defence, as space-based assets are increasingly being used to defeat an enemy's ambitions. During the Russian Victory Day parade, Russian hackers hijacked an orbiting satellite that provides television service to Ukraine and beamed parade footage from Moscow. The message was meant to intimidate and was an illustration that 21st century war is waged not just on land, sea and air but also in cyberspace and the reaches of outer space. Disabling a satellite could deal a devastating blow without any bullet being fired and it can be done by targeting the satellite's security software or disrupting its ability to send or receive signals from Earth.[2]

Therefore, to keep the Indian skies safe from new-age threats, a formidable air defence needs to be established to thwart enemy attacks on our critical military and civil installations, as well as the civil populace from the sea, air, ground or space. A well-integrated architecture to provide layered and continuous air defence promptly is a necessity. While the 'Union War Book' mandates the Indian Air Force (IAF) for the air defence of the country, Indian Army and Indian Navy (IN) also operate the air defence weapons, in large numbers, which increases durability of the defence architecture. In addition, now the Ballistic Missile Defence and Space-Based assets need to be integrated to make it a seamless protective umbrella, for which an operational and technical roadmap with an all-inclusive approach must be drawn.

Current Doctrinal Framework: Integrated Air Defence Capability

The current doctrinal framework outlines a traditional air warfare approach where control of the air is vital for executing offensive air strikes and in-depth strategic targeting. Recent operations demonstrate that offensive air defence can also provide a certain level of air control, especially when well coordinated with other offensive missions. Achieving air superiority in a highly contested airspace, particularly against adversaries with similar capabilities, is considered essential across tactical battlespaces, hostile airspace, and penetration routes, to support all joint operations. Control of the air is not only necessary for conducting air operations, but it remains a crucial joint warfighting requirement. When capabilities are matched, control of the air tends to be temporary and limited to specific areas and periods. Therefore, having effective air defence is critical to support all air operations. Integrated Air Defence (IAD) capabilities enable all air missions, including deep offensive operations, by establishing tactical conditions to penetrate the enemy's layered and resilient air defence network. The sensor and ground-based AD weapons system coverage within adversarial airspace is vital for launching attacks in enemy territory. The IAD offers layered, integrated coverage through high, medium, and low-level radars, AWACS and AEW&C, along with multi-tiered Surface-to-Air Missile (SAM) systems and fighters equipped with long-range Beyond Visual Range (BVR) missiles.[3]

The availability of long-range SAM systems, such as the S-400, enables offensive air defence operations deep within enemy airspace, making them highly potent. With such extended-range weapons and sensors, the IAD is referred to as an Extended Integrated Air Defence (EIAD) system that unifies all sensors and weapons, providing an offensive air defence capability deep inside enemy airspace. Extending the 'Sensor-shooter' reach with a powerful EIAD system across India's large, varied terrains and environmental conditions, is a vital national security imperative during wartime and equally important during peacetime to safeguard our sovereign airspace over the mainland and islands. The IAF's EIAD system, integrating airborne and ground-based sensors, multi-tiered SAGW systems, and extended-range air defence fighters equipped with visual range missiles, operates within a sophisticated and seamlessly connected network to deliver comprehensive air defence coverage across all IAF operations. A potent Indian EIAD will deny the enemy's Air Force operational freedom and reduce the effectiveness of its offensive air operations against our ground and maritime forces. The balance between the EIAD capability and the strategic offensive air power capability plays a defining role in India's multi-domain national security construct.[4]

The integration of all elements of air defence into a central command and control system is a critical necessity, which is provided by the Integrated Air Command and Control System (IACCS); the brain behind the air defence architecture of the IAF. Round-the-clock air defence surveillance of the entire Indian airspace and extended battlespaces, control, reporting, and employment of SAGW systems and interceptors are conducted by the sector-wise IACCS nodes of the IAF. The trained specialist fighter controllers and battle managers on the ground and in the air make use of the integrated system to closely control all offensive and air defence operations. Other networks, like the Indian Army's Akashteer and similar systems of the Indian Navy, are also integrated with IACCS to facilitate better negate the enemy's threats in tactical battle areas. The capability also exists to integrate other networks, like the civil radar network and BMD.

Conceptually and in terms of capability, while all components and integration feasibility exist for creating an effective EIAD, the quantum and volume are not adequate to cover the entire air space. With the pattern of present-day threats, every corner of our country and every target is threatened by our adversaries. The threat is also continuous, from its launch and travel through air or space and multi-directional re-entry. BMD and other air defences in respective silos, therefore, cannot deal the threat in isolation. There is a requirement to build architecture for cooperative engagement. It is in this direction that our capabilities need to be enhanced, in terms of scope and volume. Integration of various networks also needs streamlining, to facilitate smooth flow and sharing of information and coordinated functioning, through various operational layers of decision-making.

Glimpses of Advanced Air Defence Architectures

The air defence architecture of the US and China provides a good basis for study and analysis, to visualise and plan the futuristic air defence architecture for India. Besides the advancement in integration at various levels, the quantum and spread of the air defence weapons and systems provide interesting insights.

The US uses a multi-layered air and missile defence architecture, designed to protect the homeland, deployed forces, and allies from air-breathing threats (fighters, bombers, cruise missiles) and ballistic missiles of all ranges. The philosophy is very similar to India's IAD but on a global scale, with stronger reliance on space, cyber, and joint force integration. The early warning and space layer is the key, comprising Space-Based Infra-Red System (SBIRS), a constellation of satellites providing global missile launch detection and cueing, Over-the-Horizon Radars (OTHR) and other multi-level integrated sensors. Command & Control Battle Management and Communication (C2BMC) integrates all sensors and shooters globally, linking NORAD, NORTHCOM, STRATCOM and allies. NORAD provides the homeland air defence using ground-based radars, AWACS and fighters on alert.

The National Capital Region Integrated Air Defence System (NCR-IADS) is a permanent system around Washington for its air defence. For Ballistic Missile Defence, there is Ground-Based Midcourse Defence (GMD) to counter limited ICBM attacks, Aegis BMD, a sea platform-based interceptor, the Terminal High-Altitude Area Defense (THAAD) for terminal phase interceptor batteries for forward bases and homeland, and Patriot PAC-3 MSE for point and area defence for high-value sites/ bases and forces. The US Strategic Command (USSTRATCOM) exercises command and control for missile warning and global strike coordination. The Integrated Fire Control links the THAAD, Patriot, and Aegis for cooperative engagement. To counter cruise missiles and air-breathing targets, air defence uses the Fighter CAP and AWACS, SAMs and SHORADS. Non-kinetic weapons are also used for defence against drones.

China's air defence architecture, often referred to as its Integrated Air Defence System (IADS), is considered one of the most sophisticated and dense in the world. It is designed to protect the mainland from air-breathing threats (fighters, bombers, cruise missiles) and ballistic missiles, as well as to create Anti-Access/Area-Denial (A2/AD) bubbles around critical regions such as the Taiwan Strait, South China Sea, and Beijing/Shanghai economic belts. The PLAAF (People's Liberation Army Air Force) is the lead service for national air defence. The PLARF (Rocket Force) provides ballistic missile defence interceptors and long-range strike. Joint Theatre Commands coordinate air defence with the Navy and Rocket Force assets. National-level air defence C2 is networked through the National Air Defence Command Post (NADCP), providing integrated early warning and engagement control. China has invested heavily in sensors for broad coverage. Its Ground-Based Radars include: JY-27A (VHF AESA), YLC-8B, JYL-1 long-range 3D radars. It also has mobile, low-altitude gap-filler radars for the defence of cruise missile. It makes extensive use of Airborne Early Warning with KJ-2000 (based on Il-76), KJ-500 (new AESA AEW&C), and KJ-200 systems. Space-based assets like Yaogan EO/SAR satellites and missile early-warning satellites are used for the requisite air defence.

China has a nationwide network of Passive/ELINT systems for emitter location and electronic surveillance. To provide a strategic-level air defence, China uses HQ-9, S-400, and HQ-19 series missiles. The HQ-29/HQ-26 missiles are reportedly under development for exo-atmospheric interception. The HQ-16, HQ-22 and other sea platform-based missiles provide medium-range and Theatre-Level air defence. The HQ-7B, HQ-17 missiles and CIWS equipped with guns complete the short-range point defence layer of the air defence. China also has an active BMD programme with mid-course interceptors for exo-atmospheric interceptions, ASAT capability and cooperative engagement capability, linking radars and shooters across regions. China also makes extensive use of EW and cyber operations. The key features of Chinese air defence are high-density overlapping coverage, a nationwide networked IADS with redundancy and hardened nodes, and an Anti-Access/Area Denial strategy. When compared with Indian air defence, the main differences are the density of the air defence weapons, space-based capabilities for early warning of threats, and networking of all command and control centres to enable cooperative engagement of ballistic and cruise missiles.

New Age Concept: *Sudarshan Chakra* (Network of Networks)

Air power remains a vital tool of a nation's military strength, as seen in all modern conflicts. Along with the importance of the aerial domain, which provides comprehensive vertical coverage over land and sea, space power is a key multi-domain warfighting ability essential for future warfare. Therefore, India must integrate air and space power fully with land and sea forces to adopt a multi-domain strategy in its military and security policies.

Fighter and bomber aircraft have traditionally been the main platforms for delivering offensive air power. While they will continue to be the primary means for deep strikes, the spread of advanced area denial systems and various tactical surface-to-air missile systems has increased the vulnerability of all aerial platforms. Therefore, standoff targeting and long-range air-launched weapons that can be deployed outside the air defence threat envelope have become more important for aerial weapon delivery. The other alternatives to manned platforms for penetrating deep into enemy territory are air and surface-launched cruise missiles and long-range advanced UAVs/drones, besides ballistic missiles.

Creating a comprehensive shield to protect every asset and individual in the country is a monumental task, given the vast airspace and the complexities of enemy weapons. A carefully designed, layered network of sensors, command and control centres, and interceptors that provides depth, redundancy and graceful degradation, is essential to defend national interests from all aerial threats. Such a system must account for geography, scattered strategic assets, a doctrine that emphasises joint efforts, and an evolving threat landscape featuring high-performance aircraft, precision-guided standoff weapons, cruise missiles, ballistic threats and increasing numbers of unmanned systems. Instead of relying on a single "perfect" system, a layered and integrated air defence network with overlapping capabilities around key assets is vital. These layers should include different detection mechanisms, engagement altitudes, and kill mechanisms (kinetic versus non-kinetic), all coordinated through a unified command and control system. To develop such a resilient multi-layered system, it is important to analyse new threat spectrums, the necessity of multi-domain awareness, integration challenges, and the role of AI in various processes and solution generation for effective air defence.

New-Age Threat Spectrum

Currently, India's air defence is designed mainly for the conventional threat spectrum of air-breathing targets, despite technologically proven capabilities to counter the threat outside this spectrum. However, to provide an impregnable aerospace shield against futuristic targets, there is a need to develop, field and integrate various capabilities. Offensive air power is no longer exclusive to bombers and fighter aircraft. The present day and the future will include a wide range of manned and unmanned combat and weapon delivery platforms, as well as an increasing range of weaponry, which will use the vertical domains of air and space for launch or transit. Future offensive air power capabilities will include manned-unmanned teams, advanced hypersonic missiles, cruise missiles, a wide range of drones, advanced long-range standoff air and surface-launched weapons, etc., irrespective of service-specific ownership, and will become integral to the military's joint application of offensive power.

Manned-Unmanned Teaming

Drones have already made their mark in various conflicts around the globe and will pose problems in future with many advancements in the field. The development of advanced drones that operationally complement fighter jets, relying on direct control of their manned peers or on-board AI, is being completed as the Manned-Unmanned Teaming (MUMT) concept. It can scout the battlefield, engage the enemy and sacrifice itself to shield manned aircraft. The US Valkyrie XQ 58A and the Sukhoi S-70 are expected to provide cost-effective unmanned team solutions. Korean Aerospace Industries (KAI) is also developing a two-tiered combat MUM-T concept involving the formation of four unmanned fighters paired with a single KF-21 fighter aircraft, with an additional three to four smaller air-launched effects designated by KAI as Adaptable Aerial Platforms (AAPs) for providing additional support. The AAPs are attached to the larger unmanned fighter, and will be used for roles such as jamming, decoying, intelligence collection and attack to reduce the risk to the fighter aircraft.[5]

Many other such systems are on the anvil around the globe, including India. Being almost as capable as manned fighters in specific roles, but with the advantage of being cheap and easily replaceable, such systems allow large numbers of the type to saturate enemy defences.

Swarm Drones

At the lower spectrum, because of the inherent advantages that accrue by employing cheap drones, swarm drones are now becoming one of the preferred options to saturate enemy defences and hit tactical targets at will. The US, Russia, China and India are developing autonomous low-cost drone systems that can be used as independent swarms or under the control of manned aircraft. Employment of drones in conflicts and warfare has proliferated as they have found their place in all the warfighting domains – air, land and sea. The use of cheap drones is a tremendous financial burden on air defence resources. The use of drones by armies and navies across the globe, particularly in the Indian context, has also enhanced the complexity of the tactical battle area. Now, cheap drones are also being used as decoys by simply fitting a Luneburg Lens, a radar decoy that tricks the air defence system into believing it to be a much larger aerial target. According to Ukrainian researchers, such small drones have been used by Russia to paint the radars as Geran-2 (Shahed-136) drones through deception. The use of conventional missiles and interceptor aircraft can be a tremendous financial and operational strain on the air defence systems. Hence, there is a requirement to find counters to drone targets with relatively affordable economics.[6]

Stealth Bombers and Fighters

Stealth bombers and fighters are certainly one of the biggest challenges that air defence of the future is likely to face, given the continuously improving stealth technologies, and more such aircraft being developed and deployed. Lockheed Martin's F-22 Raptor and F-35 Lightning II are two of the best in the category, which use cutting-edge stealth technologies to remain elusive in hostile airspace. These technologies minimise the Radar Cross Section (RCS) of an aircraft. The F-22 radar signature is comparable to that of a bumblebee and is thus extremely difficult to detect. Other aircraft currently operating in this category are China's Chengdu J-20, Russia's Su-57, and, to an extent, the Eurofighter Typhoon and the French Rafale.[7]

The development and deployment of the J-20 in particular poses serious challenges to India's air defence. With almost 200 aircraft already in active service, the number, at the present production rate, could be almost 800 aircraft in PLAAF's inventory by 2030, surpassing all of India's combat aircraft. The stealth features of the J-20 and other air superiority capabilities will certainly provide China with an edge, with almost 40-plus squadrons expected to be ready by 2030.[8] India's dilemma is compounded by Pakistan's pursuit of fifth-generation fighter capabilities with countries like Turkey and China, for their aircraft, the KAAN and FC-31, respectively. Pakistan is reportedly collaborating with China for the development and deployment of J-35. According to a recent report, the J-35 is gaining attention for its advanced stealth capabilities and carrier-based functionality comparable to the US' F-35. The warplane is reported to have RCS, 'smaller than a human palm'.[9] The Chief of the US Air Force, recently, announced that Boeing is developing the F-47, a sixth-generation fighter with MUMT capability with a UCAV wingman. The initial flight of the fighter is expected in 2028.[10] There are also reports of China developing the J-50 (J-XDS) with advanced stealth, AI-assisted flight control, and tailless futuristic design.[11]

Another development programme of China that could alter the world dynamics is the H-20 bomber. If Chinese media is to be believed, its development is close to fruition. To America's discomfort, the aircraft is similar in design to the B-2 bomber, with flying wing design and stealth features. The aircraft is likely to have a range of 8,000 miles with a payload of 40 tons. The payload is expected to be land-attack cruise missiles in addition to bombs.[12]

There are also reports of sixth-generation J-36 aircraft having undertaken test flights in December 2024. The aircraft boasts a tailless, diamond-shaped design for enhanced stealth and aerodynamic efficiency. It also features AI integration, advanced sensors and hypersonic capabilities.[13] These developments are particularly concerning for India, and Indian air defence needs to cater for such threats in the future.

Hypersonic Missiles

The Russians have reportedly used hypersonic missiles in Ukraine, and there is not much defence against such a threat as of now. China has developed these missiles and India is developing this new-age, precise, potent and high-speed threat, which is difficult to counter through conventional air defence. The intercept geometry of such missiles is very complex, even when we have the means to neutralise them. There would also be a need for space-based satellites for timely detection. Over-The-Horizon (OTH) radars like the Russian Konteyner and the Chinese J 27-A can reportedly detect such threats almost 3,000 kilometres away. But it would be difficult to ascertain the target from such distances. Delayed detection and a complex intercept geometry make the task of intercepting these missiles very difficult. Hypersonic weapons can travel between five and 25-times the speed of sound. There are two types of hypersonic weapons: Hypersonic Glide Vehicles (HGVs) and Hypersonic Cruise Missiles (HCMs). HGVs glide through the atmosphere at high speed following the initial ballistic launch, while the HCMs use air-breathing engines to reach high speeds. As per a RAND study, HGVs would be detectable only six minutes before impact, which would create uncertainty. Some of the Russian hypersonic weapons include the 3M22 Zircon, advanced HGV, and Kh-47M2 Kinzhal. The Kinzhal can be launched from MiG-31 and Su-34. China, too, has a very advanced hypersonic weapons programme. It demonstrated that the DF-ZF HGV mounted on the DF-17 could fly at hypersonic speeds. India, too, has successfully tested a domestically developed hypersonic missile on 17 November 2024.[14]

Aerospace Domain Awareness

In the future, the range of threats will include everything from ballistic missiles to nano-drones, and from the ground up to space. Given that the air defence system's targets will be in continuum, domain awareness, which includes the target's awareness of their movement across the air and space must likewise, be in continuum. Effective air defence, therefore, requires domain awareness that integrates both air and space objectives. Therefore, "Aerospace Domain Awareness" must form the foundation of the new air defence system. Also, despite having different qualities, air and space media constitute a continuum that has become a global national security issue due to the growing military exploitation of space by nations such as the US, China, and Russia.

Fundamental to aerospace control is the necessity of real-time three-dimensional multi-domain aerospace situational awareness. Given the differences between air and space domain characteristics, a fusion of awareness across both domains is an extremely challenging task but is a future-relevant necessity. For over a decade, extensive air domain awareness already exists, with the IAF's IACCS, which networks all IAF airborne and ground-based sensors together with air defence shooters under regional nodes. The current combat-tested and proven IACCS of the IAF will have to be upgraded to an 'Integrated Aerospace Command and Control System (IASC2S)' to serve as a platform that will network and weave all these elements into a cohesive and integrated system of systems.[15]

Inclusion of Cyber Security, Intelligence and Space Assets into the Realm of AD

The modern air defence systems, from radars, weapon systems, command and control nodes and satellites, are all connected through secure data links, and thus the digital dependency is huge. All air defence functions, from sensor fusion to threat evaluation and fire control solutions, are data flow-dependent in real time. In addition, the linkages through various layers enable remote operations. These capabilities open possibilities for network intrusion and espionage, data manipulation or spoofing, disabling attacks, malware attacks and satellite and GPS jamming/hacking. Any modern system, therefore, must cater for safety from such threats. Building cyber-resilient air defence is therefore a necessity to ensure seamless, continuous and effective air defence. End-to-end encryption ensures confidentiality. Future systems must leverage post-quantum encryption standards and seamless key management across distributed platforms. Technology roadmaps should address dynamic encryption adaptation, secure inter-sensor communication protocols, and practical on-the-fly cryptographic upgrades as threats evolve. Incorporation of intelligence of all kinds –operational, technical and human – is critical for strategic planning and seeking solutions for air defence battles. Most of the advanced systems in the world have enmeshed the intelligence from satellites in generating air defence solutions and shrunk the sensor-to-shooter loop drastically.

Space-based assets are now a reality as a threat as well as a solution for creating an effective air defence umbrella. These capabilities, therefore, need to be catered for while planning and operating our air defence systems. Satellites contribute across five operational functions: Early Warning and Missile Launch detection, persistent wide area ISR, SIGINT/ELINT, robust and secure communication and data relay, and Positioning, Timing and Navigation (PNT). Taken together, these functions shorten the sensor-to-shooter timeline, improve target discrimination, and allow a more economical employment of costly interceptors by enabling graded responses. India's announced plans for a robust military satellite constellation and ongoing launches of EO, SAR and SIGINT payloads, indicate a conscious drive to embed space as a core element of joint air defence capability. Space platforms and long-range weapon trajectories increasingly utilise the near space for transit. Air defence needs to expand its overall architecture to encompass both air and space, moving towards a more comprehensive 'Aerospace Defence' that holistically includes advanced air defence, ballistic missile defence, and ASAT technology. It is high time India changed its current air defence paradigms of the past to look at 'Aerospace Defence' holistically to include air and space, like the US, France, Russia, and China.

Anti-Access/Area Denial and Offensive Defence Concept

The potent air defence systems across the globe are no longer reactive in nature. With improved weaponry and command and control capabilities, air defence systems have a more offensive posture and complement offensive firepower. Such fusion of air defence with offensive air operations is now an operational necessity of all professional air forces worldwide. The IAF is no exception, with its Integrated Air Defence (IAD) capability that synergises all air defence operations with practically all air operations, including depth offensive air operations. Such an offensive posture of air defence is critical to the IAF's strike operations, as it creates advantageous tactical conditions to penetrate the adversary's Anti-Access – Area-Denial (A2/AD) defence systems and multi-layered robust air defence network. The extent of the IAD sensor and ground-based air defence weapon system cover that extends adversarial airspace is critical to achieve the intended objectives in future warfare. A multi-layered combination of high, medium and low-level radars and multi-tiered Surface-to-Air Missile (SAM) systems with long, medium, short, and close-in weapons systems, which comprise an IAD, needs to be bolstered with extensive long-range SAM systems to enable offensive air defence operations as deep inside enemy airspace as possible, to classify it further as Extended Integrated AD (EIAD).[16]

A potent EIAD capability that synergises all sensors and weapons and provides an 'Offensive' AD capability deep inside the adversarial airspace, is a strategic necessity for not just the IAF but indeed other services as well, given their overarching criticality in all offensive and defensive operations. Extending the 'Sensor-shooter' reach with a potent EIAD capability across India's large continental spaces of varied terrain and environmental conditions is a vital national security requirement for the air defence of the sovereign airspace of our mainland and island territories. EIAD serves as a counter to the enemy A2/AD, as it enables friendly air power to penetrate deep inside the enemy's airspace for executing offensive strikes and air defence operations. Against Pakistan, with its strong air defence system and air power, a potent Indian EIAD will serve to deny the enemy air force operational freedom and reduce the effectiveness of its offensive air operations against our ground forces. An EIAD capability deployed in the island territories on the east and west in the maritime domain will provide offensive air defence cover over India's strategic areas of interest. A balance of future-relevant EIAD capability and strategic offensive air power capability will play a definitive role in India's future multi-domain national security construct. Such an umbrella, facilitated by EIAD, can virtually create multiple no-fly zones and corridors with requisite freedom to long-distance air defence weapons for an offensive defence concept.

AI-enabled Processing of all Air Defence Functions: Technology and Industry Roadmap

With the complexity of the threat spectrum and the multiplicity of air defence weapons and systems, faster processing and rapid generation of an air defence solution are required for an enabling prompt response. All core air defence functions such as Detection, Identification, Interception, and Destruction, demand the integration of AI for high-speed computation. With the induction of drones, the classification of targets has also become a critical air defence function to ensure weapon-to-target matching while engaging the aerial targets. Threat classification entails the construction of sophisticated mathematical models that predict and distinguish between various threat characteristics, including drones, high-endurance UAVs, fighter aircraft, precision-guided cruise missiles, ballistic and quasi-ballistic missiles, anti-ship missiles, underwater-launched weapons, anti-satellite missiles, amphibious weapons, and both short-range and long-range artillery systems. By analysing velocity and trajectory data, threats are identified as either missiles or aircraft. The application of AI enables further sub-classification, allowing identification of missile types and the prediction of possible trajectories, including mid-course changes to enhance response accuracy. The system needs to reliably classify swarm attacks and assign unique identifiers to each platform. In the case of saturation attacks, powerful computation resources are required for mathematical and physical analysis, enabling precise threat identification and rapid filtering of decoys and low-priority threats. The resulting information should be instantly transferred to a command-and-control (C2) centre with multi-sensor data fusion to ensure reliable, real-time decision support. The speed of delivering accurate inputs to C2 significantly increases available reaction time, which is crucial for launching effective countermeasures.

Whether it involves advanced radars, sophisticated weapons, user-friendly displays in command-and-control centres, or high-end algorithms for threat evaluation and identification, AI and other suitable tools are necessary to facilitate a real-time air defence response. Since a broad range of capabilities need to be enhanced and integrated, a thorough review of existing systems and requirements for additional functionalities is essential, to develop a roadmap and involve industry stakeholders. Given that the IACCS backbone is already established and proven, it can serve as the foundation for further enhancements and layers to incorporate additional capabilities and networks. An AI-enabled, multi-domain, integrated sensor fusion of air and space monitoring systems, is the way forward and must be prioritised as a key research and development area. In order to create three-dimensional aerospace combat situational awareness for India's national security, surface, aerial, and space-based sensors, as well as new-generation aerial enabler platforms such as AEWC aircraft and AWACS, future Joint Tactical Information Distribution System platforms, multi-sensor ISR systems, satellites, and more, must be integrated and networked.

Modern threat environments demand increasingly powerful computational capabilities to handle large sensor datasets and complex algorithms in real time. The adoption of next-generation multicore processors—including quantum or neuromorphic chips—can accelerate analysis and decision-making, especially under saturation scenarios. Future roadmaps should align with developments in AI processor architectures, energy efficiency, and low-latency processing for mobile command centres. Development and deployment of indigenous photonic radars, quantum radars, integrated RF and photonic radars and other such sensors, focusing on stealth aircraft, small drones, and low-RCS (Radar Cross Section) projectiles, must be prioritised.

Since a large number of technologies and institutions would be involved in the process, a comprehensive road map for the identification, fusion and integration of all these capabilities needs to be chalked out to formulate a robust architecture. India must accelerate its R&D efforts to build a comprehensive aerospace domain awareness architecture, which will require proactive support and synergy between India's space and aviation industries. The Department of Space and the Ministry of Defence must lead these efforts aggressively to enhance India's air and space situational awareness of its sovereignty and strategic interests.[17]

Multi-Level Multi-Layer Integration of Effectors, Sensors and Decision Enablers

To make an effective air defence shield as envisioned by the Prime Minister of India, a network of networks needs to be created, with additional capabilities incorporated. The IACCS's architecture, though almost a decade old, had already catered for various other networks to be integrated including BMD, civil radars and the networks from other services. The operational and technical architecture of *Sudarshan Chakra* can be created by integrating all capabilities as indicated above, and superimposing various layers of air defence from ground to space. The integration can be at the Strategic, Operational, Tactical, and point defence levels for the integration of weapon systems, sensors, and command and control systems, ensuring a clear flow of decisions and control orders across all levels in real-time, and in a smooth manner. The planned architecture should be modular, adaptable, and scalable to ensure quick operational response. The suggestive architecture at various levels is indicated in subsequent paragraphs.

Strategic Level Integration of Weapons and Command and Control Systems

The highest level of decision-making for engagements involving the launch of long-range vectors and defence against long-range vectors like ballistic missiles and ASAT operations, would originate from strategic centres such as the 'National Command Centre/Post' or the related Strategic C2 Centre. In the proposed architecture, the NCP would serve as the core for all strategic decisions and would connect to other strategic C2 layers of warfighting, including Strategic Weapons (Long-Range Vector) C2C, BMD C2C, and Space Assets C2C, as well as Aerospace Defence C2C. The NCP would need to be equipped with a fused picture from all ground, air, and space-based sensors. Inputs from space-based assets, long-range radars, airborne early warning aircraft, and strategic-level intelligence would feed into these national and strategic-level C2 nodes. The purpose of this outermost air defence layer is to launch a strategic offensive, detect cruise and ballistic missiles and provide long-lead cueing to lower layers and decision-makers. This layer offers the initial "look" at approaching threats, assesses tracks based on intent and value, and reserves high-end, scarce interceptors for the most valuable engagements. Its main role is to transform surprise into warning by detecting incoming raids or missile launches early enough to alert decision-makers. The integrated picture must be appropriately filtered both upwards and downwards, with decision flows and warnings transmitted in real time to maintain continuous engagement through all air defence layers until the threat is fully neutralised.

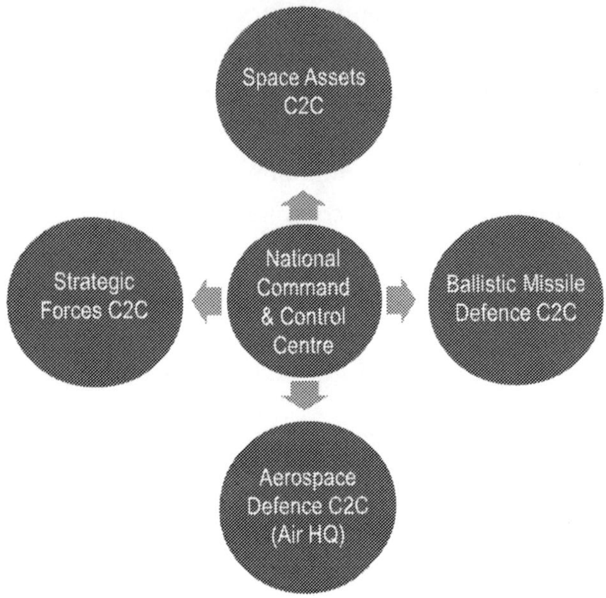

Figure 5.1: Strategic Level Command and Control Architecture

Besides space-based assets, sensors include long-range radars such as Swordfish LRTR and other trackers, High-Power Radars (HPR), OTH radars, VHF and VLF radars, space/ELINT inputs, AWACS, and AEW&C systems. All emerging anti-stealth technologies, like quantum radars and HF and VLF radars, need to be operationalised as a priority. The long-range weapons available for this layer include all BMD weapons, ASAT weapons, long-range missiles such as S-400 and similar systems like Kusha and Long Range SAM (LRSAM). Strategic decisions regarding offensive defence to engage enemy aircraft deep into hostile territory would primarily originate from this level. ASAT weapons aim to disable or destroy orbiting satellites, crippling adversary communications, navigation, reconnaissance, and early warning capabilities essential for modern military operations.

ASAT operations would be conducted at the highest strategic layer because of their disruptive potential. The development focus includes kinetic kill vehicles with enhanced targeting accuracy, directed energy weapons such as lasers and microwaves capable of incapacitating satellites without generating debris, cyber-attack methods to degrade satellite functions non-kinetically, and countermeasures to satellite defence.

Operational Level Integration of Weapons and Command and Control Systems

This level addresses all conventional threats. The air defence battle would be orchestrated by respective geographical operational air commands of the IAF through various regional air defence nodes, regardless of the warfighting structure. This would be linked to the strategic layer through Aerospace C2C at the Air Headquarters level, more for policy-level decisions than minute-to-minute battle. The operational layer provided at this level converts strategic warning into local denial by countering enemy threats through layered air defences equipped with interceptor aircraft and missiles of various ranges.

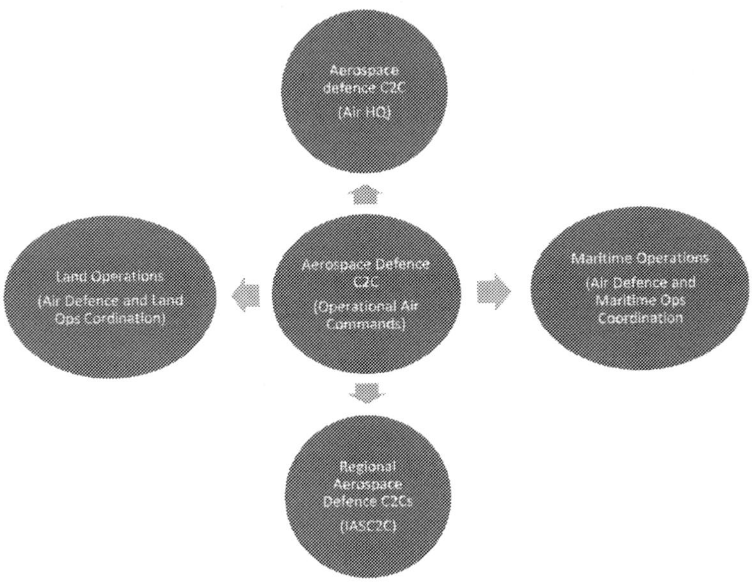

Figure 5.2: Operational Level Command and Control Architecture

The operational level systems are typically held in echeloned groups like fighter aircraft equipped with BVR and long-range missiles for long-range interceptions to provide area defence, medium-range surface-to-air systems and mobile missile systems to protect airbases, logistics hubs and critical corridors, and finally the point defences for the most critical targets. The purpose of this layer is to provide defence in depth, with key weapon systems like fighter interceptors, MRSAM, medium/long-range systems used by the Navy, IAF and Army (land MR-SAM variants), Akash family missiles (Akash, Akash-NG/Akash-Prime). These command and control centres are the brain of the air defence system, which controls the entire range of air defence weapons and manages the airspace in its entirety. The command and control centres below this level are also provided with overarching control orders either directly or through pre-decided procedural control. The integration of all sensors, weapon systems, and other networks is orchestrated at this level to generate a composite air picture, which is then shared upwards or downwards on an as-required basis.

Other networks at the operational level would be for the SSM controlled at respective service HQ, out-of-area contingency and blue operations over the sea. An Out-of-Area Contingency network could be developed as an independent networked Command & Control Centre (C2C) with airborne assets like AWACS and long-range fighters, complemented by rapidly deployable ground-based resources. The aerospace defence C2C of island territories could be linked with blue operations to facilitate long-range aerospace defence operations to safeguard our Sea Lines of Communication (SLOCs) and other maritime interests. The C2C of all these networks will interact for coordination and smooth control of respective weapon systems.

Sub-Conventional Operations (Low-Level CUAS) Network

Considering the employability of drones in recent warfare and the advancement in drone and counter-drone technologies, it can be assumed that drone swarms are no longer going to be isolated attacks in frontline areas. These are certainly going to be employed for deep penetration strikes and therefore would travel through our airspaces for a longer duration, like the conventional low-level strike aircraft. The IAF, therefore, should not only plan to engage these swarms at respective bases and other tactical targets, but also while they are flying towards various strategic targets, just like the deep penetration strikes. The targets in future could be population centres and other critical infrastructure spread across the country. To provide all-round defence in such a scenario, a dedicated low-level integrated grid comprising the CUAS radars and systems, therefore, is a necessity of the future air defence system. Indian armed forces conducting regular large drone exercises to hone the air defence capabilities is an indication that this, for sure, is going to be one of the most important layers of the *Sudarshan Chakra*. Before the advent of IACCS, the IAF used the Control and Reporting Centre (CRC) concept to tackle the low-level threat, primarily due to very little warning of such raids. With drones, the warning is going to be even less, and a dedicated automated system needs to be established, which can be further integrated with the mother network (IASC2S), like all other networks. Some autonomy to deal with the drones through soft kill options to LL CUAS Centres in consultation with IASC2S would help early destruction of such swarm raids. This will also provide much-needed early warning to depth VAs/VPs.[18] The core equipment for these systems should be a large number of highly mobile vehicles, preferably in single or two-vehicle configurations, equipped with radars and Directed Energy Weapons to neutralise the drone threat to cover the large area of responsibility of such centres. In addition, certain hard kill options should also be available with the LLCUAS Centre. The erstwhile ADDC/GCI radar operations room (Non-IACCS node) canbe converted into Sub-Con C2 nodes.

Point Defence/VSHORAD/MANPADS, Guns & Counter-UAV/Non-kinetic Layer

The innermost ring comprises very-short-range air defence (VSHORAD), man-portable air-defence systems (MANPADS), rapid-fire guns, counter-UAS systems, and non-kinetic measures such as electronic warfare and directed-energy weapons, to provide the point defence to important assets like airbases and critical infrastructures. The control centres for such point defence will coordinate with the mother network to neutralise the raiders as per the laid-down norms for weapon control. This close-in weapons defence comes into effect when the defended base/assets are directly threatened. Tactically, the point-defence layer is optimised for saturating and asymmetric threats like drone swarms or other conventional threats. The purpose of this layer is to provide last-mile local defence against UAVs, helicopters, low-flying aircraft and cruise missiles and drone swarm threats. Against such attacks, a layered response could combine electronic warfare to disrupt command links, guns for area denial, and MANPADS for select kinetic kills. The weapons would comprise MANPADS/VSHORAD units, radar-guided AA guns (upgraded L/70, ZU-23 variants), dedicated counter-UAS radars and EO suites, emerging Directed-Energy Weapons (DEW/lasers) and other electronic warfare soft-kill systems.

Networking and Integration of Effectors and Sensors: Deployed Forces (Army and Navy).

For the protection of deployed forces, mechanised formations and tactically mobile elements over land and sea, tactical short-range systems provide rapid-response air defence under the respective service. Mobility and quick reaction time are the defining features of this layer. Weapons are designed to keep pace with moving columns and to engage low-flying threats in the limited reaction-time windows that accompany close combat. Tactically, this layer is frequently integrated into force manoeuvre: mobile medium/short-range launchers and vehicle-mounted radar/EO suites accompany columns and create a protective bubble. All weapon systems and sensors of such land or sea forces are integrated into regional joint air defence centres, which provide the requisite control orders to all the deployed air defence weapons in consultation with the mother air defence network at the operational level. The key weapons systems for this layer would be QRSAM (Quick Reaction SAM) for mobile column protection; Akash batteries used in shorter-range engagements; and integrated fire units with multi-sensor cueing. The Indian Army's Akashteer and similar integrated systems of the Indian Navy, facilitate the integration of various air defence systems within their respective area of responsibility, and reduce the sensor-shooter response drastically. These systems are integrated upwards with the operational network (IACCS). The to-and-fro flow of tactical information, early warning, and appropriate control orders between systems like Akashteer and IACCS, is critical.

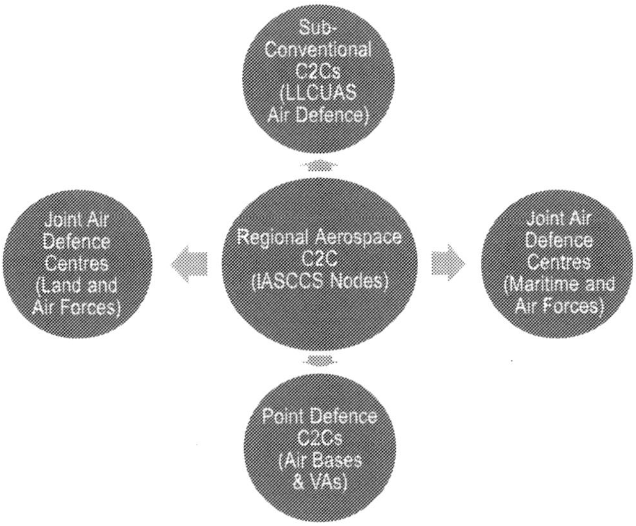

Figure 5.3: Networking with Deployed Forces and Sub Con (LLCUAS) Nodes

Command and Control Centres and Their Integration

The integration of various command and control centres is the key to an effective air defence system to facilitate real-time track correlation, shooter allocation, and deconfliction (blue-on-blue avoidance) between various layers. The Integrated Aerospace Command & Control System (IASC2S) at the operational level would serve as the nerve centre, as the majority of the functions will be executed from this centre against all aerial targets. The Recognised Air Situation Picture (RASP) would also be generated at this level after integrating all sensor inputs, which will then be appropriately filtered and passed upwards to Strategic C2 Centres like the national command post and downwards to the tactical C2 centres like army and navy C2 centres and other point defence centres at the tactical level. The weapon control orders for all weapons would originate from this centre, either directly or in an alreadydecided procedural control format. The early warning and engagement of strategic targets' information would flow from strategic C2 centres to operational C2 centres to facilitate continuous engagement of the target. Enhanced scope of air defence, as deliberated above, would need upgradation of all these command centres, in scope as well as the expanse, particularly at the operational level. Integration between the strategic and operational level, in particular, would need detailed deliberation and spelling out the specific system requirements.

The integration and functioning at various layers is summarised below:

Table 5.1: Integration and Functioning of Command and Control Centres

Layer/Level	*Key Components*	*Purpose*	*Data Flow*
Strategic	National Command Post/Strategic Command C2C, Space Asset C2C, BMD C2C, BMD weapons, extended long-range Missiles, long-range radars (LRTRs, OTH, VHF, VLF), anti-satellite systems. Aerospace defence C2C, other strategic networks.	Early Warning and cueing, engagement of Ballistic Missile threat and space-based threat, creation of A2/AD bubble, long-range engagements.	Requisite warnings, Radar feeds and inputs from space-based assets to Operational Network.
Operational	Operational/Regional C2 Nodes, Out of Area Contingency C2C, Blue Ops C2C, Fighter Interceptors, LRSAM/MRSAM, Akash family SAM, all airborne and ground-based radars integrated in a single network.	Layered Denial, Area Defence.	Filtered Recognised Air Picture to Strategic Level. Decision and Recognised Picture to Tactical Levels.
Tactical- Sub-Con (Low Level CUAS)	LL Radar chain with enhanced capability to detect drones, DEWs, LLUAS CRC.	To tackle low-level raids of drone swarms and other LL threats.	Tactical decisions coordinated from operational level.
Tactical- Point Defence	VSORADS, MANPADS, DEW systems, Akash family SAMs, Base Air Defence Centres.	Base Defence and air defence to critical national assets.	Tactical decisions coordinated from Operational Level.
Tactical- Deployed Forces	Army and Navy air defence Assets, QRSAM, Akash family SAMs, Joint Air Defence Centres.	Air Defence of Deployed Forces in TBA.	Tactical decisions coordinated with Operational Level.

Requirement of Additional Resources

Most of the organisations suggested above are already existing in some form and need only capability enhancement and rechristening. The human resources for operating these institutions already exist. However, the induction of new technologies and equipment may necessitate additional resources on an as-required basis. The creation of sub-conventional nodes for mitigating drone swarm threats would need rearranging of manpower to existing sensor units and change their role to combat air defence units rather than merely a sensor unit. The C2Cs at the strategic level would need to be manned as per the requirements of the respective vertical from within the organisation.

Challenges of Integration

The challenges of integrating various components and networks of air defence would be on two fronts: technology and operations. At the technological front, differing protocols and the systemic architecture of multiple elements pose the main challenge during integration. With many sensors with varied protocols and formats, multi-sensor fusion remains the biggest challenge. The C2 systems must analyse enormous volumes of sensor data in real time for rapid threat assessment and decision-making. High-speed multi-core processors enable parallel data processing, greatly reducing latency. AI techniques enhance data storage efficiency and enable intelligent retrieval of relevant information, supporting situational awareness and predictive analytics. The communication backbone on which each network rides also needs to be synchronised for the smooth flow of data, once integrated. Redundancy of sensors, weapons and systems in such a large architecture is another huge requirement, as each system becomes critical in the integrated architecture. Ensuring cybersecurity for such a huge system also becomes very critical, as even a small breach can weaken or compromise the system. Upgradation of the identification, classification and threat evaluation module of the system with a suitable AI algorithm for quick processing, prompt solution and right decision making would necessitate fresh developments. Collaboration between services and industry would be the key to developing such a system. A good example is the development of IACCS, where the IAF and BEL collaborated for its successful and timely development.

At the operational front, one of the main challenges would be the methodology and the quantum of data for exchange between various networks and the overlap of responsibility in certain areas that would need detailed discussion. Inter-service deconfliction for the engagement with clear, pre-agreed rules and shared situational pictures, would be critical to prevent incidents of fratricide and allow seamless use of different weapon systems as part of the layered shield. In the present context, the economy of force is the biggest challenge to match the cost of the defensive response to the value of the incoming threat. It is in this regard that the classification of threats is very important, to enable the use of electronic warfare or short-range guns against low-cost drones while reserving the fighter and surface-to-air interceptors for cruise missiles or operated platforms. Smart mobility of air defence weapons quickly after firing to ensure unpredictability and deception with the use of decoys and signature management for high-value static sites, would be a critical necessity. Effective integration of kinetic and non-kinetic weapons to ensure economy of effort would be another operational challenge. Since the air defence battle is fought at different levels and comprises varied professionals across the services, a robust and comprehensive training framework would also need to be established, rehearsed and exercised, to orchestrate an efficient air defence battle.

Conclusion

The new air defence framework, as envisioned by the Prime Minister, must be more than just a collection of radars and missiles. It needs to be a doctrinally coherent, networked, resilient aerospace defence system that integrates a full range of sensors, C2 nodes, fighter and SAM interceptors, along with non-kinetic options, and embeds and integrates space power into the existing conventional air defence architecture. For both air defence practitioners and citizens, the value of a robust, integrated air defence system lies not only in deterring aggression but also in shaping conflict dynamics in a manner that escalation becomes costly, unattractive, and strategically untenable. The air defence system that aspires for future-readiness, must integrate space as a core pillar rather than just an adjunct. Satellites for early warning, wide-area ISR, SIGINT, resilient communications and PNT, materially change how air defence senses, decides and acts. Embedding space capability increases reach and persistence, shortens Observe-Orient-Direct-Act (OODA) loops and permits more discriminating, cost-effective defences, provided resilience and counter-space contingencies are explicitly planned. As India expands its dedicated military satellite capacity, space will move from a supporting role to being central in the integrated air defence architecture.

The integration of sensors and effectors at various levels needs to be carefully orchestrated so that each layer becomes complementary to the other, with a smooth flow of data and decisions. Deconfliction between the services and decision layers must be fool proof to ensure optimum utilisation of national resources. While IACCS is battle-proven and does provide the fundamental platform, it would need to be upgraded and upscaled with the requisite addition and modification of modules, to provide the desired air defence architecture. The key enablers of this system would be Aerospace Domain awareness, AI-enabled processing and decision support system, cyber resilience, extended Integrated Air Defence (EIAD) for offense-defence synergy and robust R&D, industry-military collaboration and integration of relevant DRDO projects.

Recommendations

To prepare and implement the road map for the development of the *Sudarshan Chakra,* the following is recommended:

- Establish an inter-ministerial and inter-departmental committee to define the architecture.
- Define the overarching architecture, inclusive of all strategic, operational and tactical layers.
- Define various C2C nodes and their inter-relationship and hierarchy.
- Identify the challenges and roadblocks for integration and work out the modalities to overcome the same.
- Identify the technologies that need to be incorporated to enhance the overall system capability.
- Define a step-by-step implementation strategy.
- Define the strategy for industry engagement for inducting various technologies and capabilities.
- Define the formats and protocols for various integrations.
- Define scalability for every module and technology enhancement within the architecture.
- Define the communication backbone for each layer to enable uninterrupted and real-time exchange of information between various C2C nodes.

NOTES

1 Tara Copp, "Trump Selects Concept for $175 billion 'Golden Dome' Missile Defense System", AP news.com, 21 May 212025.

2 David Klepper, "Hijacked Satellites and Orbiting Space Weapons: Space is the New Battlefield", AP news.com, 18 August 2025.

3 Air Mshl Diptendu Choudhury, *Future Employment of Air Power: Strategic Inference for India* United Service Institute of India and Vij Books, 2024 at https://usiofindia.org/pdf/M-5-2024%20-%20AIR%20MSHL%20DIPTENDU%20CHOUDHURY.pdf

4 Ibid.

5 Akhil Kadidal, "KAI Updates MUM-T Concept for KF-21", Jane's ADEX 2023 at https://www.janes.com/defence-news/news-detail/adex-2023-kai-updates-mum-t-concept-for-kf-21

6 Boyko Nikolov, "Russia Floods Ukraine with Drones Mimicking Large Radar Targets", Bulgarian Military.Com, November 18,2024. Retrieved at https://bulgarianmilitary.com/amp/2024/11/18/russia-floods-ukraine-with-drones-mimicking-large-radar-targets/

7 "Top 6 Most Advanced Fighter Jets in the World", NI.Com, July 15, 2024. Retrieved at https://www.ni.com/en/solutions/aerospace-defense/aircraft/top-advanced-fighter-jets.html#:~:text=The%20F%2D35%20Lightning%20II%2C%20often%20hailed%20as%20the%20most,tailored%20for%20specific%20mission%20requirements.

8 Ibid.

9 Arun Nair, "Is US Losing Stealth Supremacy? China's J-35 has Stealth 'Smaller than a Human Palm'," Times Now World, 30 September 2025 at https://www.timesnow news.com/world/is-the-us-losing-stealth-supremacy-chinas-j-35-has-stealth-smaller-than-a-human-palm-article-152918695

10 Stephen Losey, "First F-47 now being built, will fly in 2028: US Air Force Chief", Defense News, 22 September 2025 at https://www.defensenews.com/air/2025/09/22/first-f-47-now-being-built-will-fly-in-2028-us-air-force-chief/

11 "Fighter Pilot Exposes Critical Intel on China's J-50's New Images", YouTube Video at https://www.youtube.com/watch?v=ZoGM0N47Anc.

12 Brent M Eastwood, "China's New H-20 'Stealth' Bomber", 19fortyfive.com, 28 November 2024 at https://www.19fortyfive.com/2024/11/chinas-new-h-20-stealth-bomber-can-be-explained-2-words/

13 Vijainder K. Thakur, "Akin to B-21 and B-2's Broad Spectrum Stealth, China's 6th Gen Aircraft Set to Rattle the US", *Eurasian Times,* 27 December 2024 at https://www.eurasian times.com/akin-to-b-21-raiders-broad-spectrum-stealth/?amp

14 Anil Chopra, "Aircraft Carriers: Can they Fight Lethal New Age Weapons", *The Eurasian Times*, 1 December 2024 at https://www.eurasiantimes.com/aircraft-carriers-after-surviving-bombers/#google_vignette

15 Air Mshl Diptendu Choudhury, no. 3.

16 Ibid.

17 Ibid.

18 Sivam Patel, "India to hold Biggest Drone Exercise Seeking Air Defence Boost", Reuters, 23 September 2015 at https://www.reuters.com/world/india/india-hold-its-biggest-drone-exercise-seeking-air-defence-boost-2025-09-23/?utm_campaign=fullarticle&utm_medium=referral&utm_source=inshorts

6

Sudarshan Chakra: A Warfighting System of Systems

Wg Cdr M V N Sai (Retd)

Mission Sudarshan Chakra is conceptually an omnipresent System of Systems considered to be eternally in existence and operation. The system is a new networked abstract node that can be brought to bear, as a union of nodes, at any point of time and space, to enforce the will of the nation. The system spans both offensive and defensive operations, without making major changes to the current operational doctrine of pre-existing node infrastructure. Each distinct type of operational role envisaged hereafter would be driven from a differentiated node, with a well-defined developmental mission. The end state demands that all existing nodes and all nodes developed hereafter would be so designed to be able to share awareness with the Sudarshan Chakra layer. The design of the Sudarshan Chakra must cater to the tenets of being always in operation, invisible till brought to bear, always connected and operable from any physical infrastructure (any node).

Sudarshan Chakra would work as a multi-function node, involving modular, extendable and scalable architecture. This would require segmenting the node's functionality, managing task concurrency and establishing clear communication protocols between different operational nodes. The broad architectural pattern of the Sudarshan Chakra would comprise distinct role-based nodes, layered architecture, defined responsibilities and a clear distinction between command and control. The event-driven multi-function nodes in the Sudarshan Chakra would handle numerous concurrent, tasks making it highly effective. The core concept of operations would be triggered by events rather than asynchronous sequence of function calls. The proposed nodes would be designed to manage asynchronous operations, making it a natural fit for conduct of such complex but concurrent operations. The idea behind such a model is that, nodes would interact with each other and at the same time would function independently. This would require a robust communication mechanism.

Types of Operations and Nodes

Considering the ever-expanding operational roles, changing geopolitical scenarios and the necessity to re-invent the national warfighting resilience narrative,Sudershan Chakra would comprise nine types of nodes as depicted hereunder:

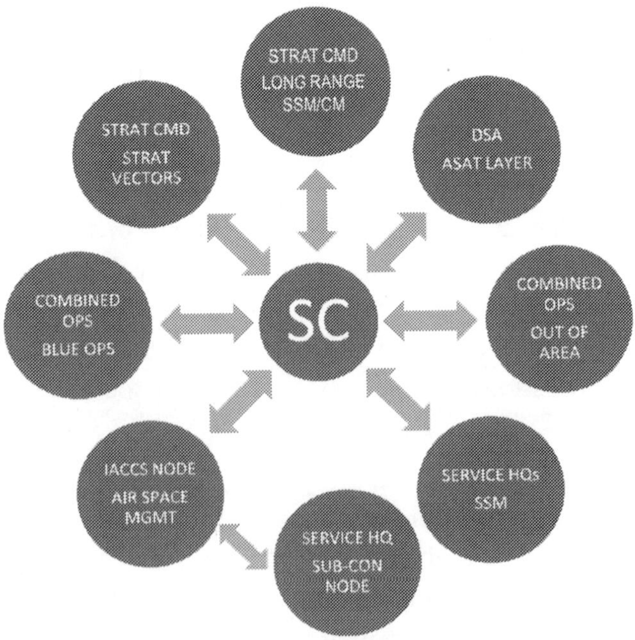

Figure 6.1: Schematic of Node Connectivity

Need for Different Types of Nodes

A multi-disciplinary approach to the project would be necessary. It is envisaged that operations could be brought to bear from the nine nodes above. Each node would run through a dedicated service; in certain cases by associating more than one service.

It is envisaged that nine distinct nodes would make up the Sudarshan Chakra ambit. Each of these nodes is designed to have a distinct and non-overlapping operational envelope. The essential purpose of each is detailed below.

Type I: SSM Nodes

Respective Service Headquarters would be empowered to utilise SSMs in support of the battle plans. However, as these occupy the same airspace and would necessarily transit through the Air Space Management (ASM) and the near-space layer, information exchange with other nodes usually to the extent of "Information Only" would be in order, to minimise unnecessary and "man in the loop" decisions. As these are tactical in nature, their employment would be well defined in the offensive doctrine. As such, the offensive operations for all the Services transit seamlessly with the existing ASM layers, thereby adding another layer of information to the same, to complete the air picture.

In a conflict situation, the node responsible for coordinating surface-to-surface missile launches would be part of our larger Command, Control, Communications, Computers, and Intelligence, Surveillance, and Reconnaissance (C4ISR) architecture. This node is not a single entity, but a highly redundant and distributed system that ensures accurate, timely, and secure execution of a missile strike.

The requirements for coordinating operations from such a node include:

Data and Intelligence Fusion

Target identification. The node must receive real-time intelligence from multiple sources, such as satellites, drones, radar, and other reconnaissance assets, to identify and verify targets.

Threat analysis. It must analyse intelligence to assess potential threats from enemy defences, such as air defence systems and electronic warfare capabilities, that could impact the missile's flight path.

Target vulnerability. The node must process information to determine the optimal time and method of attack to maximise the probability of success against a hardened or mobile target.

Command and Control

Secure communication. The node requires a resilient and secure communication network, like the Defence Communication Network (DCN), to transmit and receive sensitive data and commands. This prevents interception and spoofing by the adversary.

Authorisation and Decision-Making. It must have a clear chain of command for receiving launch authorisation from higher command levels, such as Service Headquarters Theatre Command.

Launch Sequencing. The node must manage the synchronised launch of multiple missiles to overwhelm enemy defences or achieve a specific time-on-target objective.

Planning and Operational Management

Trajectory Planning. The node uses sophisticated software to calculate and plan targeting, considering factors such as terrain, enemy air defence zones and potential counter-measures. For cooperative launches, this includes planning the missile trajectories to ensure they arrive at the target simultaneously.

Logistics Co-ordination. It must have a system to coordinate with launch platforms (fixed, mobile, or naval) and ensure their readiness, including fuel, missile status, and launch procedures.

Battle Damage Assessment (BDA). The node must coordinate with ISR assets after the strike to assess the success of the mission and determine if follow-on strikes are necessary.

System Security and Resilience

Electromagnetic pulse (EMP) hardening. To withstand the effects of nuclear conflict, critical components of the coordination node must be hardened against EMP.

Redundancy and fail-safes. The architecture must include redundant systems and clear fail-safe procedures to ensure operational continuity in case of system damage or failure.

Cybersecurity. The node must be protected from sophisticated cyberattacks that could compromise the system, alter data, or issue false commands.

Human Interface

Crew roles and procedures. The node must be manned by trained personnel with specific roles, such as the Missile Combat Crew Commander (MCCC) and Ballistic Missile Analyst Technician (BMAT), who follow strict, multi-step procedures for authorisation and launch.

Clear display and visualisation. It must feature command consoles that present clear, real-time data on targeting, missile status, and the battle situation to support rapid, informed decision-making.

Type II: Sub-Con Node

The advent of sub-conventional warfare has been the most striking over the past years if not more. A paradigm shift in the approach and address is necessary. This threat manifests itself whenever and wherever the perpetrators feel the need for it. The counteracting systems also need to keep up with this need and must be instituted without undue delays. Wide area low RCS detection, surveillance, electronic scanning and passive interoperable-based detectors must be employed. Weapons that have the ability to take down incoming drones, swarms, loiters, UCAVs and improvised projectiles at the smallest possible cost, need to be developed. These nodes must be agile and deployable both at an area level as well as in relation to a VA/VP or a Situation of Chance. These sub-con nodes would have great autonomy and would operate under pre-decided rules of engagement. Often times, micro-management of these layers is attempted, much to the detriment of air defence.

In a conflict situation, a "sub-conventional node" is a separate, decentralised unit necessary for coordinating air defence and airspace management at a tactical, localised level. This is especially critical in sub-conventional warfare, which blurs the lines between front and rear, combatants and non-combatants.

The node is required to manage the unique challenges posed by asymmetrical threats like small drones, loitering munitions, and low-flying aircraft that often operate outside of conventional radar detection.

Challenges in Sub-Conventional Conflict Zones

Decentralised operations. Unlike conventional warfare, where airspace is centrally managed, sub-conventional threats require a decentralised approach with local commanders managing their own tactical airspaces against sub-conventional transient threats.

Sensor limitations. Sub-conventional aerial platforms, such as visually sighted mini-drones, are difficult to detect with conventional radar systems, requiring supplementary detection methods.

Electronic warfare (EW). The prevalence of EW makes constant communication with central command and control centres unreliable, necessitating local, independent nodes to manage immediate threats.

Overlapping airspace. During an asymmetrical conflict, a battle zone's airspace, controlled by local forces, overlaps with the national airspace, which is under the central control of the Air Force and civil authorities.

Proliferation of users. In a modern battlefield, numerous air assets like drones, helicopters and tactical aircraft operate simultaneously, requiring local coordination to prevent collisions and friendly fire.

Requirements and Functions of a Sub-Conventional Node

The node addresses the challenges of sub-conventional conflict through several key functions:

Autonomous Command and Control. The node allows for decentralised execution of air defence. It receives centralised planning and verification of friendlies, through an advanced AI based application set, from systems like India's Integrated Air Command and Control System (IACCS), but can make its own tactical decisions in case of compromised communication.

Integrated Sensor Fusion. It integrates data from a variety of sensors suited for low-altitude surveillance in the locallised conflict zone. These can include:

a) Forward troops and observation posts
b) Low-RCS radars
c) Electro-optical and infrared sensors
d) Wide area Passive systems
e) ESM-based detection systems

Kinetic and Non-Kinetic Weapon Control. The node is configured to direct both kinetic weapons, such as Man-Portable Air-Defence Systems (MANPADS), laser-based Directed Energy Weapons (DEWs), and non-kinetic tactics like electronic countermeasures to neutralise low-flying threats.

Real-Time Airspace Picture. It creates a real-time, consolidated air picture of the local battle zone. This allows local commanders to distinguish between hostile, friendly, and civilian aerial platforms.

Coordination with Higher Command and Other Nodes. The node maintains connectivity with a higher-level command, such as the IACCS/ Divisional Air Defence Centre, using secure and ruggedized communication networks. This ensures its operations align with the overall strategic air defence plan.

Civil-Military Coordination. The node is crucial for coordinating with civil aviation authorities. It helps restrict civilian air traffic in the conflict zone and manages any air traffic near military installations to avoid safety hazards.

Seamless C3 Integration. It ensures seamless integration with other branches of the armed forces, like the Army and Navy, as demonstrated by the Indian military's joint exercises, which involve the coordination of special forces and air assets.

Integration. Intended integration has been achieved in the following:

Akashteer System. The Indian Army's Akashteer is an example of a system that functions as a node for Army Air Defence. It connects and coordinates Army air defence units in the battle zone, managing low-level airspace and controlling ground-based weapon systems.

Integration with IACCS. Akashteer operates by integrating its battlefield information into the Indian Air Force's Integrated Air Command and Control System (IACCS). This creates a single, national air defence grid while allowing for decentralised tactical execution. This needs to be expedited.

Type III: Airspace Management Node (Existing IACCS, Akashteer, INCCS)

We are fortunate that decades of continuous work has been put into our ASM frameworks, the bedrock of situational awareness rural route ASM nodes (IACCS). Recently another layer of tactical nodes in the IB and LoC sector has been added in the form of Akash-teer. These two assets have helped us maintain a high degree of situational awareness and control over our air defence assets. The IACCS ASM node has also enabled us to manage our counter-offensive campaigns. There would be a necessity to further strengthen the survivability of these nodes, improve redundancies both at the sensor level and communication layers as well as diversify and improve the sensor set. These nodes are currently manned and operated by respective Service Headquarters, and relevant information as per matrix shared, needs to be implemented. Security of our networks and all efforts to improve data security non-traceability and modularity as suggested, needs further work.

During a conflict, an airspace management system such as the Integrated Air Command and Control System (IACCS) nodes, provides a unified, real-time air picture and enforces dynamic airspace control to prevent friendly fire and response to threats. The following are the requirements to coordinate air operations and airspace management through IACCS nodes during a conflict.

Integrated Air Picture

Sensor Fusion. Data from multiple sources, including ground-based radars, airborne sensors like AWACS and AEW&C aircraft and civilian radar systems, must be fused to create a single, recognised air situation picture (RASP).

Centralised display. This RASP needs to be displayed in real time to commanders at various levels (strategic, operational, and tactical) through the IACCS nodes.

Command and Control

Centralised Control and Decentralised Execution. The system must allow for centralised control at higher command levels for coordinated planning while enabling decentralised execution by tactical units.

Automated Decision Support. IACCS nodes should provide automated decision support to help commanders make quick and accurate decisions on identifying and assessing threats and directing air defence assets for engagement.

Multi-Service Integration. The system must be fully integrated with the air defence networks of other services, such as the Indian Army's Akashteer system and the Indian Navy's Trigun network, to ensure seamless joint operations and prevent fratricide.

Dynamic Airspace Management

Flexible use of Airspace (FUA). Airspace should be managed flexibly and allocated dynamically, rather than being permanently designated for a single user. This allows for time-sharing and segregation as needed, minimising the operational impact.

Automated De-Confliction. The IACCS must automatically de-conflict airspace for different users, including fighter aircraft, transport aircraft, and surface-to-air weapon systems. This includes preventing friendly fire by ensuring ground-based weapons hold fire when friendly aircraft are in the area.

Responsive Airspace Management. The system needs the ability to accommodate short-notice and unplanned airspace changes in response to the dynamic tactical situation.

Survivability and Security

Redundancy and Robustness. IACCS nodes and the underlying communication network, like the Air Force Network (AFNET), must have redundancy to ensure continuous operation under intense electronic warfare and physical attack.

Security. The network must be secure, providing converged voice, data, and video services over a protected system to prevent enemy interception and compromise.

Threat Response

Layered Defence Coordination. IACCS coordinates India's multi-layered air defence, including long-range, medium-range and short-range surface-to-air missiles, as well as fighter aircraft. The system guides the most appropriate weapon system to engage an identified threat.

UAV and Drone Management. With the proliferation of unmanned platforms in modern conflict, the system must effectively monitor and control low-level airspace over battle areas to manage friendly drone operations and counter hostile ones in conjunction with sub-conventional nodes.

Type IV: Out-of-Area Operation Node (Blue Ops and OOAC)

The need for intervention and engagement, in aid of foreign power, or solely to secure India's international interests, could be classified as Out-of-Area Operations. These operations could be pre-defined (conventional OOAC), as has been the case thus far, or might simply occur at distant locations across the globe (Blue Ops), with defined or undefined contexts. These two operations are distinct, both in terms of context and complexity, as pre-defined operations have well-defined force assignments, while for the Blue Ops, the context, force levels involved, other friendly foreign powers aligned with us, and arraigned against us, all need definition.

Considering the increasing levels of uncertainty in international alliances, extremely widespread supply chain arrangement, increasingly vulnerable Sea Lanes of Communications (SLOC), there exists a need for expeditionary force that will decisively influence the outcome of any future Blue Ops intervention. Most often, there is adequate planning for the enablers, such as warships, fighter planes and such. However, the binding force for such operations lies in a ready-to-go Operational Blue C2 node. These nodes can only come into operation when we can ensure, secure on-board computing, data back haul when necessary, local compute to close out computational problems, C2 framework for localised decision-making over a secure interoperable intranet, between all elements that may be brought to bear on this operation.

Out-of-Area Operations Node

In these times of stress and in exercise of India's soft power, we may often times be called upon to operate for extended periods in aid of a foreign bar either in a standalone configuration or as a collaborative effort. In such cases, based on the declared national policy, intervention operations may be carried out. In order that such pre-designated operations maybe conducted in a seamless manner, this mode will need to be equipped with all necessary displays, overlays, planning, dispositions, intelligence, real-time transmission, communication and execution aids. This node could be multi-disciplinary and will need to be kept ready to take on operations in all designated theatres of national "out-of-area" interests.

Therefore, establishing two types of operating nodes – one for well defined, closer-to-home contingencies that may involve all three Services as well as intelligence agencies as well as another for a newer type of threat that is fast emerging and likely to be the new normal in the global scheme of things for India, with inbuilt connectivity to a rearward network – is crucial for both types out-of-area contingency operations. The process involves several strategic, operational, and tactical considerations to ensure command and control (C2), logistical support, and communications for deployed forces.

Establishing the Forward Node. The initial phase focuses on selecting, deploying, and securing a Forward Operating Location (FOL) or Forward Operating Site (FOS).

Site Selection and Reconnaissance

Strategic location. Choose a site that supports the mission and provides tactical advantages, such as proximity to the area of operation and defensible terrain.

Host-nation agreements. Secure diplomatic and legal permissions from the host country for entry, access, and support activities.

Infrastructure assessment. Evaluate existing infrastructure, including airfields, ports, communication lines, and water and power sources, to determine the necessary deployment assets.

Initial Deployment of Forces

Rapid Response Teams. Insert an initial expeditionary force with security, logistics, and communications capabilities to establish the base and secure the area.

Modular Deployment. Deploy force modules designed to support specific missions, which can be scaled up or down based on operational needs.

Base Development

Secure Perimeter. Establish a multi-layered security perimeter with surveillance, access control, and force protection measures.

Basic Life Support. Create initial infrastructure for personnel, including billeting, sanitation, water, and power and buttoned-up operational capabilities.

Logistics Hub. Set up a reception and staging area for equipment and supplies. The site must be able to receive, store, and redistribute resources effectively.

Rearward Networking of the Node

Connecting the forward node to strategic command centres is critical for maintaining situational awareness and controlling operations.

Communications Architecture

Initial connectivity. Use rapidly deployable, high-bandwidth satellite communication (SATCOM) links to establish immediate command and control. Commercial networks where available, can supplement these

Resilient network. Build a redundant communications architecture to ensure connectivity even in a contested, congested, degraded, or disconnected (C2D2) environment. This can involve using multiple communication paths and technologies, such as SATCOM, terrestrial microwave links, and high frequency (HF) radio.

Cybersecurity: To plan for data integrity at the node level, robust cybersecurity measures to protect the network from interference and disruption.

Information Management

Data synchronisation. Ensure effective and secure data synchronisation between the forward node and rearward command structures. As far as possible, the node must remain self-contained as much as possible with backward connectivity restricted to situational awareness, higher command flow and intelligence, logistics, and operational support related flows.

Information Sharing. Establish protocols for information sharing with coalition partners, which is crucial in multinational operations. Also, establish protocols that consume minimum bandwidth, through standardisation of entities' nomenclature.

Logistics Network

Strategic Supply Chain. Integrate the forward node into a larger, strategic supply chain that extends back to depots, arsenals, and national manufacturing centres.

Joint Logistics Nodes. Coordinate with joint logistics nodes (JLNs) to secure and streamline the supply of fuel, ammunition, food, and other materials.

Multi-Modal Transport. Establish air, sea, and land transport corridors to and from the node. This provides flexibility and redundancy in the supply lines.

Integrating Intelligence and Command

A successful contingency operation requires a seamless flow of information and a clear command structure.

Command and Control (C2)

Exercise Authority. A designated commander exercises authority and overall direction on assigned and attached forces to accomplish the mission.

Command Centres. Link the forward node's tactical operations centre (TOC) with strategic-level command centres, such as a Joint Task Force Headquarters.

Intelligence Integration

All-Source Intelligence. Continuously gather and analyse intelligence from multiple agencies and platforms to maintain situational awareness in the operational area.

Real-Time Information. Use networked sensors, unmanned aerial vehicles (UAVs), and other systems to provide real-time battlefield information to the forward node and strategic commanders.

Table 6.1: Summary of Key Elements

Element	*Description*
Forward node	A temporary or semi-permanent operating location in or near the area of operations. It provides a secure base for forces and a platform for projecting power.
Rearward network	A logistical and communication infrastructure that connects the forward node back to a nation's home territory or a regional hub.
Logistical support	The supply and maintenance chain that provides resources, equipment, and personnel to the deployed forces.
Communications and Information Systems (CIS)	The hardware and software that enable command and control, intelligence sharing, and overall coordination.
Command and Control (C2)	The exercise of authority and direction by a commander over assigned forces.

Type V: Blue Ops Node

Blue Ops

The advent of a multipolar world and transient partnerships juxtaposed with India's growing stature as a world leader demand an agile force, capable of executing India's blue water strategy. For the first time since the Second World War, the need for maintaining and monitoring SLOCS has increased manifold. As a strategic importer of goods and raw materials and with the rapid diversification of our supply chain sources, India needs blue water presence. This force must ensure continuous supply to arguably the top three economies of the world. India's blue forces could comprise elements from multiple disciplines often brought together by a need or planned operations. This mode could be onshore or offshore, on board an aircraft or a carrier, or even on an isolated landmass. Equipment necessary for such operations, both in terms of compute and communications, must be easily portable and operable. Iot devices cross computers edge devices and highly portable communication equipment that are air and sea portable, need to be developed such as "such as the C2 in a box" concept.

Establishing a "blue operations node" refers to creating a centralised hub for managing activities in faraway regions. This node will often comprise a multiple disciplinary expeditionary force, that would be tasked, often on the move, with securing national interests, ranging from securing supply lines, to intervention to aid friendly forces, or simply a show of strength. This node needs to be so established that it is brought to bear at any point with any or all components of the force. The basic tenets of this node would be similar to the Out-of-Area node.

Key Requirements for Establishing a Blue Operations Node

Organisational and Doctrinal Requirements

Clear mandate and purpose. The node must have a clearly defined mission, whether it is for military strategy, commercial logistics, or geopolitical security. This includes delineating its objectives for different operational scenarios, from peacetime monitoring to high-intensity conflict.

Integrated Command and Control (C2). The node must be integrated into a joint, multi-domain command structure, operating in tandem with air, land, and space components. This requires a common lexicon and defined guidelines for effective planning and execution of joint military operations.

Inter-agency and international cooperation. A blue operations node is most effective when it fosters robust information-sharing agreements and collaborative frameworks with other national agencies and international partners. This expands situational awareness and operational reach beyond sovereign waters.

Trained Personnel. The node requires personnel with specialised skills in data analysis, intelligence interpretation, and operational planning. Training programmes should cover the use of advanced simulation software, international law, what if analysis tools and knowledge of international protocols.

Technological and Infrastructure Requirements

Information Fusion Centre (IFC). The core of the node is an IFC that collects, processes, and fuses data from a variety of sources to generate a Common Operational Picture (COP). This includes both military intelligence and civilian intelligence.

Advanced Sensors and Platforms. To ensure comprehensive MDA, the node requires a network of sensors and data-gathering platforms. These include:

> **Space-based assets**. Surveillance satellites equipped with Automatic Identification System (AIS) receivers, radars and Synthetic Aperture Radar (SAR), to track hostile threats.
>
> **Airborne platforms**. Surveillance aircraft and helicopters, EW assets, ELINT and COMINT capability, AEW and C capabilities and Unmanned Aerial Vehicles (UAVs) for localised and extended-range operations.
>
> **Surface and subsurface assets**. Naval ships, submarines, and unmanned underwater systems to provide precise classification and identification of contacts.

Expeditionary force. An assault force, trained and capable of operations off/from austere forward posts, capable of quick deployment and survival under hostile conditions.

Robust data and communication network. A resilient and secure communication system is essential to ensure a low-latency flow of information. This includes reliable, jam-resistant networks, and standardised data-sharing mechanisms to enable the seamless exchange of intelligence.

Artificial intelligence and machine learning. AI-powered tools crucial for analysing vast amounts of data, detecting anomalies and predicting patterns of behaviour to help identify emerging threats more effectively than traditional methods.

Integration with Other Operational Domains

Seamless C2 integration. The blue operations node must be able to interface directly with the Sudarshan Chakra node.

Data interoperability. To create a true multi-domain COP, the node's systems must be interoperable with those of air, land, and space components. This ensures a unified understanding of the battlespace across all services.

Operational synchronisation. The node is to facilitate the coordinated application of force across domains by providing real-time intelligence for operations.

Logistics coordination. The node could also be used to integrate and optimise logistics across the sea, air, and land. This supports the efficient movement of personnel and supplies, reducing duplication and improving supply chain resilience.

Type VI: ASAT Node

ASAT C2

ASAT operations would be run by specialists from a dedicated C2 system. It is suggested that this be primarily run at DSA (Defence Space Agency) with experts drawn from various associated Services. Information from this system as a series of overlays and what if analysis can be shared with the Sudarshan Chakra. ASAT operations being highly confidential, needto be run from dedicated operations centres. The operation centre needs to be equipped to be able to track and identify the orbital position of all space-based objects that would be of relevance to our area of operation (15000 km) on either side of the Indian boundaries. The operations must be equipped to direct and launch necessary weapons to take out any inimical object.

Establishing an Anti-Satellite (ASAT) node and integrating it with national operations is a complex process with significant strategic, technical, and organisational requirements. Such a node is necessary to provide a country with the capacity to neutralise an adversary's space-based assets, defend its own satellites, and ensure space superiority during a conflict.

Key requirements for establishing an ASAT node

Foundational infrastructure

Space surveillance network. An ASAT node covers a robust network of ground-based radars, optical telescopes and other sensors to maintain continuous Space Situational Awareness (SSA). This network must track enemy satellites, identify their orbital patterns and detect pre-positioning of ASAT weapons.

Command and control (C2) system. A secure and resilient C2 system is essential to receive intelligence, authorise missions and issue commands to ASAT effectors. The system must coordinate with terrestrial military forces and national command authorities to ensure proper mission execution.

Threat analysis centre. This facility uses intelligence data and SSA to analyse threats, assess adversary capabilities, and plan counter-space operations. During a contingency, it would provide real-time threat analysis and targeting information to operational units.

Anti-Satellite Capabilities

The node must be equipped to manage both kinetic and non-kinetic ASAT effectors.

Kinetic-Kill Weapons (KKW). Missile-based systems designed to destroy a satellite in orbit. These are launched from the ground, air, or sea.

Directed-Energy Weapons (DEWs). Use of lasers or microwaves to damage or blind a satellite's sensors or electronics without creating debris.

Electronic Warfare (EW). Capabilities for jamming and spoofing signals are critical for non-kinetic engagement to overwhelm a satellite's communication link or spoof a satellite's navigation systems.

Cyber Warfare: An ASAT node is to integrate with a national cyber force to enable attacks that can hijack, disable, or destroy satellites by exploiting vulnerabilities in ground stations, control links, or the satellite's software.

Integration with Joint Military Operations

A standalone ASAT capability is ineffective without deep integration into a nation's multi-domain operations (MDO) strategy.

Multi-Domain Operations Centre. This centre combine intelligence from space and other domains (land, sea, air, and cyber) to provide a comprehensive operational picture for commanders. Integrating the ASAT node here ensures that space assets enable terrestrial military objectives.

Joint Task Forces. The ASAT node must be able to deploy specialised personnel and equipment to support joint task forces as needed during a conflict. This includes expertise on satellite vulnerabilities, targeting and the effects of ASAT operations.

Standardised Protocols. Creation of common procedures, terminology and data formats necessary to ensure seamless information flow and coordination between the ASAT node and SC.

Personnel and Training

Interdisciplinary Teams. The ASAT node must be staffed by professionals from diverse backgrounds, including military officers, space scientists, cyber warfare specialists, and engineers.

Joint Training Exercises. Regular joint military exercises that simulate multi-domain conflicts are essential to train personnel, test procedures and refine operational tactics in a realistic setting.

Expertise Development. Specialised knowledge is required for satellite tracking, space environment analysis and the unique challenges of space warfare, which differs greatly from traditional terrestrial warfare.

Policy Frameworks

Rules of Engagement (ROE). Since the use of force in space is controversial and risks rapid escalation, the ASAT node must operate under strict, clearly defined rules of engagement. These rules should be consistent with national policy and international law.

International Diplomacy and Norms. The node must also adhere to international treaties, such as the Outer Space Treaty, which govern activities in space. Its establishment should be part of a broader diplomatic effort to shape international norms for responsible behavior in space and deter an arms race.

Debris Mitigation Strategy. Any plan to use destructive ASAT capabilities must include a strategy to minimise space debris and its long-term effects on the global space environment.

Type VII & VIII: Strat Command Node

Establishing a strategic command node for integration during national contingencies requires addressing several key requirements:

Defined Command and Control (C2) Structure

A clear hierarchical structure outlining lines of authority and responsibility within the strategic node and its relationship with other operational and tactical nodes.

Defined roles and responsibilities for personnel within the strategic node, ensuring efficient decision-making and task execution.

Robust Communication and Information Systems

Secure, resilient and interoperable communication systems capable of connecting with all relevant nodes across different services and agencies.

Advanced information sharing platforms to facilitate real-time data exchange, situational awareness, and collaborative planning. This includes robust cybersecurity measures to protect sensitive information.

Interoperability and Standardisation

Standardised protocols, procedures and equipment to ensure seamless integration and communication with other nodes, minimising friction and delays during critical operations.

Compatibility of systems and data formats across different branches of the armed forces and other government agencies involved in national contingencies.

Shared Understanding and Common Operating Picture

Mechanisms for developing and maintaining a shared understanding of the operational environment, threats, and objectives among all integrated nodes.

Tools and processes to create and disseminate a common operating picture, providing all stakeholders with accurate and timely information.

Training and Exercises

Regular joint training exercises involving personnel from the strategic node and all integrated nodes to practice coordination, communication, and decision-making in a simulated contingency environment.

Development of standard operating procedures (SOPs) and battle drills to ensure a consistent and effective response during actual contingencies.

Strategic Command Node for Long Range Vectors and Counter Measures

STRAT C2: Strategic operations could be classified into two sub-divisions each, operating out of their respective nodes. The first type of operation would pertain to the control and launch of long range SSMs and CMS, while orders for and assessment thereof would need to be exchanged between the node and the NCP. Once the decision is made, all operational directions and real-time control over the operations would be exercised from these nodes. What-if analysis tools would be a notable departure from existing equipment stacks. Mid-course tracking and end-game monitoring tools, telemetry, advanced communication and powerful simulations would be needed to enable these operations. Strategic operations need space-based and HAPS dedicated communications. Launch, monitoring and management of both conventional and tipped vectors would need to be managed from these nodes. There would be different nodes for management of tipped and untipped vectors, under the control of different agencies.

A strategic command node is essential for coordinating the use of long-range vectors (Un-tipped as well as tipped) along with the processes involved for initiating countermeasures, particularly during national contingencies, to provide decision-makers with a unified, real-time operating picture. Integration with other nodes is crucial for ensuring synchronised, multi-domain operations across air, sea, land, space, and cyberspace.

Core requirements for such a strategic command node are enumerated below:

Command and Control (C2)

Delegated Authority. It must possess a clear, delineated chain of command-and-control with authority delegated by a nation's top decision-making body, such as India's Nuclear Command Authority (NCA).

Operational Planning. The node must have the capability to create and execute contingency plans for the employment of strategic assets, such as long-range ballistic and hypersonic missiles.

Target Selection. The process for target selection must be calibrated and cumulative, involving multiple levels of approval before action is authorised.

Communications and Computing

Secure networks. Resilient and secure communication networks are necessary for the uninterrupted exchange of voice, data, and video. These networks may include satellite and encrypted digital radio links.

High-speed processing. Powerful computers are needed to process the immense volume of data from multiple sources in near real-time. This processing must turn raw data into actionable intelligence.

Cyber resilience. The node requires robust cybersecurity to protect its C2 systems from cyberattacks, which can disrupt communications, steal information, or manipulate data.

Intelligence, Surveillance and Reconnaissance (ISR)

Common Operating Picture. The node must fuse information from thousands of sensors across multiple domains to build a comprehensive, real-time view of the battlespace.

Multi-Source Intelligence. Data must be gathered from a variety of platforms, including space-based systems, long-endurance drones, and naval and ground-based sensors.

Predictive Analytics. The node should use data analytics and artificial intelligence to anticipate events, predict the adversary's movements, and provide decision support.

Long-Range Vectors and Countermeasures

Vector Management. The node needs the systems to manage amid course and terminal phases, including capability for tracking and disengagement.

Targeting and Engagement. Integration with targeting systems for precision strikes. The node must enable rapid assessment and coordination of countermeasures against incoming threats.

Counter-Measures Deployment. Counter-measures, including missile defences and electronic warfare capabilities, must be coordinated with offensive vectors to ensure force protection.

Integration with the National Nodes

All data necessary for higher order of command is to be exercised through integration with the Sudarshan Chakra node.

Major Tenets of the Sudarshan Chakra System

The major tenets of the system can be encapsulated as under:

a) Omnipresent.

b) Invisible.

c) Non-interfering.
d) Can be brought to bear at any place at any time.
e) Seamlessly connected.
f) Highly autonomous at each layer.

Command and Control

There is a need for reimagining the entire Sudarshan Chakra as having no specific form factor with fixed locations. The system must be manifestable "at will" in any form factor that it may be needed without having to move "men and material". That is, the system must be brought to life at an instant's notice.

To enable this, the basic tenets of development must cater for the following:

a) Each node that constitutes the system needs to be self-sufficient in its concept and execution.
b) All nodes must be linked to each other seamlessly.
c) Layer data approach should be followed with different levels of exposure for data transactions.
d) The system should be modularly constructed, with each node coming into its own keeping in mind the technological challenges of achieving each of them.
e) The interface control documentation should be well defined, to cater to the interface at each node.
f) PULL-based authority level approach needed, assigned to the operator at the Sudarshan Chakra level, with high levels of authentication and validation, considering that any operation could be initiated from this node.
g) Photonics-based data transfer within and between nodes is necessary.
h) New-Age encryption systems needed to enable data security and integrity.
i) Master-less operations with takeover possible from any node, either on land/air/water.

j) Redundant connectivity plan, through widespread mesh creation and maintenance of at least four operational grids.
k) Minimising communication between nodes, using standardised data transfer language/protocols/scripts.
l) Development and commissioning of new-age middle-ware, that facilitates data-storage, data-transfer and data-retrieval within the theatre of operations itself, without needing to access mainland backup, and are archival backup systems.
m) Development of Indian switch and communication gear.
n) Development of Indian waveforms for space communications.
o) Development of long-range data-communication modems for undersea communication.
p) Seabed communication hardware needed to support seabed mesh network.
q) Amphibian craft and aeroplanes that could be converted and used for communication bridges, airborne C2, communication and signal jamming Elint/Comint stations, airborne C2 stations.
r) C2 in a container system for use as a floating node.
s) Battlespace observation systems for FLOT and FEBA management.

Technological Overview

The overall system architecture demands a multitude of technological interventions. This system-of-systems intervention needs a major revamp and revoke in the following spheres. Some suggestions are indicated:

Communications

a) Tactical communications Infrastructure.
b) Satellite-based communications.
c) Modern Over-the-Horizon Communication.
d) Mobile satellite phones (secure).
e) Other-side-of-the-earth connect (using mirror satellites).
f) Leo constellations for tactical handover.
g) Photonics-based data transfer.
h) Widespread mesh radio network.
i) Omnipresent terrestrial mesh.

j) Communication in a box.
k) Multi-mesh backup planning.
l) Minimum of four secure grids with interconnect.
m) Last-mile tactical communication inbox.

These interventions need to cater for the following:

a) Multi-mesh inland support.
b) Blue-operations using satellite communication.
c) OOAC using modular communication.
d) Strategic operation hotlines across land/water/space/underwater.
e) LEO must for far-earth connectivity.
f) Use of near space as a communication mirror for strategic reach from mainland.
g) Miniaturisation of wearable communication for last mile soldiers' weapon connect/control.

Recommendations

The chapter outlines a comprehensive, multi-layered command and control (C2) system for India's strategic, blue water and out-of-area operations. It emphasises autonomous, modular nodes linked via secure, photonics-based communication, enabling real-time data exchange, simulation and decision-making. Key operational domains include ASAT, SSM, ASM, Sub-Conventional Warfare and joint service coordination. The system demands advanced middleware, encryption and mesh networks to ensure seamless, omnipresent functionality.

Thus, it is recommended that we develop a decentralised, scalable C2 architecture with indigenous communication waveforms and secure data links to support all envisaged and hitherto un-attempted operations. It may also be understood that each of the sub-systems would come into force in their own time frame, and Sudarshan Chakra can come into existence with all available elements at that point of time.

Conclusion

The Sudarshan Chakra architecture envisions a modular, event-driven, multi-domain command and control system capable of managing complex, concurrent operations across strategic, tactical, and sub-conventional layers. Its success hinges on robust communication protocols, secure data fusion and seamless integration of diverse nodes. The institution of this multi-disciplinary system of systems is imperative, considering the vast scope of the Sudarshan Chakra. It must be borne in mind that with this thought process outlined in the chapter, the net has been cast far and wide. To operationalise this vision, several innovative solutions have been suggested. As an emerging global economic power, with a need to protect our economic and political independence, the institution of an all-encompassing system that helps decision-makers, make the most appropriate and informed decisions, is an imperative. Past successes in the field of net-centric operations, are but a precursor to the end state we would like to reach. The past is a clear indication of the capability. The future is full of challenges that calls for both technological and operational maturity, and we in India are ready to rise up to the challenge once more.

Table 6.2: Data Transaction Overview Flow of Information

ASAT OPS	
ASAT HQ to NCP	*At NCP*
Location information	Suitable Display for Record of
Readiness	Information and Simulation
Progress	
Go – No Go Criteria	What-If Analysis
Recall	
State-Status	
Simulation and analysis	
Executive Orders	
STRATEGIC OPS	
STRAT HQ to NCP	*At NCP*
Location information	**Comprehensive System**
Weaponisation Information	**To Transact**
Readiness Profile	
Range & Effect Simulation	Status & State
Target Information	Location
BDA plus Analysis	Analysis & Simulation
Launch Command	Post Analysis & Display
Mission Progress	Strat Communication
Mission Progress	
Strategic Recall	
Executive Orders	

<table>
<tr><td colspan="2">LONG RANGE COUNTER MEASURES</td></tr>
<tr><td>Strategic HQs and NCP</td><td>At NCP and Strategic HQs</td></tr>
<tr><td>Executive Orders.
Tracking Information.
Simulated and What If.
BDA Plus Analysis.
Mission Progress.
Space Picture.
Offensive & Defensive Ops (Op Updates)
Recall & Emergency Orders.</td><td>Comprehensive system
to receive all relevant updates
to and from Strat HQ to NCP</td></tr>
<tr><td colspan="2">BLUE OPS</td></tr>
<tr><td>Joint Ops Command to NCP</td><td>At NCP</td></tr>
<tr><td>Fleet State & Status.
Order of Battle (Orbat) and Disposition.
Augmentation Requirement.
Diplomatic Brief.
Operations Progress.
Reconnaissance, BDA and Analysis.
Recall and Updates</td><td>Blue ops layer to depict and transact Commands
Communications & Hot Lines
Diplomatic Out reach</td></tr>
<tr><td colspan="2">OUT-OF-AREA OPS</td></tr>
<tr><td>Joint Ops Command to NCP</td><td>At NCP</td></tr>
<tr><td>Mission readiness.
Mission Progress.
Executive Order.
Overlays and Displays.
Augmentation Requirement.
Diplomatic Outreach.
Interlocution.
Intelligence Inputs.
Rollback & Pullback.</td><td>Data layer for Institution of suitable
Communication, C2 & Display System</td></tr>
<tr><td colspan="2">CONVENTIONAL AIR OPS</td></tr>
<tr><td>Services to NCP</td><td>At NCP</td></tr>
<tr><td>(IACCS, Akashteer, INCCS)
Filtered RASP
Asset State
What If (Aperiodic)
State of Battle (Periodic)
Snap Shots
BDA + Recce (For Briefing)
Enemy ORBAT
Intelligence</td><td>Receiving
Collating
Layering
Communication
Any Higher Order info flow</td></tr>
</table>

SUB CONVENTIONAL OPS	
Sub- Con Node to NCP	***At NCP***
Events of Importance Saturation Situation Rocket Attacks Air Situation Picture Important Snap Shots (a periodic) EMP and Area Weapon activation Emergency Controls	Receipt and Display of Relevant Situation Updates
SSM NODES	
SSM Nodes to NCP	***At NCP***
Activation Info Affected Area of Ops Targeting Overlays Impact Analysis Emergency Controls	A Request based layer of Info

SECTION III

Space Based Systems

7

Space, War and Security: A Strategy for India

Prof S Chandrashekar

The Role of Space Assets in Addressing Indian Vulnerabilities

India shares land borders with seven other countries. Her large coastline also results in maritime borders with six other countries, some of whom like Pakistan and Bangladesh also share land borders. India's location along major maritime routes makes her an important player in the geopolitics of the Indo-Pacific region and the world.

Because of India's size and economic dominance, relationships with neigbours have seen ups and downs. Despite the protection offered by the Himalayas, India has been subjected to several invasions from its Northwest borders. Maritime supported military occupation has also resulted in several centuries of suppression and humiliation because of colonial rule.

After India became independent, border wars with China and with Pakistan have been major concerns. The close nexus between them have posed specific threats to India's sovereignty and security. Though on occasions India has been helped by the major powers, she has often had to face these crises on her own.

In more recent times these border skirmishes, have been compounded by other geopolitical factors that include US power, the rise of China, the resurgence of Russia and the relative decline of the western lead alliance. Navigating an independent path through this complex maze of global politics has been fraught with economic, political and technological consequences.

Though neigbours and the neighbours of neighbours remain major sources of concern, India's size and location make her vulnerable to the larger geopolitics of the world power order. As an emerging power, India needs to straddle this world to grow and transform herself so that she can take her rightful place in the comity of nations.

In this dangerous and interconnected world of today, though geographic barriers still do matter, the threats to security can emanate from very distant and constantly moving platforms located on land, the air, the sea and increasingly in space. Whilst India has responded to these vulnerabilities in varying degrees, there has not been, an articulated and clearly outlined strategy as to how the country proposes to deal with them.

Recent developments have clearly revealed the fragility and cracks in the often ad hoc approaches that the Indian nation state has adopted. Dependence on other more technologically advanced countries in strategically important areas have derailed Indian efforts substantially. The nuclear and space arenas bear mute testimony to the various problems that the country has had to face in the absence of national capabilities in key areas of technology.

The call by the Prime Minister for a "Sudarshan Chakra" or a protective shield around the country both to defend itself and if necessary, to attack adversaries, provides an opportunity to take stock of the current situation and outline an approach that could take the country forward.

To make the idea of a Sudarshan Chakra work there is a need to look well beyond defending key assets with limited range terminal defense systems. Economics dictates that we cannot spend a lot of money defending the tens of thousands of targets that are vulnerable to drone and missile attacks in the world of today. Prudence dictates that we deal with these threats long before they reach the target. Space assets are the key to winning wars in the era of information dominance.

It is evident that to preserve the country's sovereignty, India needs the capabilities to look well beyond its neigbours and the neighbours of neighbours. In simpler terms India needs to look over horizons to identify threats well before they can reach her borders or shorelines. India also needs the capabilities to deal with these threats before they can do significant damage to the country.

This view of threat assessment should encompass the land, the maritime, air and space domains that provide access to the country. In the world of today this would require assets of various kinds to access and use space for the defence of the country.

Platforms in space cover very large areas on the earth. This offers great benefits in several ways. The most important of them is of course the collection of information from all over the world and the real time transmission of this information to intelligence analysts and decision makers within the national security complex of the country. These ongoing trends have shaped the national security strategies of all countries since the 1991 Gulf War.

This paper provides an outline of the architecture of the space assets needed to preserve the integrity and sovereignty of the Indian nation state that includes defending the country from missile and drone attacks.

The Information Collection and Movement Mission

The Intelligence, Surveillance and Reconnaissance Function

The first major requirement is the collection and movement of information from over Indian horizons to locations where they could be analysed and used.

Constellations of Intelligence, Surveillance and Reconaissance (ISR) satellites in various orbits are needed for collecting the information. The key requirement for these are Electronic Intelligence (ELINT) Satellites.

These have been used by the superpowers for ocean surveillance since the days of the Cold War. China has in place an operational system that uses two kinds of ELINT constellations. One constellation uses a triangular formation of satellites to locate an emitter.

The Yaogan ELINT Triplets – Position Location of Emitters

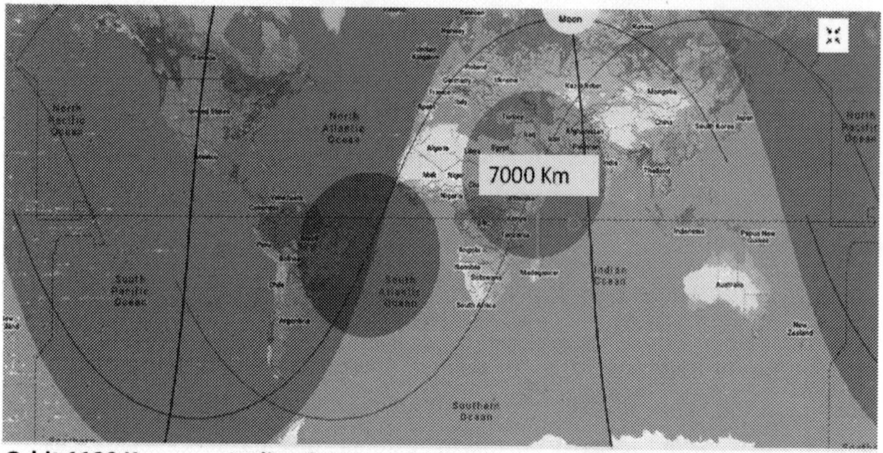

Orbit 1100 Km **Inclination 63.4 degrees** **Triplets Triangulation**

Current satellites: Yaogan 31 series – 12 operational satellites – Coverage Circle 7000 Km

Location accuracy about 25 Km

Figure 7.1: The coverage area of an ELINT triplet to locate radio emitters

As shown in the figure, the triplets cover a very large area on the surface of the earth. They can also fix the location of a military target by triangulation via its radio emissions. These ELINT satellites are spread out across the equator in four to six different planes. As the earth rotates one triplet is replaced by another so that the target can be tracked again.

Whilst this approach is adequate for targets that are far away, more frequent location and tracking may be needed as the target approaches closer to the country's borders.

For this purpose China has in orbit another constellation of ELINT satellites. Unlike the triplet ELINTs these do not fly in a triangular formation. There are six satellites flying in the same orbital plane. As one satellite covers the emission source and goes over the horizon this architecture ensures that another satellite takes its place. So the target is continuously tracked. These orbit the earth at about 600 Km altitude with an inclination of 35 degrees.

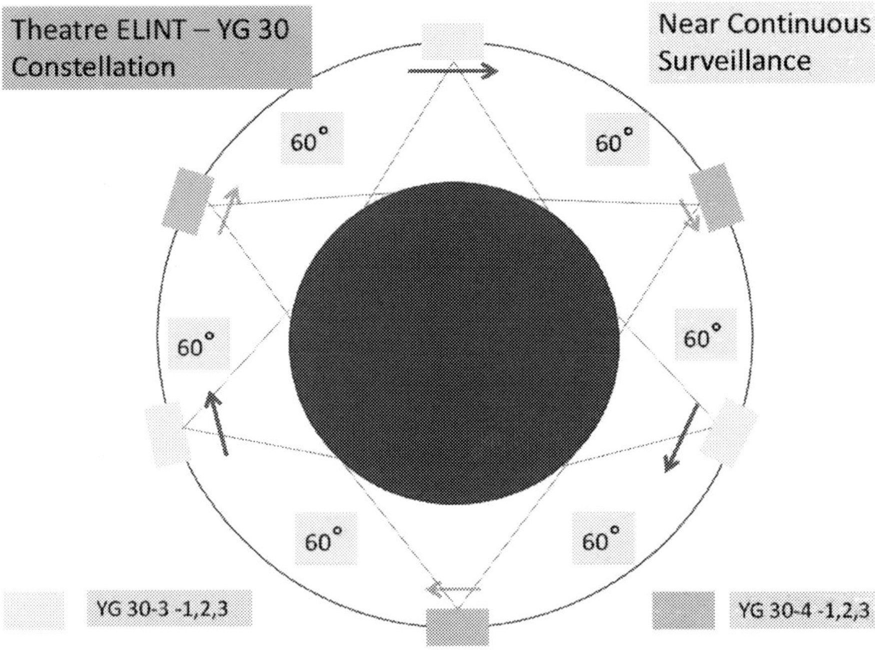

Figure 7.2: The architecture of the continuous tracking ELINT constellation

Once again as the earth rotates one constellation of six coplanar satellites goes outside the visibility of the target and is replaced by a second set of six satellites.

The current configuration that China uses has between three to four of these six satellite ELINT constellations. The position location provided by the triangular ELINT constellation is used by these coplanar ELINT satellites. Figures 2 and 3 provide details of this architecture.

To ensure that the targets never go out of sight, China also has in place several electro-optical and Synthetic Aperture Radar in different orbits. These can be cued by the ELINT satellites to provide an accurate location that facilitates continuous tracking and targeting information.

A propagation of the orbits of these Chinese satellites in a detailed study at the National Institute of Advanced Studies in 2024 suggest that China would have all areas between 35 degrees North Latitude and 35 degrees South Latitude under near constant surveillance. It is likely that this information could be used by its missile and drone arsenal to target the assets of the adversary.

The New Yaogan 30 Surveillance ELINT Constellation

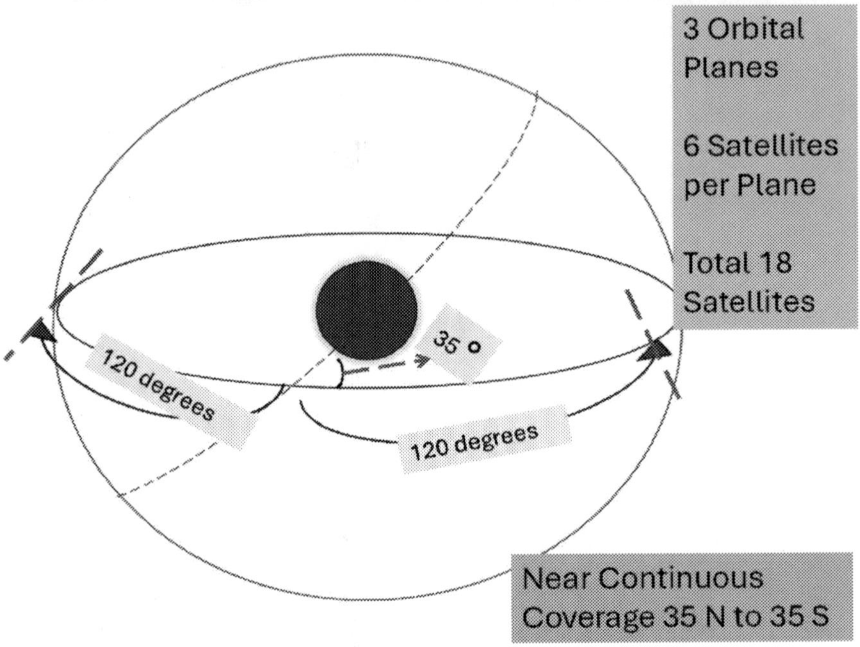

Figure 7.3: The distribution of these coplanar constellations across the equator

More recently India has signed up with a US company Hawkeye 360 for an Electronic Intelligence Service under a contract worth a reported $ 131 million dollars. Though this uses a slightly different architecture than the Chinese constellations they do use the same triangular formation as the Chinese ELINT. The US satellites are however significantly smaller than the Chinese ones.[1]

India could of course choose other possible architectures than the ones outlined here. Irrespective of this choice India would need about 30 to 40 operational ELINT satellites for its ISR mission along with their associated launch vehicles. A dedicated set of between 10 to 15 electro-optical and SAR satellites would also be needed. A total of between 40 to 55 satellites would be needed for the ISR mission.

The Command, Control, Communications and Computer (C4) Function

Once the information has been collected it has to be moved around to the required places where it can be used. These require communications satellites.

Though India does possess dedicated military communications satellites, these may not be sufficient to take care of situations where the movement of relevant information must take place over large, dispersed geographic areas. While it is difficult to quantify this need without more detailed studies, drawing upon examples from other similar countries, an operational architecture would need between six to ten dedicated military satellites in Geostationary Orbit.

Ground stations are needed to collect data from the ISR constellations. Such facilities may not always be available as the satellites move away from ground stations located in India. To address this problem, India would require a minimum of three Tracking and Data Relay satellites (TDRS) located in the GSO. To ensure that the data collected by the ISR satellites reach India in real time, they must relay the data via the TDRS satellites to ground stations on the mainland. A minimum of three such satellites would be needed to meet this requirement. These satellites are very similar to the large communications satellite mentioned above.

Between ten to fourteen large communications satellites in Geostationary Orbit would be needed for the movement of the collected information to the right locations.

Small Satellite Constellations for C4ISR

There has been a revolution in the use of smaller satellite constellations in Low Earth Orbit for carrying out imaging and communications functions. India has so far not fielded such systems.

Two constellations of six small satellites each, making a total of twelve, are needed to establish the viability of this approach for C4ISR use. India could of course hire such services from international vendors. This would increase vulnerabilities during a crisis.

The Space Situation Awareness Mission

Keeping Tabs on all the satellites and other objects in orbit

With the advent of small satellite constellations like Starlink, the number of satellites being launched has increased exponentially. There are many other discarded components of satellites, non-functioning dead satellites, debris from earlier experiments and ASAT testing. There have also been examples of physical collisions between satellites. A key requirement to handle any potential threats to the Indian state is to keep track of all of them and their orbits.

Though functioning satellites can be tracked via their radio emissions, dead and defunct satellites require a network of Long-Range Radars and Optical and Laser tracking telescopes.

Apart from ISRO and DRDO the expertise to track and keep track of all the satellites in orbit does not exist within the country. Many of the better Universities and Engineering colleges can be co-opted for a national capability building effort. These could also be used to study satellites of specific countries in search of trends and insights into functions like proximity operations and maneuvers. Astronomy faculty and associated telescopes could also be a very useful resource for this purpose.

Recent developments also suggest that satellites in orbit can provide information on other satellites in orbit. These will call for some test satellites to explore the feasibility and the algorithms needed to convert the information provided by the satellites into workable trajectories and predictions.

A minimum of two operational satellites in suitable orbits must be available for this purpose. A total of ten satellites may be needed for this over the next decade.

Keeping tabs is not enough – you need more details on some of them

Based on the assessment of their orbits and other auxiliary information an analyst or even a properly trained AI can identify satellites that could be of special concern. To deal with potential threats from them more information on their specific characteristics are often required. These would require satellites in both LEO and GSO to be able to move around in both regions, approach these satellites, and gather more information on them. This could include not only their physical features and shape but also their radio emission and telemetry characteristics. It is also useful to signal to potential adversaries that you can get close to some of the critical nodes in their space information networks in case of a crisis or a conflict.

At least two such satellites must be available operationally to perform these functions. Since they must move around quite a bit **these proximity and rendezvous satellites** need to carry a lot of fuel. They provide the technical teeth that can communicate an ASAT capability (potential or real) to the adversary.

At least ten such satellites may be needed for performing this function after an initial period of experimentation.

Performing the Missile Defence or the Sudarshan Chakra function

Recent conflicts have emphasised the need to protect high value targets with terminal defence systems. In this approach incoming planes, drones or missiles are destroyed by a self-contained system located on suitable platforms that can track and direct attacks against them. As mentioned earlier these systems, while very effective, cannot be deployed all over the country to protect all sensitive installations and our cities.

In principle a missile can be destroyed as soon as it is launched. If this does not work it could be destroyed during its midcourse ballistic phase after its warheads and decoys are deployed. It could also be dealt with during its terminal phase as it moves in towards hitting its target. While ascent phase missile defence is very difficult since launch sites could be located deep inside countries, both mid-course and terminal defence systems are feasible. Terminal phase defence systems are the most advanced.

Ideally if a threat can be identified early enough, and its trajectory established, it may be easier for the defence to be able to locate and destroy them much earlier before they come close to their targets. During the cold war years both the superpowers had satellites in GSO or high altitude orbits that could track the hot flame of the rockets as they came out of the atmosphere. Using this data they were able to predict the trajectory and should the situation arise alert suitable terminal defence systems on the ground. China has also experimented and fielded satellites in GSO for this purpose.[2]

After the initiation of the Star Wars programme by President Reagan, the notion of moving from terminal defence to mid-course intercept gained ground. This involves the discrimination of the warhead from the decoys as they are deployed during the ballistic phase of their trajectories. A series of satellites created a data bank of signatures for this purpose. The Chinese too have experimented and possibly created a data base of signatures that could be used by satellites in LEO to detect such threats and track them.

Together these early warning satellites in GSO and the mid-course intercept satellites in LEO add to the terminal phase defence capabilities in taking care of threats well before they reach the target.

The accomplishment of this task requires a minimum of two satellites located in GSO equipped with the infrared detectors that can detect the hot plumes of the missiles as they arise out of the atmosphere. After experimentation with the collection of needed signatures, this needs to be operational. About four large satellites in GSO may be needed over the next ten years.

Another set of at least two operational satellites in LEO orbit may be needed for the mid-course interception function. Once again after some experimentation this needs to become operational. About ten medium size satellites may be needed for this over the next ten years.

It is worth recapitulating that India has already performed some experiments regarding missile plume detection from GSO. The Geosynchronous Satellite (GSAT) 7A launched on GSLV in 2018 was tracked by a Geoimaging High Resolution Camera (GHRC) carried by the GSAT 29 geostationary satellite located at 55 degrees East Longitude. This has apparently been used to demonstrate the detection of missile plumes once they reach a certain altitude.[3] It must be possible to track the hot end of the rocket stage which would be at a temperature of about 3000 degrees Kelvin.

India may not have experimented with satellites in LEO for the collection of signatures needed for tracking the deployed payload.

Space Support for Military Operations

Positioning, Navigation, and Timing Services

India does have in place a regional navigation constellation in place called Navigation with Indian Constellation (NAVIC). Many advanced systems such as missile guidance or drone coordination may require a more advanced and global system. India may have to move towards a 35 satellite constellation of navigation satellites in Medium Earth Orbits (20000 Km) and in GSO. Designing and Building a high accuracy atomic clock for space use remains a major challenge.

Weather Services

The INSAT weather satellites have provided yeoman services for over three decades. This of course will hopefully continue as a part of the civilian public good service.

These may have to be augmented by some LEO orbiting weather satellites. Two operational satellites with a select set of optical, infrared and microwave sensors may be needed for this. About six satellites over the next ten years may be needed for this purpose.

Creating the Ground and Organisation Infrastructure

Creating the Ground segment for each one of these missions and integrating them to work as one is of course a major challenge. This may also require a re-look and a reorganisation of the division of work and the coordination of work within the national security system of the country.

R&D in Key Areas

Annexure 1 provides a list of some key technologies that may need to be developed on a priority basis by the country.

Overall Assessment

Table 1 provides an estimate of the required number of satellites and launch vehicles to meet the challenge of realising a Missile shield or Sudarshan Chakra.

More detailed technical studies would be needed to refine the estimates.

India would need to build and launch a total of 155 satellites over the next ten years to be able to better protect its citizens from missile and drone attacks.

These would require about 50 PSLV and 62 GSLV launchers.

This does not include other human flight, civilian, and science missions that India needs to undertake.

A major partnership with industry is needed along with a significant augmentation of the launch infrastructure that would involve the creation of at least two more launch sites. All the satellites and launchers needed for this task should be built and launched by industry with oversight from government entities. This is the only way that these ambitious targets can be realised. The great challenge facing the nascent Indian space ecosystem is the transfer and scaling up of the capabilities that have been built-up within Government to industry. Without proactive support for this transformation this formidable task cannot be realised.

Since the entire effort for meeting these needs must be funded by the Government it provides an opportunity for the Government to create a mechanism through which the key technologies developed in Government institutions with public funding are transferred to Indian industry for large scale deployment and use. There is no reason to believe that such a trajectory of partnership and co-evolution cannot be made to happen.

A strong partnership supported by the government with the academic and think tank communities regarding Space Situation Awareness studies is needed. Whilst geopolitical understanding is important, there is no awareness of the technological and science base in many of the areas related to space. India needs a talent pool of technology led studies to redress major imbalances of knowledge within the national security ecosystem. Unless these are linked to geopolitics in closer ways there will be a knowledge gap in the taking of decisions.

The division of work and the coordination of work within the National Security Complex needs to be reevaluated and reorganised. The reality of fighting and winning the information based wars of this century should form the basis for this reorganisation.

There are several key space related technologies that India needs to address. A few of them are listed in Annexure 1. These should be supported on a crash basis and linked to the development process followed for various products and services needed for this programme.

Continuous tracking of technologies and their evolution should feed into the projects and programmes of the national security complex.

Figure below provides an overview of the status and capabilities in the country. The areas highlighted in red are those of special concern.

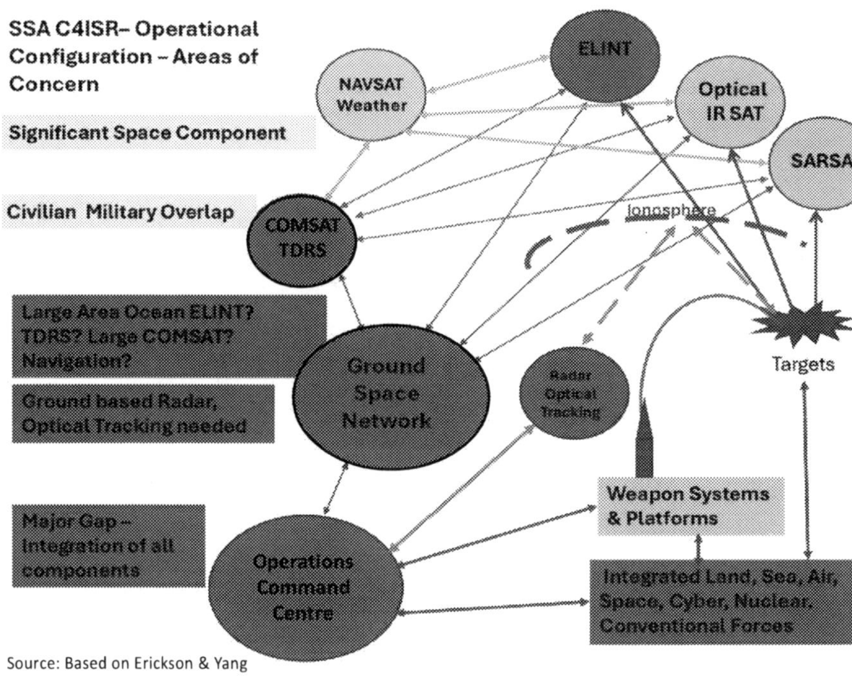

Figure 7.4: Key Focus Areas marked in red

References

S Chandrashekar, "Space, War & Security – A strategy for India," NIAS Report R36 – 2015, National Institute of Advanced Studies, 2015.

S Chandrashekar, "China's Space Programme From the Era of Mao Zedong to Xi Jinping, Springer Nature NIAS publication, 2022.

Table 7.1: Satellite and Launcher Requirements for Defending India 2025-2035

Function	*Satellite*	*Mass (Kg)*	*Orbit*	*Nos*			*Launchers Comment*
				PSLV	*GSLV*	*Small*	
ISR Functions							
Dedicated ISR military services	500–1000 Kg	SSO LEO	40	20			ELINT, SAR, EO capacity needed
ISR Small Satellite development	150–200 Kg	LEO	6	2			Ion Propulsion
Sub-Total 1			*46*	*22*			*Industry Delivery*
Communications C4 Function							
C4 System Military	2000–4000 Kg	GSO	10		10		Ion Propulsion GSLV launch
Data Relay Satellites	2000–4000 Kg	GSO	3		3		Ion Propulsion GSLV launch
LEO constellation - development	150–200 Kg	LEO	6	2			Ion Propulsion PSLV
Sub-Total 2			*19*	*2*	*13*		*Industry Delivery*
Space Situational Awareness							
Keeping Tabs - satellites & orbits	200–500 Kg	LEO	10	5			National effort with academia
Proximity, Rendezvous, ASAT	1500–2000 Kg	GSO LEO	10	5	5		Detailed threat assessment
Ballistic Drone Missile Defence	1000–4000 Kg	GSO LEO	14	5	4		Data bank of signatures for decoy
Subtotal 3			*34*	*15*	*9*		
Weather Services							Important support service
Orbiting satellites	500–1000 Kg	LEO / SSO	6	6			Polar satellites
Subtotal 4			*6*	*6*			
GSO Weather Services	The Civilian Public Good services with some augmentation may be adequate to meet military requirements						

Function	*Satellite*	*Mass (Kg)*	*Orbit*	*Nos*			*Launchers Comment*
				PSLV	*GSLV*	*Small*	
Navigation Services							
GSO, IGSO & MEO constellation	1500–2000 Kg	GSO, MEO	35		35		Ion Propulsion – GSLV launch
Sub-Total 5			*35*		*35*		***Government-Industry Partnership***
R&D test satellites	100–1000	LEO, GSO	15	5	5		Emerging trend
Sub-Total 6			*15*	*5*	*5*		***Government-Industry Partnership***
Total			155	50	62	some	**Industry role vital in scaling up**

Notes: C4 – Command Control Communications & Computers, **ISR** – Intelligence Surveillance & Reconnaissance, **DRS** Data Relay Satellite
ELINT – Electronic Intelligence, **EO** – Electro-optical, **SAR** – Synthetic Aperture Radar, **GSO** – Geostationary Orbit, **SSO** – Sun Synchronous Orbit
MEO – Medium Earth Orbit, **LEO** – Low Earth Orbit, **PSLV** – Polar Satellite Launch Vehicle, **GSLV** - Geostationary Satellite Launch Vehicle

Annexure 1

Critical Infrastructure & Major Areas of Concern

Critical Infrastructure & Areas of Concern	*Comment*
Space Situation Awareness	
Radar Network for Tracking Space Objects & Debris	Major Gap area for Immediate Action
Optical & Laser Ranging Facilities for Tracking Space Objects	Major Gap area for Immediate Action
Capabilities & Capacities for Monitoring the Space Environment	Major Gap area for Immediate Action
Ship borne TTC stations for space missions	TDRSS is an alternative for future
Orbit based Scientific Studies (International Collaboration)	Geodesy, Astronomy, Global Tracking
C4 & Related Areas	
Ion Propulsion for satellite applications	Critical to redress launcher satellite gaps
Satellite to Satellite Radio Links	Need for switching via satellite
Satellite to satellite Laser Links	Need for optical switching
Secure Communications	Encryption, Frequency hopping, Anti-jamming
C4 Network Operations	Connectivity within C4 commands + Civilian
LEO C4 Internet Constellations	Architecture, Design, Validation key areas
Antennae Beam forming Beam Shaping	Major area for Advanced C4 TDRSS Satellites
ISR Related Areas	
ELINT Technology Development	Major Gap Area for Immediate Action
Infrared Technologies and Imaging Sensors	Needed for military & BMD applications Gaps
Improved Integrated Optics for Imaging Sensors	Capabilities may need enhancement
SAR weight reduction initiatives	Benchmarks show Scope for improvement
ISR Small satellite development	Need for Catch up
TDRSS related Compatibility capabilities	Interface issues – compatibility issues
Data Processing especially SAR data Processing	Need for speedier processing of Satellite Data

Critical Infrastructure & Areas of Concern	*Comment*
Use of commercial or open source data for strategic applications	Improve National capabilities to use Data
Space Based Support Services	
TDRSS related	Technology development compatibility issues
Infrared Microwave imagers and sounders for weather	Need to improve complement of sensors
High precision clocks for time measurement navigation	Alternatives for time measurements
Small Satellites	
A National Initiative on Small Satellites – Multiple Centers	Emerging area for military and civil use
Launchers	
Scale up Improvements PSLV	Need to produce in numbers. Industry role
Operationalisation GSLV Mark 2 – Scale up for Production	Launcher production and launch by industry
Operationalisation GSLV Mark 3 - Scale up for Production	Need for industrial capacity
Agni 5 modifications for Space Launch	Useful Complement – small satellite initiative
Space Weapons	
Retain Develop Technology Options for BMD, ASAT	Link to good SSA – Midcourse BMD extension
Technology Development Early Warning Satellite	Option for a Possible Future
Monitor Space Geo-political Environment – other Space Players	Link to good SSA – technology assessments
Integrated SSA & C4ISR Capabilities	
Need to restructure and re-organise operational capabilities	Integrated Mission mode network operations
Strengthening the Planning & War Strategy capabilities	Link to threat scenarios wars and conflicts
Strategy & Doctrine Related	
Restructuring of the National Security Complex	Major challenge to recognise new realities

NOTES

1 "US approves sale of Hawkeye 360 technology to India to boost the country's surveillance capabilities", https://www.newsonair.gov.in/us-approves-sale-of-hawkeye-360-technology-to-india-to-boost-the-countrys-surveillance-capabilities/

2 S Chandrashekar, "China's Space Programme From the Era of Mao Zedong to Xi Jinping", Springer Nature, 2022, pp. 217-243.

3 Mehul R Pandya, Rohit Pradhan, "A Study of rocket exhaust plumes in the lower atmosphere using Geo-Imaging High Resolution Camera (GHRC) onboard Indian Geostationary Satellite", https://www.researchgate.net/publication/355481704_A_Study_of_Rocket_Exhaust_Plume_in_the_Lower_Atmosphere_using_Geo-Imaging _High_Resolution_Camera_GHRC_On-board_Indian_Geostationary_Satellite

8

Propulsion as Strategic Leverage: Building Dynamic Spacepower in India's Sudarshan Chakra Architecture

Sai Susmitha Guddanti

Introduction

On 15 August 2025, Prime Minister Narendra Modi announced an ambitious national defence initiative: Mission Sudarshan Chakra, a multi-layered and integrated air and missile defence architecture designed to protect critical military, civilian, and infrastructure assets from aerial threats.[1] Described as a "*powerful weapon system*," the Mission aims to not only neutralise attacks but also enable precise counter-action, with research, development and manufacturing conducted domestically, ensuring it remains a fully indigenous capability.[2]

At its core, Mission Sudarshan Chakra seeks to integrate existing systems such as the S-400, along with homegrown interceptors and surface-to-air missile families like Akash Medium-Range Surface-to-Air Missile (MRSAM), and Quick Reaction Surface-to-Air Missile (QRSAM), while incorporating emerging technologies such as directed-energy weapons, hypersonic interceptors, and other long-range systems into a seamless, networked defence grid.[3] If realised, it would represent one of the most comprehensive and technologically sophisticated defence architectures ever prepared by India. Achieving this level of integration demands unprecedented coordination across multiple domains such as land, air, sea, undersea, and space. It requires resilient and secure C4ISR (Command, Control, Communications, Computers, Intelligence, Surveillance, and Reconnaissance) infrastructure, Space Domain Awareness (SDA), along with real-time data fusion, autonomous decision-making, and interoperable communication links between sensors and shooters. The roadmap envisions testing and early deployment beginning around 2026, with full operational capability targeted by 2035.

India's security landscape is shaped by a complex mix of regional rivalries, emerging counterspace capabilities, and the increasing militarisation of technology. With China's demonstrated anti-satellite (ASAT) capabilities and Pakistan's evolving missile programmes, India faces a dual-front challenge that extends beyond traditional borders into the orbital domain.[4] Modern warfare now hinges on the seamless integration of space-based communication, navigation, and surveillance systems, where the disruption of even a few satellites could cripple decision-making and deterrence.[5] As regional adversaries pursue space denial and electronic warfare strategies, the ability to protect, manoeuvre, and sustain India's space assets has become indispensable. This makes propulsion, Space Domain Awareness (SDA), and C4ISR not just technical enablers but instruments of strategic survival – defining how India anticipates, responds to, and recovers from threats in the multi-domain battlespace.

C4ISR is the eyes and ears of any defence system, linking sensors, shooters, decision-makers, and support elements across every domain. Within Mission Sudarshan Chakra, the space-based C4ISR component becomes especially critical. Modern space-based sensors span a wide range of modalities – optical, radar, infrared, and multispectral imaging systems, collectively known as Imagery Intelligence (IMINT). These operate alongside Signals Intelligence (SIGINT) and Electronic Intelligence (ELINT) satellites, as well as early-warning, target acquisition, and tracking systems, including emerging hyperspectral sensors. Together, these are not merely data-collecting instruments but integral parts of an information ecosystem that must translate raw data into actionable intelligence.

It is worth emphasising that data is not the same as intelligence. Collecting data is only the first step; its real value lies in how it is processed, fused, interpreted, and linked to decisions. Without this analytical pipeline, more sensors only generate more noise and potential brittleness in the decision loop. Space-based ISR holds true value only when it informs operational timing and strategic choices.[6] These systems must also interface seamlessly with communication, navigation, and weather satellites, ensuring the architecture operates as a cohesive, dynamic defence ecosystem. Such cross-domain synergy will ultimately determine whether Mission Sudarshan Chakra fulfills its intended promise.

Such an undertaking inherently depends on a high-fidelity Space Domain Awareness (SDA) network. Traditional Space Situational Awareness (SSA) focuses primarily on tracking and cataloguing space objects, predicting trajectories, preventing collisions, and maintaining orbital safety. SDA, however, represents the strategic evolution of that concept. It extends beyond positional awareness to encompass behavioural interpretation, threat attribution, and intent analysis.[7] In essence, SDA is not only about *what* is happening in orbit but *why* it is happening, *who* is responsible, and *how* a State should respond. Any manoeuvre in space signals intent, and the ability to recognise, predict, and react to such manoeuvres defines strategic advantage. Mission Sudarshan Chakra, by design, should rely heavily on such an awareness layer, not only to safeguard its space assets but also to integrate space-derived intelligence into its terrestrial and aerial defence networks.

However, awareness without mobility is incomplete. To interpret and respond to orbital manoeuvres, a nation must also possess the propulsion capacity to act, to reposition, evade, or counteract threats in real time. Awareness without mobility is incomplete; propulsion provides the capacity to translate knowledge into action. Propulsion systems determine how satellites and other space assets can alter orbits, evade threats, reposition for surveillance, or maintain persistence in contested environments. In this sense, propulsion is not merely an engineering function but a strategic instrument, one that underwrites deterrence, responsiveness, and survivability in the space domain. Without reliable, efficient, and flexible propulsion architectures, no integrated defence system, whether in the atmosphere or beyond it, can claim true autonomy or resilience.

To achieve this, India will require multiple propulsion systems with varying capabilities depending on each mission profile. For example, low-Earth orbit (LEO) constellations, supporting communication or tactical data relay, can benefit from electric propulsion, which is efficient and capable of long-duration station keeping. Geostationary (GEO) satellites, by contrast, rely on chemical or hybrid propulsion for orbital insertion and station maintenance. However, the traditional approach of launching satellites into fixed orbits for the entirety of their operational life will not be sufficient for the dynamic C4ISR and SDA needs of the coming decades.[8] We increasingly need agile and manoeuvrable satellites, space assets that can reposition as required by mission demands, shifting vantage points to track moving threats, replace disabled systems, or fill temporary coverage gaps. The limiting factor, however, is propellant. Every orbital manoeuvre, station-keeping adjustment, or attitude correction consumes propellant, and propellant mass is among the most restrictive constraints in spacecraft design. Due to payload and launch cost limitations, most satellites carry just enough propellant for the lifetime of their planned mission.

Propellant is not only limited but expensive, both in economic and operational terms. Once expended, it directly determines the end of mission life, even if the satellite's sensors and communication systems remain functional.[9] As defence missions become more dynamic and unpredictable, this constraint becomes unacceptable. Future SDA and C4ISR networks will require space assets that can sustain manoeuvring capability over longer periods, which in turn calls for on-orbit refueling, life-extension systems and modular satellite designs capable of servicing or upgrading components in space.[10]

Beyond fuel replenishment, maintaining system resilience also requires redundancy. If one satellite fails or is disabled, another must seamlessly replace it to avoid operational blind spots. Dynamic satellites with independent propulsion capacity can be repositioned to fill these gaps rapidly, minimising time lost in surveillance coverage. In high-tempo defence operations, time is as critical a variable as thrust and propulsion;

therefore, it becomes the ultimate determinant of responsiveness. To make such responsiveness meaningful, manoeuvring satellites must operate on real-time data pipelines that link propulsion control with situational intelligence. This fusion of propulsion dynamics with intelligent decision-support effectively turns mobility into strategy, ensuring every manoeuvre aligns with broader defence objectives.

In a dynamic defence architecture like Sudarshan Chakra, propulsion, SDA, and C4ISR together form a mutually reinforcing triad. Propulsion confers mobility, SDA provides awareness, and C4ISR ensures actionable control. Each element supports the others, without propulsion, awareness is inert; without SDA, propulsion lacks direction; without C4ISR, both remain uncoordinated. Building this trinity also demands a robust industrial ecosystem. The development of advanced propulsion technologies like chemical, electric, solar, and nuclear, cannot rest solely on ISRO or DRDO. Private companies and startups must be integrated into the national framework, fostering innovation in reusable launchers, modular satellite buses, and in-space servicing systems. Reusable first and second stages will be essential for cost-effective replenishment and deployment of defence constellations.

While Mission Sudarshan Chakra is an ambitious vision, realising it requires closing critical technological gaps – particularly in propulsion diversity, refueling infrastructure, and adaptive satellite architectures. The transition from static, single-orbit systems to a responsive and manoeuvrable constellation will define India's strategic flexibility in both defence and deterrence. In summary, the credibility of Mission Sudarshan Chakra as a future-ready defence system will not rest solely on its interceptors or radars, but on the invisible yet decisive power of propulsion – the means through which India's space assets can move, survive, and act in an increasingly contested domain.

Building on this premise, this article examines the role of propulsion as the strategic enabler of India's *Mission Sudarshan Chakra*. It argues that propulsion, alongside Space Domain Awareness (SDA) and C4ISR, forms the foundation of a dynamic defense architecture capable of sustained mobility and deterrence in orbit. The article proceeds in two parts: the first outlines the technological and operational context of propulsion within Sudarshan Chakra, while the second situates these insights within a broader strategic discussion that integrates propulsion, SDA, and C4ISR as the trinity of deterrence shaping India's emerging spacepower.

Propulsion and Strategic Leverage

Propulsion refers to the systems that generate thrust and control motion of space vehicles, determining how satellites or any space objects can accelerate, decelerate, or alter their trajectory in space. Beyond its physical function, propulsive power represents strategic agency – the ability to act, react, or reposition a space asset in a contested domain. In short, propulsion is the hidden currency of spacepower. India must view propulsion not just as an engineering subsystem but as strategic leverage, determining where and how fast we can act in space.

With Sudarshan Chakra's multi-domain design, there is a clear need for dynamic, manoeuvrable space assets for real-time intelligence, surveillance, reconnaissance (ISR), and defence. Regular static, fuel-limited satellites confined to fixed orbits are no longer enough. Positional space operations, where satellites occupy predictable "parking spots" determined by Keplerian dynamics, belong to an earlier era when threats in orbit were minimal and motion was costly. In today's contested domain, the advantage shifts to the force capable of sustained manoeuvre – maintaining initiative, achieving surprise, and out-manoeuvring an adversary over time.[11] For India, this means propulsion must enable satellites to chase, evade, or outlast competitors, ensuring survivability and responsiveness within Sudarshan Chakra's networked defence grid. Dynamic, manoeuvrable space assets are no longer optional; they are the operational hinge between deterrence credibility and technological obsolescence.[12]

Current Limitations and Operational Realities

Propulsion determines what kind of leverage a nation has in space, what orbits can be accessed, how quickly debris can be avoided, and how a satellite can escape or pursue a potential threat. India will need at least a few dynamic space assets that can change orbits, increase or decrease speed, and reposition quickly without losing significant time.

However, current satellite systems are highly limited once launched. Except for attitude control or small debris-avoidance manoeuvres, satellites operate under tight ÄV (change-in-velocity) constraints that restrict major orbital shifts. A satellite's orbit is largely fixed at injection, with only a small propellant margin reserved for station-keeping or collision avoidance. Each kilogram of fuel directly limits mission life, and large plane changes or altitude adjustments are generally infeasible.[13] Bowen connects this physical rigidity to strategic exposure, noting that predictable orbits make satellites easy to monitor, target, or disable.[14]

Changing orbit also takes time if fuel is conserved, which is often the case because propellant is expensive and limited. It is like owning a car with a full tank but no option to refuel, every trip must be weighed against the risk of running empty. The same logic applies to satellites, each orbit-change decision trades short-term responsiveness for long-term survival. Therefore, satellites are typically designed around specific mission requirements such as orbit altitude, payload, lifetime, and propulsion type are fixed at the design stage. This rigidity makes dynamic manoeuvres difficult; every manoeuvre consumes propellant, and when fuel runs out, the mission ends. Even when using orbital mechanics for passive repositioning, the process can take weeks or months, often too slow for real-time defence or ISR needs. Hence, propulsion efficiency and flexibility are not just engineering preferences but operational necessities.

Various Propulsion System Options

Propulsion technologies can be grouped into chemical, electric, solar-electric, and nuclear systems, each with trade-offs between thrust, efficiency, and mission suitability.[15]

- Chemical propulsion uses combustion to generate high thrust but at the cost of efficiency. It is ideal for rapid manoeuvres, orbital insertion, or evasive actions, drains fuel quickly but saves time.
- Electric propulsion (EP) converts electrical energy into kinetic energy, offering high efficiency and long endurance but low thrust; major orbit changes can take weeks or months.[16]
- Solar-electric propulsion (SEP) relies on solar power to drive electric

thrusters, sustainable but limited by sunlight availability and power density.

- Nuclear propulsion exists in two broad forms: Nuclear Thermal Propulsion (NTP), which heats a propellant using a reactor to produce high thrust, and Nuclear Electric Propulsion (NEP), which generates electrical power to drive Ion or Hall thrusters. NTP is better suited for interplanetary missions that need short bursts of high thrust, while NEP offers long-duration operation for cis-lunar or Earth-orbit applications, where sustained power is critical. NEP can power large assets such as space stations or defense platforms without dependence on sunlight, requiring only propellant for the electric thrusters themselves, making them much efficient than chemical-based systems.

Each propulsion type thus fits a specific layer of Sudarshan Chakra's architecture. For communication or navigation constellations in low- or medium-Earth orbit, electric propulsion offers longevity and efficiency, using minimal propellant for station keeping. But for military or strategic satellites that need to move quickly, whether to avoid anti-satellite (ASAT) threats or debris, electric propulsion alone is inadequate. Low thrust means slow orbit changes, sometimes taking months, which is unacceptable when reaction time determines survival. These missions need high-thrust chemical systems for immediate manoeuvring.

The trade-off is that every rapid burn consumes significant fuel, reducing mission duration. Constantly replacing large satellites is economically and logistically unsustainable. Therefore, the only practical path is to extend operational life through refueling and modularity.

Extending Life: Refueling and Modularity

The sustainability of dynamic space operations ultimately depends on the ability to refuel or service satellites in orbit. Without this capability, even the most advanced propulsion remains single-use. Recognising this, several defence programmes now integrate on-orbit refueling requirements into next-generation architectures.

The US Space Force, for instance, is considering refueling capability for its forthcoming Space Domain Awareness constellation. Maj. Gen. Stephen Purdy emphasised that manoeuvrable, refuelable satellites are essential for long-term agility, with plans to leverage commercial technology to replace legacy GSSAP systems.[17] This approach reflects a global shift from "launch-and-leave" satellites towards serviced, sustainable architectures – more efficient to refuel in orbit than to replace once fuel is exhausted. Designing for refueling from the outset reduces cost and strengthens deterrence through persistence.

For India, the lesson is clear. Refueling must be treated as a baseline design parameter, not an advanced feature. Sudarshan Chakra's layered defence network will require constellations capable of on-orbit life extension, particularly for high-value ISR and command satellites. This could involve:

- Standardised docking ports compatible with robotic or autonomous refueling vehicles.
- Fuel depots stationed in geosynchronous orbit or cis-lunar space, possibly operated by public-private partnerships.
- Modular satellite designs that allow replacement of thrusters, sensors, or power modules without de-orbiting the entire asset.

India can draw from global examples such as Northrop Grumman's GAS-T platform, which uses an ESPAStar-D bus to add propellant and extend the life of in-orbit satellites – a model showing how commercial platforms can directly support military needs.[18] There are also other private companies like Orbit Fab that are actively looking into refueling.

Moreover, refueling and servicing technologies are not purely technical, they reshape strategic planning. A refuelable satellite changes the cost calculus of deterrence, instead of losing a system once fuel runs out, nations can sustain manoeuvring capabilities longer, provided they have the logistical chain to support it. This also enhances redundancy, when one satellite fails, another can reposition quickly without risking the loss of long-term coverage.

Refueling, however, is only part of the solution. In the long run, fuel alone cannot guarantee functionality. Satellites are complex systems with multiple subsystems such as sensors, communication modules, power systems, and thrusters that degrade or fail over time due to radiation, thermal stress, simple wear or debris hit. A refueled satellite with a failed sensor or processor still remains operationally blind. Therefore, future defence satellites must be designed with true modularity in mind, allowing replacement or upgrade of specific components rather than deorbiting the entire system. Such modularity would enable robotic or autonomous servicing spacecraft to replace malfunctioning sensors or thruster units in orbit, without human intervention or long downtime. This requires common mechanical and software interfaces, as well as precision docking and handling systems capable of operating in microgravity. The goal should not just be to extend fuel reserves, but to extend the total life and performance of the satellite itself – maintaining functional continuity, not just orbital persistence. In essence, India must move from thinking about refueling architectures to thinking in terms of life-extension ecosystems, where hardware, software, and energy replenishment all converge to keep strategic assets operational for decades.

Refueling also demands policy and standardisation. Currently there are challenges involved because commercial vendors use different fuel types and interface designs. India will need early coordination between ISRO, DRDO, and private companies to develop common refueling interfaces and propellant standards. Without such standardisation, orbital logistics could become fragmented, undermining the very efficiency refueling aims to provide.

Finally, modular and refuelable architectures align with India's push toward indigenous, reusable systems. Private startups like Skyroot Aerospace, Agnikul Cosmos, and Bellatrix Aerospace are already experimenting with reusable launch vehicles and advanced propulsion modules.[19] Integrating their innovations into a national propulsion roadmap under Sudarshan Chakra can accelerate progress towards sustainable, responsive, and deterrence-ready space operations.

In summary, propulsion determines how India's space assets move, survive, and assert presence within the Sudarshan Chakra framework. Current systems, bound by limited ÄV and finite propellant, restrict flexibility and shorten mission lifetimes. As emerging propulsion technologies like chemical, electric, solar, and nuclear diversify, their integration must be guided by mission type, operational tempo, and strategic value. Ultimately, on-orbit refueling and modularity will define the next era of defence space power. The ability to sustain manoeuvre, rather than merely achieve it, is what will separate static capability from enduring deterrence.

Discussion

Technological progress without strategic alignment can be wasteful. Within the *Sudarshan Chakra* framework, technology and strategy must advance together. Propulsion, Space Domain Awareness (SDA), and C4ISR must therefore be integrated to achieve maximum operational effect. SDA provides situational awareness, C4ISR enables control and decision-making, and propulsion grants the mobility that translates information into action. Their synergy determines how effectively India can sense, decide, and act across domains.

Propulsion and Strategic Leverage in Space Power Thought

Propulsion functions not merely as a technological enabler but as a determinant of strategic behaviour in space. As E.C. Dolman observes in *Astropolitik: Classical Geopolitics in the Space Age*, control of movement in orbit is analogous to control of maritime sea lines; the actor capable of manoeuvring freely dictates the terms of engagement.[20] In this view, propulsion transforms access into advantage, without the capacity to reposition or sustain orbital presence, even the most sophisticated satellites remain passive observers rather than active instruments of policy. Bleddyn Bowen, in the *Original Sin: Power, Technology and War in Outer Space*, extends this argument by identifying propulsion as part of the "material basis of spacepower," emphasising its role alongside sensors and communications in enabling states to project, sustain, and contest power beyond Earth's atmosphere.[21] Similarly, John Klein, in *Fight for the Final Frontier: Irregular Warfare in Space* underscores manoeuvre and positional advantage as central to deterrence, contending that mobility, enabled by reliable propulsion, introduces strategic uncertainty and shapes both operational outcomes and political signaling.[22] Collectively, these perspectives converge on a central proposition: propulsion embodies agility. It grants a nation the freedom to determine when, where, and how to act in orbit, thereby transforming spacepower from a static possession into a dynamic instrument of statecraft.

For India, these insights are directly relevant. *Sudarshan Chakra's* layered defence depends on translating propulsive capability into strategic leverage. As Dolman's framework implies, control of orbital "sea lines" will determine initiative in space.[23] India's current propulsion assets – largely chemical and limited-electric – grant access but not manoeuvrable dominance. To progress from possession to control, propulsion must become an instrument of strategy, enabling dynamic repositioning and sustained presence. In this sense, *Sudarshan Chakra's* success will rest not only on interceptors or command networks, but on the propulsive freedom of its space assets, the capacity to act, adapt, and endure as a reflection of national will.

Transforming Space Power: From Positional to Dynamic

Refueling stations, modular satellites, and sustained maneuver capabilities collectively transform spacepower from being positional to persistent and dynamic. Traditional "launch-and-leave" systems project presence but not adaptability, once the propellant runs out or a subsystem fails, capability decays. By contrast, architectures that can refuel, repair, and reposition create endurance – the ability to maintain, recover, and reconstitute power over time.

Refueling allows satellites to remain active far beyond their original design life, directly translating into strategic persistence. This ensures continuous coverage and deterrence without costly replacements. When combined with modular design, refueling extends not just fuel capacity but functional life, allowing upgrades or replacements of specific subsystems rather than full deorbit and relaunch cycles. This modularity enhances strategic flexibility, as assets can be reconfigured or serviced in response to operational needs or emerging threats.[24]

By allowing satellites to be refueled in orbit, nations can avoid the costly and time-consuming process of launching new satellites when existing ones run low on propellant. This not only extends the utility of existing assets but also supports longer missions and the potential for sophisticated in-orbit manoeuvres.[25] The economic implications of operational endurance through refueling stations are significant. Modular spacecraft equipped for refueling ensure that valuable resources are utilised efficiently, allowing for continuous adaptation and upgrading of orbital infrastructure, similar to how traditional vehicle servicing stations sustain terrestrial fleets.[26] Such strategic infrastructure can enhance a nation's global reach and influence by ensuring that its satellite assets remain functional and responsive to immediate requirements.

Additionally, these servicing capabilities can be leveraged for dual military-civilian applications, reinforcing national governance and control over space assets. Nations possessing advanced in-space servicing and modular capabilities can exert leadership in international space governance, technology transfer, and cooperative frameworks vital for future space endeavours.

Strategic Mobility and Deterrence

Strategic mobility, the ability to reposition satellites quickly and effectively, is a transformative aspect of national security. Advanced transportation methods for satellite relocation allow nations to respond dynamically to both routine operational needs and emergent threats.[27] Enhanced mobility disrupts adversaries' strategies by allowing rapid deployment of assets where they are most needed. In military contexts, such adaptability provides tactical advantages where satellites can be repositioned to maximise observation or coverage while minimising vulnerability. Nations with strategic mobility capabilities can enhance their reconnaissance and surveillance functions, turning orbit into an active operational domain rather than a passive medium. This multi-dimensional projection of power becomes increasingly significant in a global environment characterised by great-power competition, where control over space translates directly into terrestrial influence.

China is reportedly preparing to field a nuclear-powered fleet of spacecraft by 2040, with plans for hybrid and reusable carriers by mid-century.[28] Such systems would offer immense endurance and manoeuvring capability, allowing continuous operations far beyond Earth orbit. Access to nuclear propulsion would therefore be a decisive advantage, granting sustained reach, faster orbital transfers, and independence from conventional fuel constraints. For other nations, this marks a pivotal shift; those limited to chemical or electric propulsion risk strategic asymmetry in both space mobility and deterrence.[29]

The Trinity of Deterrence: Propulsion, SDA, and C4ISR

Propulsion, SDA, and C4ISR together form a "trinity of deterrence" in space operations. Propulsion supplies the physical capacity to act; SDA provides the cognitive awareness of movement and intent; C4ISR furnishes the organisational control that converts knowledge into timely action. None can function in isolation. A manoeuvrable satellite is ineffective without intelligence to guide it, just as awareness is futile without the means to respond. Deterrence therefore rests on the continuous ability to detect, decide, and dynamically act. Integrated effectively, this trinity can transform India's spacepower from reactive monitoring to active control, enabling both protection of assets and assertion of strategic freedom in orbit.

Institutional Integration and the Road Ahead

Realising this trinity requires institutional coherence and technological alignment in areas where India still faces significant gaps. DRDO, ISRO and private industry, each advance propulsion and satellite technologies, yet their efforts remain parallel rather than integrated.[30] The absence of a unified propulsion roadmap connecting research, production, and operational doctrine, limits efficiency and slows innovation. Export control regimes and dependence on imported materials for advanced thrusters further constrain autonomy.

In contrast, Sudarshan Chakra demands synchronised progress across laboratories, launch providers, private sector and defence command centres, where propulsion development is guided not only by engineering milestones but also by doctrinal and operational priorities. India's strategic community must treat propulsion not as an isolated R&D pursuit but as part of a national defence ecosystem, coordinated and responsive to both civilian and military needs. Only such integration will convert technological capacity into sustained strategic leverage.

Conclusion

Mission *Sudarshan Chakra* represents one of India's most ambitious steps towards an integrated air, missile, and space defence architecture. It embodies both technological aspiration and strategic foresight, a recognition that future security will depend as much on the ability to manoeuvre and persist in orbit as on traditional terrestrial strength. This study examined the propulsion dimension of that mission, exploring how propulsion technologies, modular architectures, and refueling capabilities together shape India's evolving space power.

The analysis demonstrated that propulsion must be understood not merely as an engineering function but as strategic leverage. It determines a nation's freedom of action in space, what orbits can be reached, how quickly satellites can respond to threats, and how long they can sustain operations. Drawing on space power theories by Dolman, Bowen, and Klein, the discussion underscored a common premise: mobility defines mastery. Applied to India's context, this means propulsion forms the operational backbone of *Sudarshan Chakra*. The Mission's success depends on translating technological capability into strategic agency, shifting from possession of assets to control of orbital dynamics. While India has advanced in chemical and limited electric propulsion, manoeuvrable dominance remains constrained by fuel supply and efficiency. To move from being a static to a dynamic space power, India must therefore develop systems capable of sustained mobility, modularity, and endurance.

A key insight of this study is that refueling, modularity, and in-space servicing are no longer secondary design features but structural enablers of long-term space power. Refueling extends energy life, modularity extends functionality, and servicing restores resilience. Together, they transform satellites from expendable units into maintainable infrastructure, allowing space power to evolve from a static construct to a regenerative ecosystem where assets adapt, upgrade, and recover. Integrating refueling stations and servicing platforms also redefines economics: nations can sustain strategic presence without constant replacement, redirecting resources towards innovation rather than replenishment. This transition demands institutional and doctrinal alignment. India still lacks a propulsion roadmap linking research, production, and operations. *Sudarshan Chakra's* vision of multi-domain integration will succeed only if propulsion development is coordinated across agencies and industry, with shared standards for refueling interfaces and servicing protocols. Bridging this divide is among the most urgent requirements for realising credible deterrence in space.

While India's ground-based tracking and data fusion capabilities are improving, the dynamic linkage between those insights and manoeuvrable assets is still evolving. Building this combined system must therefore be treated as a national security imperative, not merely a technological goal. From a policy standpoint, the largest gap lies in standardisation. India lacks a clear doctrine for refueling and servicing infrastructure, including common propellants, docking mechanisms, and control interfaces. Without these, in-space logistics will remain fragmented and unsustainable.

Despite the strong theoretical and operational foundation of this work, certain limitations remain. The analysis focused primarily on propulsion and its immediate interfaces, without deeper treatment of supporting enablers such as power systems, AI-based trajectory optimisation, or cyber resilience. The reliance on open-source data also leads to biased findings towards observable indicators rather than operational realities. Future research could expand the comparative scope to include China, Japan, and Europe for a broader perspective on propulsion architectures.

Looking ahead, India must prioritise technologies that enhance endurance, autonomy, and flexibility in orbit. Advanced electric and hybrid propulsion systems will enable persistent low-thrust manoeuvring for surveillance networks, while nuclear electric propulsion (NEP) can support long-duration missions in geostationary and cis-lunar space. Parallel efforts should advance robotic servicing, modular component replacement, and AI-driven trajectory optimisation to enable predictive manoeuvre planning. Together, these innovations will extend operational life, strengthen responsiveness, and build the foundation of sustainable space power.

In essence, propulsion is the quiet determinant of space power. It turns awareness into action and possession into control. When integrated with SDA and C4ISR, propulsion grants India not just the means to operate in orbit, but the freedom to shape events there. Mission Sudarshan Chakra's success will therefore depend not just on the number of interceptors it fields but also on how effectively its satellites can move, adapt, and endure. The future of deterrence will not be decided by who reaches space first, but by who remains manoeuvrable longest.

NOTES

1 DD News, 2025.

2 English Rendering of the Text of Prime Minister Shri Narendra Modi's Address from the Ramparts of Red Fort on the occasion of 79th Independence Day, 2025.

3 "Mission Sudarshan Chakra: How India Aims to Develop an S-400 Style Defence System, Starting with 2026 Missile Trials", *The Economic Times*, August 2025 at https://economictimes.indiatimes.com/news/defence/mission-sudarshan-chakra-how-india-aims-to-develop-an-s-400-style-defence-system-starting-with-2026-missile-trials/articleshow/123538439.cms

4 A. Lele, "Indian Space Force: A Strategic Inevitability", *Space Policy*, 65, 2023, at https://doi.org/10.1016/j.spacepol.2022.101526

5 B.E. Bowen, *Original Sin: Power, Technology and War in Outer Space*. Oxford University Press, 2022.

6 Ibid.

7 Space Training and Readiness Command, *Space Doctrine Publication 3-100: Space Domain Awareness* (Doctrine Document SDP 3-100), US Space Force 2023 at https://www.starcom.spaceforce.mil/Portals/2/SDP%203-100%20Space%20Domain%20Awareness%20%28November%202023%29_pdf_safe.pdf

8 J.E. Shaw, "Dynamic Space Operations: The New Sustained Space Maneuver Imperative, *Æther: A Journal of Strategic Airpower & Spacepower*, 2, 2023.

9 B. Cabrières, F. Alby, and C. Cazaux, "Satellite End of Life Constraints: Technical and Organisational Solutions", *Acta Astronautica*, 73, 2012, pp. 212–220.

10 C. Albon, "US Space Command seeks maneuverable, refuelable satellites by 2030", C4ISRNet 20 April 2023 at https://www.c4isrnet.com/battlefield-tech/space/2023/04/20/us-space-command-seeks-maneuverable-refuelable-satellites-by-2030/; *On-Orbit Satellite Servicing Study: Project Report*, Goddard Space Flight Center, NASA, 2010 at https://www.nasa.gov/wp-content/uploads/2023/10/nasa-satellite-servicing-project-report-0511.pdf

11 J.E. Shaw, no. 8.

12 Ibid.

13 Wertz et al. (Ed.), *Space Mission Engineering: The New SMAD*. Microcosm Press, 2011.

14 B.E. Bowen, no. 5.

15 S.S. Guddanti, and M. Fernandez-Tous, "Propulsion Systems for Mars Mission: Alternatives and Opportunities", IAF Space Propulsion Symposium, 75th International Astronautical Congress (IAC), Milan, Italy, January 2024 at https://doi.org/10.52202/078371-0146

16 S. Chandrashekar, *Space, War and Security – A Strategy for India*, NIAS Report No. R36-2015.

17 Mikayla Easley "Space Force's Next-Gen Space Domain Awareness Satellites will Require On-Orbit Refueling Capability", *DefenseScoop*, 24 September 2025 at https://defensescoop.com/2025/09/24/space-force-rg-xx-refuel-on-orbit/

18 "Northrop Grumman Satellite-Refueling Technology Selected as First Preferred Refueling Solution Interface Standard for Space Systems Command (SSC)", News, Northrop Grumman (n.d) at https://news.northropgrumman.com/satellites/northrop-grumman-satellite-refueling-technology-selected-as-first-preferred-refueling-solution-interface-standard-for-space-systems-command-ssc-6899294?utm_source=chatgpt.com (Accessed 18 October 2025).

19 "Skyroot Aerospace: Pioneering India's Private Spaceflight Revolution", Asia Tomorrow, February 2025 at https://www.asiatomorrow.net/articles/skyroot-aerospace-pioneering-indias-private-spaceflight-revolution;

"Bellatrix Aerospace's next-generation propulsion systems accomplish Space", Bellatrix Aerospace, 4 January 2024 at https://bellatrix.aero/updates/arka-shines-rudra-roars; "IIT Madras Startup Agnikul, Maker of 3D-Printed Engine, Eyes Reusable Rocket", October 2025 at https://www.indiatoday.in/education-today/news/story/iit-madras-startup-agnikul-maker-of-3d-printed-engine-eyes-reusable-rocket-2802741-2025-10-14?utm_source=chatgpt.com

20 E.C. Dolman, *Astropolitik: Classical Geopolitics in the Space Age*, Routledge. 2005.

21 B.E. Bowen, no. 5.

22 J.J. Klein, *Fight for the Final Frontier: Irregular Warfare in Space*, Naval Institute Press, 2023.

23 E.C. Dolman, no. 20.

24 A. Ali, H. Ali, J. Tong, M.R. Mughal, and S.U. Rehman, "Modular Design and Thermal Modeling Techniques for the Power Distribution Module (PDM) of a Micro Satellite", *IEEE Access*, 8, 2020, 160723–160737; J. Morton, G. Hodges, M. Pankow, and L. Lamberson, (2025). Hypervelocity Impact Investigations of Composite Truss Tubes for In-Orbit Assembly Risk Assessment", *Journal of Composite Materials*, 59 (3), pp. 331–342.

25 Z. Sun, S. Li, H. Zhang, H. Lei, and X. Song, (2022). "Design and Analysis of a Novel Floating Docking Mechanism for On-Orbit Refueling", *Aerospace*, 9 (7), 2022, p. 365.

26 *On-Orbit Satellite Servicing Study: Project Report*, no. 10.

27 B. Xu, X. Su, Z. Liu, M. Su, J. Cui, Q. Li, Y. Xu, Z. Ma, and T. Geng, "Analysis on BDS-3 Autonomous Navigation Performance Based on the LEO Constellation and Regional Stations", *Remote Sensing*, 15 (12), 2023, p. 3081.

28 "China to Achieve 'Major Breakthrough' in Nuclear-powered Space Shuttle Around 2040: Report", Chinese Academy of Sciences, 2017 at https://english.cas.cn/newsroom/archive/china_archive/cn2017/201711/t20171121_186363.shtml

29 S.S. Guddanti, Francisco Del Canto Viterale, Marcos Fernandez-Tous, Brian Urlacher, Chonglin Zhang, and Pranika Gupta, "Geopolitical and Geo-Economic Implications of Recent Advances in Space Propulsion and Hypersonic Technologies", *International Cooperation, Challenges, and New Horizons*, 2025, pp. 50-64 at https://doi.org/10.52202/080552-0007

30 A. Lele, no. 4.

SECTION IV

Technology

9

Integrated Area Defence System – A System of Systems: A Brief Overview and Possible Technology Road Map

Y. Sreenivas Rao

1.0 Introduction

India is a vast nation characterised by its diverse and strategic geographic boundaries. The northern region features mountainous terrain extending across 15,200 kilometres, while the eastern and western land borders span approximately 4,100 kilometres and 3,220 kilometres, respectively. The country also boasts an extensive peninsular coastline measuring about 7,520 kilometres, in addition to the Andaman and Nicobar Islands and Lakshadweep, which are critical from both strategic and security perspectives.

Evolving Threat Landscape

Modern warfare is undergoing rapid transformation, largely propelled by advancements in technology and autonomous weapon delivery systems. As a result, threat profiles are becoming increasingly dynamic, unpredictable, and multi-dimensional. India faces external threats along its borders as well as covert risks such as surprise attacks from sleeper cells operating within its territory. The emergence of cyber warfare and sophisticated electronic countermeasures further complicates the national defence scenario. Addressing these challenges demands a holistic, integrated approach to area defence.

2.0 The Need for Advanced Defence Systems

Given the complex spectrum of threats, it is imperative to develop and deploy a fully automated, network-centric intelligent area defence system. Such a solution must be capable of safeguarding vital national assets located on land, at sea, and in space. The system should account for various threat scenarios – including both traditional military aggression and unconventional attacks like cyber intrusions – and support seamless, real-time operations for comprehensive protection.

3.0 *Sudarshan Chakra* Programme

In line with these requirements, the Government of India's *Sudarshan Chakra* programme envisions a sophisticated, intelligent, and network-centric area defence architecture. Key features of this programme include modularity, adaptability, and scalability to ensure quick operational response. The system is designed to serve a dual purpose: defence against saturation attacks and the capability to execute rapid counterattacks. Operational readiness hinges on effective implementation, commissioning, and continual system upgrades to sustain its ability to deliver simultaneous, multi-weapon engagements that can saturate enemy sensors and defence structures.

4.0 System Capabilities and Objectives

To achieve superior defence outcomes, the recommended area defence system should exhibit the following attributes:

4.1 Automated Network Operations

Facilitate real-time data exchange and situational awareness across land, sea, and space domains.

4.2 Modularity and Scalability

Allow for incremental upgrades and rapid deployment in diverse threat environments.

4.3 Adaptive Response

Enable quick transition between defence and counterattack modes using advanced weapon delivery mechanisms.

4.4 Saturation Attack Handling

Defend against large-scale, simultaneous attacks while maintaining the ability to launch counter-saturation offences targeting adversary sensors and weapon systems.

5.0 Integration of Cyber and Electronic Warfare

Incorporate counter- measures for evolving cyber threats and electronic warfare tactics.

India's security ecosystem requires continuous evolution to address the fast-changing dimensions of warfare and technology. The deployment of an automated, intelligent, and network-centric area defence system under the *Sudarshan Chakra* programme will significantly enhance national strategic resilience. This approach will not only strengthen defence capabilities but also ensure adaptive, scalable, and robust protection of the nation's most vital assets in an increasingly contested environment.

6.0 Principal Components of an Area Defence System

An effective Area Defence System comprises the following essential components:

6.1 Threat Detection System

Employs advanced sensors – such as radar, optical and electronic surveillance tools – to provide early identification of potential threats across the protected area, ensuring comprehensive situational awareness.

6.2 Threat Classification System

Analyses the characteristics of detected objects using signature, trajectory, and behavioural data to accurately categorise each threat (e.g., aircraft, drones, missiles), thereby facilitating appropriate prioritisation.

6.3 Threat Path Prediction, Kinematics, and Network Command and Control

Utilizes predictive algorithms to determine the likely path and behaviour of threats. The command-and-control unit coordinates defensive actions across the network, integrating near real-time sensor feeds and weapon status, while allocating resources optimally.

6.4 Wide Area Multi-Frequency Multi-Mode Communication System

Provides secure, resilient, and uninterrupted communications – often operating across multiple frequencies and modes – to ensure robust exchange of information between all subsystems, command centres, and mobile assets.

6.5 Target Position Update System

Continuously assimilates live data from all available sensors, updating the location and status of threats for precision tracking and timely response as threats manoeuvre or change trajectory.

6.6 Integrated Wide Area Network

Establishes seamless data connectivity between sensors, effectors, and control units, uniting the distributed elements of the defence structure into a coherent, responsive whole. This network enables dynamic tasking and situational awareness at all command levels.

6.7 Weapon Launch System for Threat Neutralisation

Receives engagement commands from the central network and executes the deployment of appropriate countermeasures – such as interceptors or missiles – to neutralise validated threats with maximum efficiency.

6.8 Threat Kill Assessment

Employs sensor feedback and post-engagement analysis to verify whether a threat has been neutralised, enabling re-engagement if needed and informing immediate operational adjustments.

6.9 Redundancy and Fail-safe Measures

Integrates backup power supplies, duplicated network nodes, and fallback operational procedures to guarantee operational continuity in case of subsystem failures, cyber-attacks, or kinetic damage.

6.10 Cybersecurity Measures

Deploys specialist systems and protocols to monitor, detect, and counter potential cyber threats targeting the defence network, ensuring data integrity and secure command flows across all elements.

6.11 Training and Simulation Subsystem

Includes platforms for regular simulation exercises and scenario-based training, allowing personnel to maintain high levels of preparedness for emerging or complex threat situations.

6.12 Post-incident Analysis and Reporting System

Facilitates comprehensive debriefing, outcome analysis, and lessons-learned documentation after each engagement to enhance future operational effectiveness and system resilience.

7.0 Types of Threats

To accurately define the required technologies and establish effective deployment strategies, it is crucial to evaluate the spectrum of potential threats, anticipate technological advancements within these threats, and analyze their likely deployment patterns. The following section provides a concise overview of these factors to guide subsequent planning and development efforts.

7.1 Drones

Drones are used for covert operations, given their ability to fly silently at low altitudes, evading conventional radar and visual detection. They can carry out reconnaissance, intelligence gathering, or deliver payloads for targeted strikes. Their small size and manoeuvrability make them difficult to counter.

Technological advancements: Expect further miniaturisation enabling micro-drones with AI-powered autonomous navigation, swarming techniques allowing coordinated multi-drone attacks, enhanced stealth features such as radar-absorbent materials, and electronic counter-countermeasures that resist jamming or hacking.

7.2 Unmanned Aerial Vehicles (UAVs) with Long Range and Endurance

Larger UAVs enable sustained intelligence, surveillance, and reconnaissance (ISR) missions and can carry heavier payloads for precision strikes over hundreds of kilometres. Their endurance allows persistent presence, complicating defence planning.

Technological advancements: Advancements will include solar-powered or hybrid engine UAVs for extended flights, satellite-based beyond-line-of-sight communications, AI for fully autonomous mission planning and execution, and incorporation of stealth technologies to reduce risks of detection.

7.3 Fighter Aircraft

Modern fighter jets are designed for high-speed, High-G combat manoeuvres with the ability to deliver precise weapons accurately. Their stealth capabilities and integrated sensors allow superior survivability and lethality in contested environments.

Technological advancements: Future fighter aircraft will likely incorporate adaptive camouflage materials, onboard-directed energy weapons (e.g., laser systems), AI-assisted decision making to reduce pilot workload, enhanced sensor fusion for comprehensive situational awareness, and manned-unmanned teaming where drones operate alongside pilots.

7.4 Precision-Guided Cruise Missiles

These missiles fly low with terrain-hugging trajectories guided by advanced GPS, inertial navigation, and terrain-following radar to avoid detection and interception, enabling accurate strikes at long distances.

Technological advancements: Emergence of supersonic and hypersonic cruise missiles for reduced reaction times, improved seekers using multi-mode sensors (infrared, radar, optical) for target discrimination, and enhanced counter-countermeasure systems to overcome missile defence threats.

7.5 Ballistic and Quasi-Ballistic Missiles

Ballistic missiles follow high-arc trajectories to deliver warheads over intercontinental distances, while quasi-ballistic missiles exhibit manoeuvrable terminal phases to evade interception. Both possess strategic and tactical significance.

Technological advancements: Development of hypersonic glide vehicles capable of rapid, unpredictable manoeuvres, improved stealth coatings, and enhanced guidance systems combining satellite navigation and real-time data links to increase strike accuracy while complicating defence interception.

7.6 Anti-Ship Missiles

These missiles target naval vessels by flying close to the water surface to avoid radar detection and using sophisticated guidance for terminal homing. They pose serious threats to naval fleets and require advanced defensive measures.

Technological advancements: Advancements expected in supersonic and hypersonic anti-ship missiles for rapid engagement, AI-driven autonomous target recognition and selection, improved stealth technologies, and coordinated swarm tactics designed to overwhelm ship defences.

7.7 Underwater Launch Missiles

Submarine-launched missiles provide stealth strike capabilities against surface ships or land targets, launched from undersea platforms to evade early warning systems.

Technological advancements: Extended range and speed with improved propulsion systems, stealthier launch methods reducing acoustic signatures, integration with autonomous underwater vehicles for covert launch and targeting, and enhanced guidance algorithms for precision strikes.

7.8 Anti-Satellite Missiles

These weapons disable or destroy orbiting satellites, crippling adversary communications, navigation, reconnaissance, and early warning capabilities, vital to modern military operations.

Technological advancements: Increasing use of kinetic kill vehicles with improved targeting precision, deployment of directed energy weapons (lasers, microwaves) capable of satellite incapacitation without debris generation, cyber-attack integration to degrade satellite functions non-kinetically, and countermeasures to satellite defence.

7.9 Amphibious Weapon Systems

Systems operating seamlessly on land and water include amphibious assault vehicles capable of transporting troops, weapons, and supplies during coastal or riverine operations, enhancing operational flexibility.

Technological advancements: Autonomy-enabling unmanned amphibious vehicles, improved terrain adaptability, integration of loitering munitions for sustained fire support, and modular payload systems allowing rapid reconfiguration for diverse mission profiles.

7.10 Short-Range and Long-Range Motor Guns

These motorized weapon platforms provide direct fire support or defensive capabilities. They can range from towed artillery to mobile gun systems, crucial for both offensive and defensive battlefield operations.

Technological advancements: Introduction of smart targeting systems leveraging networked surveillance inputs, guided munitions with precision strike capabilities, unmanned and remotely operated gun platforms improving crew survivability, and integration with AI-based fire control systems, for rapid target acquisition.

7.11 Swarm and Saturation Attacks

The simultaneous coordinated deployment of large number of weapons or drones from multiple vectors creates saturation scenarios, overwhelming defence systems designed for limited threats. This tactic exploits gaps in coverage and reaction times.

Technological advancements: Enhanced swarm autonomy through distributed AI coordination, improved electromagnetic spectrum management for resilient communications within swarms, and adaptive tactics, making swarms less predictable and harder to disrupt.

7.12 Insider Threats and Sleeper Cells

The threat landscape also involves covert operatives or sleeper cells within defended territory who can launch attacks from inside, such as drone launches or sabotage, complicating detection and attribution.

Technological advancements: Advanced behavioural analytics and AI-driven insider threat detection systems, integration of biometrics and network monitoring to identify anomalous activities, and deployment of autonomous surveillance platforms for internal premises monitoring.

8.0 In view of the identified threats and their potential technological advancements, the subsequent sections address the system requirements pertaining to each element of the Area Defence System. A comprehensive overview of the necessary technical parameters is presented, considering both prevailing threat scenarios and prospective enhancements in technology, to meet future operational demands. A structured roadmap encompassing prototype development, testing, production, and deployment is delineated. Furthermore, the roles of R&D institutions, Centres of Excellence, academic establishments, and industry partners are outlined, with emphasis on integrated collaboration to ensure effective, timely, and sustainable implementation of the system.

9.0 Threat Detection System

In contemporary battlefields, protecting sensitive areas from incursions hinges on early threat sensing and real-time tracking of adversarial pathways. This enables rapid neutralisation – whether by counter-weapons, high-energy beams, or electronic jammers – before any damage occurs.

Modern warfare is characterised by multimode saturation attacks, rendering single-sensor solutions ineffective and necessitating multi-sensory deployment across multiple domains: ground, air, space (low orbital and geostationary satellites), underwater (sonars), signal intelligence, and early warning systems. Cross-domain data integration from radars, infrared (IR) sensors, electro-optic devices, SIGINT, and acoustic sensors is vital for achieving a unified and precise battlefield picture. This demands advanced processing technologies addressing detection errors and false positives. Acoustic data fusion remains especially challenging, with AI-driven prediction models offering promising approaches for future improvement.

Major technologies pivotal for next-generation threat detection, are described below, each expanded with roadmap guidance and key threats to consider.

9.1 Multi Spectral Phased Array Radars

Multi-spectral phased array radars utilise electronically steerable beams across various frequency bands, allowing simultaneous detection and tracking of diverse threats—including low-altitude aircraft, missiles, and drones – in high clutter environments.

Technology Roadmap and Future Threats

- Evolve to multi-band, software-defined array platforms for seamless integration across land, sea, and air domains.
- Integrate gallium nitride (GaN) semiconductors for increased power and resilience to electromagnetic warfare.
- Prioritise AI-supported automatic target recognition and jamming protection for hypersonic and stealth targets, given the increase in adversary capabilities in these areas.
- Prepare for rapid, modular upgrades via open system architectures for adaptability against evolving threats.

9.2 Photonic Radars

Photonic radars leverage light-based signal generation and transmission, using lasers and optical fibres to achieve wide-spectrum operation, high precision, and resilience against electronic jamming.

Technology Roadmap and Future Threats

- Increase development in indigenous photonic radar modules focused on stealth aircraft, small drones, and low-RCS (Radar Cross Section) projectiles.

- Integrate photonic sensor arrays in mobile, airborne and satellite platforms, to exploit low weight and high bandwidth for persistent surveillance.
- Research advanced photonic integrated circuits, enabling frequency agility for anti-jamming operations and multi-object detection in saturated electromagnetic environments.

9.3 RF and Photonics Integrated Radars

Combined RF and photonic radars represent a fusion of traditional electronic and cutting-edge optical detection, merging the strengths of both broad-spectrum coverage and noise-resistant operation.

Technology Roadmap and Future Threats

- Accelerate hybrid system development to counter adversaries using unconventional frequency bands or stealth technologies.
- Employ chip-scale integration for reduced size, weight, and power, increasing suitability for unmanned and space-based assets.
- Build robust EW (Electronic Warfare) modules for resilience against high-power jamming and spectrum-hopping threats.

9.4 Auxiliary (Decoy) and Secondary Radars

Auxiliary/decoy and secondary radars act as deception tools and backups, simulating high-value assets or operating in secondary channels to mislead adversaries and preserve main sensor integrity.

Technology Roadmap and Future Threats

- Advance real-time frequency modulation and AI-driven threat simulation to outmanoeuvre enemy ELINT or anti-radiation tactics.
- Deploy networked decoy radars to mask force movements during saturation attacks.
- Integrate secondary radar nodes into distributed sensor grids for redundancy against targeted strikes and cyber threats.

9.5 Long Range Wide Beam Radars

These radars provide extensive coverage with broad beam widths, tracking high-speed threats over vast distances—including ballistic missiles, swarms of drones, or hypersonic gliders.

Technology Roadmap and Future Threats

- Expand to multi-object tracking and AI-driven predictive analytics for time-critical interception decisions.
- Develop adaptive beam-shaping algorithms to counter evasive manoeuvres and cluttered operational environments.
- Integrate with satellite-based systems for persistent, global situational awareness.

9.6 Airborne Electronically Scanned Array (ESA) Radars

Airborne ESA radars deliver rapid electronic beam steering for real-time detection of high-speed aerial threats and time-sensitive battlefield engagements.

Technology Roadmap and Future Threats

- Miniaturize ESA packages for integration with UAVs, fighter jets, and drones.
- Embed AI-enabled tracking for multi-threat environments, such as UAV swarms and hypersonic missiles.
- Ensure interoperability with space-based sensor networks for comprehensive aerial threat response.

9.7 Multi-Wavelength Infrared Cameras

These cameras enable simultaneous detection across multiple IR bands, providing superior identification and tracking of targets with passive signatures or anti-radar coatings.

Technology Roadmap and Future Threats

- Enhance sensitivity and spectral resolution for stealth detection and countermeasures against low-signature platforms.

- Utilise advanced image fusion with radar and acoustic inputs for complete threat classification.
- Develop rapid processing algorithms tailored for real-time missile and drone tracking.

9.8 High-Sensitivity Thermal Detection Cameras

Advanced thermal cameras detect minute heat signatures from threats, improving nightime and low-visibility detection capabilities.

Technology Roadmap and Future Threats

- Innovate sensor materials to increase resolution and reduce noise.
- Enable distributed sensor grids for perimeter protection and automatic tracking of fast-moving threats.
- Integrate real-time analytics to counter camouflage and decoy tactics.

9.9 Long Range Low Frequency Sonars

These sonars use low frequencies to identify underwater threats at greater distances, including submarines and autonomous vehicles.

Technology Roadmap and Future Threats

- Advance sensor fusion with AI-based models for improved target discrimination in cluttered environments.
- Integrate with unmanned surface and underwater vehicles for persistent maritime surveillance.
- Research anti-stealth sonar techniques to counter adversaries' acoustic masking technologies.

9.10 High Performance Computing for Real-Time Data Fusion

Powerful computing platforms enable real-time fusion of diverse sensor data, improving battlefield awareness despite high data volume and varying formats.

Technology Roadmap and Future Threats

- Develop resilient, distributed edge computing networks immune to cyberattacks and EMP threats.

- Implement AI/ML algorithms for detection of anomalies and rapid decision-making in saturated data environments.
- Prioritise modular, upgrade-friendly architecture to keep pace with advancements in sensor technologies in the future.

9.11 Master Clock Stamping and Protocol Synchronisation

Precise time synchronisation across distributed sensors is critical for coordinated, multi-domain threat tracking.

Technology Roadmap and Future Threats

- Research quantum timing protocols for enhanced accuracy, independent of satellite-based clocks.
- Implement secure time distribution networks to resist electronic attacks and spoofing.
- Standardise protocols for interoperability across diverse platforms.

9.12 Quantum Sensor Technologies and Quantum Computing Algorithms

Quantum sensors offer unprecedented sensitivity, while quantum algorithms deliver rapid, robust data processing, vital for future-proof threat detection systems.

Technology Roadmap and Future Threats

- Increase R&D in quantum-enhanced radar, sonar, and IR sensors for next-generation detection capabilities.
- Integrate quantum-resistant cryptography in sensor networks to protect against quantum cyber threats.
- Develop quantum simulation platforms for real-time, AI-enabled battlefield scenario analysis.

This approach will ensure that the threat detection system is robust, future-ready, and capable of countering advanced and emerging threats—including stealth platforms, hypersonic weapons, electronic jamming, and cyber warfare – through continuous technological innovation and integration.

10.0 Threat Classification

Threat classification entails the construction of sophisticated mathematical models that predict and distinguish between various threat characteristics, including drones, high-endurance UAVs, fifth-generation and advanced fighter aircraft, precision-guided cruise missiles, ballistic and quasi-ballistic missiles, anti-ship missiles, underwater-launched weapons, anti-satellite missiles, amphibious weapons, and short-range as well as long-range artillery systems. For example, by analyzing velocity and trajectory data, threats can be identified as either missiles or aircraft. The application of artificial intelligence further enables sub-classification, allowing identification of missile types and the prediction of possible trajectories, including mid-course changes, to enhance response accuracy.

This methodology should be applied uniformly to all threat types mentioned. The system needs to reliably classify swarm attacks and assign unique identifiers to each platform. In the case of saturation attacks, powerful computation resources are required for mathematical and physical analysis, enabling precise threat identification and rapid filtering of decoys and low-priority threats. The resulting information should be transferred instantly to a command-and-control (C2) centre with multi-sensor data fusion, to ensure reliable, real-time decision support. The speed of delivering accurate inputs to C2 significantly increases available reaction time, which is crucial for launching effective countermeasures.

The system must be continuously, developed and should incorporate the following technology advancements, to remain effective against evolving adversarial technologies:

10.1 Fast Enhanced Multicore Processors

Modern threat environments demand increasingly powerful computation capabilities to handle large sensor datasets and complex algorithms in real time. The adoption of next-generation multicore processors – including quantum or neuromorphic chips – can accelerate analysis and decision-making, especially under saturation scenarios. Future roadmaps should align with developments in AI processor architectures, energy efficiency, and low-latency processing for mobile command centres.

10.2 Edge Computing

Edge computing places data processing at the sensor level, drastically reducing latency and bandwidth requirements. Advances in edge AI will allow the threat classification to occur locally and instantaneously, supporting autonomous sensor nodes and unmanned vehicle integration. A robust roadmap should include distributed algorithm deployment, federated learning, and resilient architectures that can adapt to disrupted communication networks or cyberattacks.

10.3 AI/ML Algorithms

Artificial Intelligence (AI) and Machine Learning (ML) algorithms form the backbone of adaptive threat classification. Continuous model training with evolving datasets, adversarial learning to counter spoofing, and explainable AI to enhance operator trust, is essential. Future developments will need to address AI hardware acceleration, adversarial robustness, and joint sensor fusion for multi-domain operations.

10.4 Real-Time Tracking Models

Accurate and rapid tracking of multiple, highly manoeuvrable threats – including hypersonic missiles and drone swarms – requires advanced tracking models based on sensor fusion, Kalman filtering, and advanced prediction algorithms. Technology roadmaps should incorporate high-precision multi-sensor integration, stochastic prediction, and self-learning edge models that anticipate evasive manoeuvres and decoy tactics.

10.5 Data Management and Security

Effective data management ensures integrity, traceability, and secure retention of sensor inputs. Future-proof systems must include automated data labeling, high-assurance storage, zero-trust access architectures, and integration with classified network protocols. Security roadmaps will require support for quantum-resilient cryptography and secure global data sharing – especially for multi-nation coalition operations.

10.6 Optimised Operating System Resource Utilisation

A bespoke operating system, designed specifically for threat classification, will minimise vulnerabilities to cyberattacks and maximise operational performance. The operating system should employ advanced sandboxing, minimal attack surfaces, and real-time priority scheduling to guarantee critical threat data is processed first. Roadmaps must cover secure kernel architectures, adaptive resource allocation based on tactical scenarios, and full operational redundancy.

10.7 Data Encryption

End-to-end encryption ensures classified threat information remains confidential from the point of collection to C2 dissemination. Future systems must leverage post-quantum encryption standards and seamless key management across distributed platforms. Technology roadmaps should address dynamic encryption adaptation, secure inter-sensor communication protocols, and practical on-the-fly cryptographic upgrades, as threats evolve.

10.8 Packet and Information Management for Command-and-Control

Optimally managing the size and content of data packets transmitted to C2 nodes guarantees timely, actionable information delivery, even in congested or contested environments. Intelligent packet prioritisation, adaptive compression, and error-free delivery mechanisms will be essential. Roadmaps must focus on bandwidth optimisation, real-time transmission algorithms, and resilient packet routing, that maintains C2 connectivity in the face of jamming, cyberattacks, or enemy interference.

The system must be adaptive and modular, allowing rapid integration of new target characteristics or threat profiles as they emerge from adversary advances. Ongoing research and development in computational technology, AI, cyber security, and sensor networking, are fundamental to maintaining strategic advantage.

11.0 Command and Control

The Command and Control (C2) station serves as the central hub of the entire area defence system. It is connected through a dedicated, secure communication system to all nodes of the integrated weapon network within the area defence infrastructure. The station receives inputs from fused sensor data, each classified with unique identification numbers.

The C2 station performs comprehensive target trajectory estimation along with predictions of likely impact locations. Based on these calculations, it designates and commands local weapon launchers to deploy countermeasures – such as lasers, high-energy electron beams, or other appropriate weapons – to neutralise the threats.

It conducts initial ground guidance computations based on launcher locations and identifies multiple launch stations to operate simultaneously in a synchronised closed-loop manner. The station also monitors system health and faults across the network, providing centralised health status and activating redundancies where necessary.

Security is ensured by an intrusion detection system coupled with alarm generation, to protect critical assets.

The key technologies to be developed and integrated include:

11.1 High-speed Multi-core Data Processing Combined with AI-based Data Storage and Retrieval

The C2 system must analyze enormous volumes of sensor data in real time for rapid threat assessment and decision-making. High-speed multi-core processors enable parallel data processing, greatly reducing latency. AI techniques enhance data storage efficiency and enable intelligent retrieval of relevant information, supporting situational awareness and predictive analytics.

Technology Roadmap

- Develop specialised multi-core processors optimised for defence sensor fusion.
- Implement AI-driven data indexing and retrieval systems trained on massive sensor datasets.
- Integrate edge computing at sensor nodes to preprocess data and reduce C2 processing loads.

- Embed machine-learning models for detection of anomalies and trajectory prediction.
- Plan upgrades for quantum computing accelerators as they mature for high-complexity computations.

11.2 Multi-layer Biometric Operational Security

Operational security must prevent unauthorised access to C2 functions using multi-factor biometric authentication (fingerprints, retina, voice, behavioural patterns). Multi-layer security ensures that even if one layer is compromised, others protect critical operations.

Technology Roadmap

- Implement biometric systems using fingerprint, iris, face, and voice recognition.
- Add behavioural biometrics (typing rhythm, gait) for continuous authentication.
- Integrate hardware security modules to store biometric data securely.
- Ensure security system resilience against spoofing attacks with liveness detection.
- Combine with cryptographic access control mechanisms and monitoring for anomalies.
- Future cyber threats may include biometric data theft and spoofing. Multi-layer biometric and AI-driven anomaly detection can mitigate these risks effectively.

11.3 Distributed Architecture Design

A distributed system architecture enhances resilience by decentralising processing, data storage, and command decision-making. It reduces the risk of total system failure and allows flexible, scalable network growth. Distributed architecture mitigates risks from kinetic strikes, jamming, and cyberattacks targeting central nodes, supporting continuous operations.

Technology Roadmap

- Design modular nodes with processing and storage capabilities at multiple layers.

- Employ decentralised consensus algorithms for unified decision-making.
- Utilise blockchain or distributed ledger technology for secure, tamper-proof data exchange.
- Develop self-healing network protocols to maintain operations despite node failure.
- Test scalability to integrate additional sensors and launchers over time.

11.4 Multiple Command and Control Stations

Multiple Command and Control Stations should be distributed – at least five across India's landmass and two on naval platforms – capable of real-time mesh network synchronisation. Each station can assume decision-making responsibilities, with a central master and several secondary stations. Any station can take over the master role if the central unit becomes non-functional during exigencies. Mesh networking enables real-time synchronisation and collaborative decision-making. Each station can operate independently or assume master control if others fail. Mesh architecture defends against localised destruction or cyber incapacitation, ensuring command continuity during multi-domain attacks.

Technology Roadmap

- Deploy at least five land-based stations and two naval C2 platforms across strategic locations.
- Develop robust mesh network protocols for secure, low-latency inter-station communication.
- Implement automatic failover mechanisms, enabling seamless master station switching.
- Conduct joint simulation exercises to validate multi-station operation under various attack scenarios.
- Incorporate satellite and terrestrial communication backups for redundancy.

11.5 A Well-structured Graphical User Interface (GUI) Dashboard

GUI Dashboard providing a comprehensive air situation picture, target trajectories, kill assessment, and system health diagnostics, should be set up. The GUI dashboard provides a comprehensive visual interface to operators, displaying the air situation, target trajectories, kill assessment, and system health with fault diagnostics. Intuitive design reduces operator workload and enhances situational comprehension. Operators need to rapidly interpret complex data against sophisticated threat patterns. Improved visualisation and AI aids are essential for timely, accurate responses.

Technology Roadmap

- Develop customisable displays with layered alert levels and interactive control elements.
- Integrate augmented reality (AR) elements for complex 3D battlefield visualisation.
- Incorporate AI-based decision support tools presenting recommended actions.
- Ensure dashboard interoperability with allied command systems.
- Regularly update interface UX based on operator feedback and emerging best practices.

11.6 A Dedicated, Resource-optimised Operating System

The C2 station requires a secure, stable, and resource efficient operating system tailored for defence environments. It should support real-time processing, minimal latency, and robust fault tolerance. Future threats are often unpredictable and multi-domain; adaptability is critical for resilient defence postures.

Technology Roadmap

- Develop or customise real-time operating systems (RTOS), optimised for high-security defence applications.
- Harden the operating system against cyber intrusions using advanced access controls and sandboxing.
- Enable modular updates to quickly remove vulnerabilities.
- Incorporate performance-monitoring tools for sustained operation under load.
- Optimise operating system for low-power consumption and high reliability.

11.7 The Ability to Adapt Dynamically to Changing Environments

The C2 must adapt to evolving battlefield conditions, including unexpected threat vectors, environmental changes, and system performance variations. Adaptive algorithms allow dynamic resource allocation and decision-making adjustments. Future threats are often unpredictable and multi-domain; adaptability is critical for resilient defence postures.

Technology Roadmap

- Implement AI-based adaptive decision-making frameworks capable of real-time adjustments.
- Integrate environmental sensors (weather, electromagnetic spectrum) for contextual awareness.
- Develop self-learning modules to improve effectiveness based on past engagements.
- Enable flexible reconfiguration of network and asset deployment on the fly.
- Establish interfaces for operator override when required.

11.8 Housings Mostly Under the Ground with Blast-proof, NBC-protected Structures that Utilise Latest Civil Engineering Models to Resist Precision Deep Strike Attacks

Naval platform models include air and naval defence systems. Physical protection of C2 stations involves blast-proof, Nuclear, Biological, Chemical (NBC)-protected structures, employing state-of-the-art civil engineering models designed to resist precision deep strikes. This ensures survivability of critical C2 infrastructure amidst escalating precision conventional and unconventional weapon threats.

Technology Roadmap

- Design structures with layered blast-resistant materials and shock absorbers.
- Integrate NBC filtration and decontamination systems.
- Include EMP hardening to protect electronics against electromagnetic pulses.

- Conduct regular structural integrity tests and upgrades based on threat intelligence.
- For naval platforms, combine structural protections with complementary air and naval defence assets.

11.9 High-level Security Systems Preventing Human or Cyber Intrusions

Security systems must prevent unauthorised physical and cyber access through multi-layered defence, including monitored entry points, encryption, and real-time intrusion detection. Need for addressing insider threats, sophisticated cyberattacks, and physical breach attempts in an era of hybrid warfare.

Technology Roadmap

- Integrate AI-driven cybersecurity systems that detect and respond to novel threats.
- Deploy continuous monitoring with automated alarm and lockdown protocols.
- Use hardened communication links with quantum-resistant encryption.
- Train personnel rigorously on operational security and cyber hygiene.
- Implement insider threat detection systems using behavioural analytics.

11.10 Efficient Data Logging, Storage, and Retrieval for Space, Air, Land, and Sea Objects

Data management incorporates deep learning for building simulation tools and digital twins. The C2 system must effectively log and store data on space, air, land, and sea objects. Deep learning needs to support simulation modeling and digital twin creation, augmenting predictive and planning capabilities. Should anticipate information overload, enabling actionable insights and proactive threat response through AI-enhanced data analytics.

Technology Roadmap

- Develop scalable data lakes with multi-domain sensor integration.
- Apply AI/ML models for pattern recognition, threat prediction, and decision optimisation.

- Build digital twins replicating battle environments for simulation and training.
- Enable real-time data sharing with allied forces for joint operations.
- Ensure compliance with data governance and security protocols.

11.11 Use of Stealth Technologies Ensuring Low Noise, Zero Emissions and Concealment to Evade Detection

C2 platforms must utilise stealth technology to minimise noise, emissions, and detectability, protecting against enemy reconnaissance and electronic warfare.

Technology Roadmap

- Implement low-noise machinery, passive cooling, and emission control subsystems.
- Use advanced materials with radar-absorbing and thermal dissipation properties.
- Adopt emission control protocols restricting transmissions to essential communication only.
- Develop electromagnetic signature management systems.
- Integrate with camouflage and deception techniques.

11.12 Rapid Mobility or Ability to Switch to Shadow Locations in Emergencies

C2 stations must have the capability to relocate swiftly or switch to shadow locations during emergencies, preserving command continuity in hostile conditions.

Technology Roadmap

- Design mobile C2 units with modular, rapidly deployable hardware and software stacks.
- Develop logistics and communication support for relocation under duress.
- Implement autonomous systems to enable remote setup and operation.
- Test mobility protocols in simulated attack and blackout scenarios.

- Establish network redundancy to maintain reach-back connectivity during moves.
- Address survivability against surprise attacks and catastrophic failures, ensuring uninterrupted command and control functionality.

12.0 Communication Roadmap for Area Defence Systems

Communication serves as the backbone and nerve centre of any area defence system. With multiple nodes distributed across vast geographical regions, establishing a robust Wide Area Network (WAN) is imperative for operational integrity. To ensure high reliability and minimal downtime, the system integrates multiple redundancies, connecting all nodes, using:

- Dedicated Fibre Optic-based WAN connectivity;
- SATCOM links;
- Point-to-point local networks via Ethernet and line-of-sight RF modes.

The rapid evolution of communication technologies and bandwidth capacity requires that networks are protected against threats such as spoofing, unauthorised intrusions, false data injections, and service disruptions. Thus, an ongoing commitment to securing terrestrial communications is vital for maintaining up-to-date systems that address load balancing, minimise latency, and prevent traffic congestion.

Given the fast-changing nature of technology, periodic infrastructure reviews are essential. The roadmap calls for developing indigenous, scalable, and adaptable communication assets, including fibre-optic grids, routers, switches, and reliable power supply systems, designed for dense, secure communication environments.

Technology Roadmap

12.1 Implement Quantum Technologies

Develop systems equipped with quantum communication solutions, quantum number generators, and quantum key distribution protocols to establish a grid secured by quantum cryptography.

12.2 Foster Collaborative R&D

Mobilise Indian R&D institutions, Armed Forces, industry, and academia to collaborate in a mission-mode framework, aligning efforts with the National Quantum Mission to upgrade the nation's communication networks.

12.3 Expand SATCOM Infrastructure

Deploy a dedicated SATCOM network using two geostationary satellites positioned strategically, complemented by approximately 100 low-cost small Low Earth Orbit (LEO) satellites. Simulation runs should determine optimal orbital orientation and satellite distribution for maximum coverage.

12.4 Establish Ground Receiving Hubs

Create appropriate ground receiving hubs to support satellite communications, with frequency bands of 60–70/Hz to ensure all-weather operation and robust security for data transmission.

12.5 Promote Indigenous Satellite Development

Task Indian industry with designing and manufacturing LEO satellites, and launch them via cost-effective, demand-driven space vehicles developed domestically to minimise overall launch expenses.

12.6 Visible Light Communication

Enables jam-resistant, high-bandwidth line-of-sight data transmission. The development of advanced photonics and the pursuit of technologies for blue laser systems will deliver efficient point-to-point line-of-sight communication, particularly within the underwater domain.

13.0 Target Update Transmitters

Target update transmitters function as extended nodes for the command and control station. They provide continuous real-time updates to airborne counter-weapon systems, sharing current target trajectory data to enable mid-course corrections and optimise weapon guidance in the endgame phase. These updates also serve as active inputs for onboard seekers or homing systems, enhancing target accuracy and adaptability.

Key Technologies

13.1 CDMA (Code Division Multiple Access) Frequencies

CDMA involves the use of unique codes to allow multiple transmitters to communicate over a shared frequency spectrum. It enables secure, jam-resistant communication through frequency hopping and advanced modulation techniques, making it ideal for contested environments.

13.2 Integrated Multiband CDMA

This technology integrates multiple CDMA bands to support seamless, robust communication across various frequencies. By leveraging several bands, the system becomes adaptable to changing operational requirements and more resistant to interference.

13.3 Spread Spectrum Transceivers

These transceivers distribute signals across a wide range of frequencies, reducing the risk of interception and jamming. Spread spectrum methods improve the security and reliability of data transmission, essential for real-time targeting updates.

13.4 High-Gain Antennas and Beamforming

High-gain antennas focus transmission/reception capabilities in specific directions, increasing range and signal strength. Beamforming further enhances this by steering beams electronically, allowing precise targeting of receivers, minimising interference, and maximising data throughput.

13.5 Software-Defined Radios (SDRs)

SDRs use programmable hardware, allowing communication systems to adapt to different protocols, waveforms, and frequencies through software updates. This flexibility enables rapid upgrades and mission-specific configurations.

13.6 Long-Range Transmission with Low Packet Loss

Achieving reliable long-distance data transmission while minimising packet loss due to atmospheric (aero) effects is critical for continuous and accurate updates, especially in dynamic or cluttered environments.

Technology Roadmap

- **AI-Driven Adaptive Communication:** Incorporate artificial intelligence to optimise frequency selection, error correction, and jamming resilience dynamically based on battlefield conditions.
- **Quantum Communication Protocols:** Research and integrate quantum-based secure communication techniques to further enhance data confidentiality and prevent interception.
- **Integration with Network-Centric Warfare:** Ensure seamless compatibility with broader sensor and shooter networks for improved situational awareness and coordinated operations.
- **Miniaturized, Low-Power Components:** Invest in advanced materials and miniaturization to reduce the size, weight, and power consumption of transmitters, enabling deployment on diverse platforms including drones and micro-UAVs.
- **Automatic Fault Detection and Resilience:** Develop self-diagnostics and auto recovery features within transmitters to ensure continuous operation even under electronic attacks or hardware failures.

14.0 Counter Weapon System

Establishing an automated C4I (Command, Control, Communications, Computers, and Intelligence) network enables highly effective target neutralisation upon receipt of a directive from the central command station. The local battery, functioning as the operational arm, comprises co-located radars (such as advanced X-band radars), secure communication terminals, a Launch Control Centre, and cutting-edge neutralisation systems.

Neutralisation Systems and Technology Roadmaps

14.1 RF Jammers

RF jammers are electronic countermeasure devices used to disrupt communication links, navigation signals, and remote controls of hostile assets, particularly drones and guided munitions. Modern RF jamming employs AI-driven algorithms to adaptively engage new frequencies, minimising adversary ECCM (Electronic Counter-Countermeasures) capabilities. The future roadmap includes cloud-based distributed jamming, miniaturised components for portable deployment, and integration with sensor fusion networks, to autonomously identify and respond to threats.

14.2 High Power Microwave Devices

High Power Microwave (HPM) devices emit bursts of electromagnetic energy to disable electronic targets, especially swarms of drones and unmanned systems. Future advancements focus on software-defined HPM weapons, improved beamforming, energy efficiency, and range extension. These systems will play a vital role in neutralising mass drone attacks by incapacitating entire swarms within seconds, and further developments will integrate adaptive control and precise targeting to minimise collateral effects.

14.3 Nets and Net Guns

Physical countermeasures such as nets and net guns offer reliable methods for neutralising low-flying drones in urban and sensitive installations. Technology progression includes automated deployment systems, integration with drone detection sensors, and re-usable net materials with low weight and high tensile strength. Future concepts may incorporate guided net launchers that can target swarming UAVs in coordinated attacks.

14.4 High-Energy Lasers and Counter-Drone Drones

High-energy laser weapons provide precise, speed-of-light engagement, effectively neutralising aerial targets by damaging sensors or causing structural failure. Counter-drone drones, operating autonomously, can intercept and disable rogue UAVs through kinetic or electronic means. The evolving roadmap will see greater power output, range increases, advanced beam steering, swarm-coordination methods, and close integration into layered defence systems.

14.5 Electromagnetic Rail Gun Launched Projectiles

Electromagnetic rail guns utilise electromagnetic acceleration to launch projectiles at hypervelocity, offering long-range area defence against high-speed threats. The roadmap involves higher energy storage densities, wear-resistant barrel materials, and smart munitions for precision engagement.

Globally, programmes are aiming to achieve effective standoff ranges well over 200 km, integrating with multi-domain defence platforms.

14.6 Air Defence Guns

Traditional and next-generation air defence guns remain a cornerstone in neutralising various aerial threats. Technology is progressing towards automated tracking, integration with radar and electro-optical systems, and guided ammunition. Future developments will enhance rapid response rates and multi-target engagement through advanced fire control algorithms.

14.7 Air Defence Missiles

Air defence missiles provide kinetic intercept solutions for fast-moving aerial and missile targets, with ongoing improvements in guidance, propulsion, and sensor fusion. The roadmap focuses on hypersonic interceptors, swarming counter-missile capabilities, and seamless integration with C4I networks, to reduce intercept times under saturation attack scenarios.

14.8 Missile Defence Missiles

These specialised systems target ballistic and cruise missiles now increasingly designed for multi-layered defence and advanced threat discrimination. Future enhancements include dual-mode seekers, networked targeting, and rapid retargeting protocols, to counter multiple simultaneous warheads and decoys. Vessels equipped with Sea-Based Missile Defence Systems offer distinct strategic advantages, particularly given our geographical positioning. Key areas for development include ship-launchable missile systems, advanced plume management technologies, co-located radar installations, and comprehensive EMI/EMC/EMP hardening, to ensure onboard operational safety and automation. Additionally, careful selection of materials and specialised surface coatings is essential to guarantee reliable performance under all-weather conditions at sea.

14.9 ASW Torpedoes (Multi-Platform Capability)

Anti-Submarine Warfare (ASW) torpedoes with capabilities for deployment from surface vessels, aircraft, helicopters, submarines, and AUVs, provide comprehensive undersea defence. Evolution will focus on autonomy, intelligent target discrimination, multi-platform interoperability, and extended range. Future systems will feature rapid data linking to the broader area defence network for coordinated undersea engagements.

15.0 The Defence Research and Development Organisation (DRDO) and Indian industry, with the active support from Indian Armed Forces, Proactive policies of the Government of India and other supporting organisations, remain committed to advancing counter-drone and area defence systems, maintaining technological superiority against emerging threats.

The analysis presented in this chapter underscores the integrated nature of modern area defence systems, emphasising that the synergy between advanced detection, classification, kinematic prediction, robust communication, and resilient command structures, is paramount for operational success. Each subsystem contributes to building an adaptive, holistic shield, capable of countering diverse aerial, ballistic, and unconventional threats – a necessity in today's rapidly evolving defence landscape. For the DRDO and Indian Industry, the technology roadmap is clear and ambitious. It calls for accelerated indigenous development of sensor arrays, predictive algorithms, and secure, multi-mode communications – blending AI, advanced electronics, and resilient network architectures. The path forward demands prioritisation of integrated wide-area networks, automated threat neutralisation protocols, and rigorous cybersecurity frameworks to guarantee uninterrupted operational capabilities even under cyber or kinetic attack. Equally, investment in training and real-time simulation ensures that personnel and systems remain prepared for emerging threats.

In essence, the future of India's area defence ecosystem (*Sudarshan Chakra*) hinges on a seamless partnership between Government agencies and private industry. By fostering innovation across sensor fusion, command automation, and adaptive engagement, the nation will not only achieve technological self-reliance, but set benchmarks in global multi-domain defence solutions. The principles and objectives outlined herein provide a robust foundation for sustained leadership in defence technology advancement.

10

The Challenge of the Cyber Domain: Enhancing Capabilities, Containing Vulnerabilities

Cherian Samuel and Rohit Kumar Sharma

'Mission Sudarshan Chakra' is India's ambitious national defence initiative to develop a multi-layered, indigenously manufactured shield aimed at neutralising enemy infiltrations, protecting critical assets, and enhancing India's offensive and defensive capabilities by 2035.[1] The shield will ensure that all critical sites – both strategic and civilian – are equipped with advanced technologies and weapon systems that will not only deter and repel enemy attacks but also deliver appropriate countermeasures.[2] The futuristic defence programme also has an element of indigenisation, with the entire system envisaged to be developed and manufactured in India.[3] The cyber domain will act as a decisive force multiplier, transforming a collection of air- and missile-defence weapons into an integrated, intelligent, and anticipatory national shield. A major pillar of the Mission is its cyber backbone: the cyber domain is expected to act as a decisive force multiplier, transforming disparate air and missile defence assets into an intelligent, anticipatory, and resilient national shield through real-time sensor fusion, secure communications, and predictive analytics.

The announcement of Mission Sudarshan Chakra followed Operation Sindoor, during which India effectively employed counter-drone systems, surface-to-air missiles, and electronic-warfare tools to repel attacks from

Pakistan. The operation demonstrated the potency of a layered, indigenously developed defence architecture and underscored the growing convergence of kinetic, cyber, electronic-warfare, and AI-driven capabilities – an integrated approach that Mission Sudarshan Chakra aims to scale to the national level.[4]

Although 'Mission Sudarshan Chakra' remains a futuristic concept, it is expected to be comprehensive in scope, integrating surveillance, cybersecurity, air and missile defence, electronic warfare, and space-based monitoring, into a single national grid.[5] Some reports suggest that the nationwide air defence shield will be created by linking 6,000 to 7,000 radars, satellites, and directed energy weapons (DEWs) that will feed into one integrated network.[6] The architecture envisions a networked system: sensors (air, land, sea, space), command & control centres, AI-enabled decision-making, and communication links. This makes cybersecurity foundational: without assured integrity, availability, and resilience of data flows, sensor fusion and weapon cueing could be disrupted or manipulated, degrading the shield's effectiveness across both military and civilian domains.

The core challenge lies in securing every element of this highly integrated ecosystem – space assets, ground-based radars, weapons systems, and the communication networks binding them. Real-time data fusion and AI-driven command systems require hardened, redundant, and tamper-resistant digital infrastructure; otherwise, the same interconnectedness that enables rapid response, may expose the system to hijacking, spoofing, or cascading failures. 'Mission Sudarshan Chakra' must also incorporate a cyber shield capable of countering hybrid and electronic-warfare threats, protecting critical national infrastructure while managing the convergence of data from land-based, airborne, maritime, undersea, and space sensors, through big-data analytics and real-time processing.

Thus, while 'Mission Sudarshan Chakra' promises a transformative leap in India's defensive posture, its reliance on deep digital integration also raises concerns about systemic vulnerabilities. A breach or data-integrity compromise in any node of the architecture could propagate across the network, undermining situational awareness, misdirecting interceptors, or degrading decision-making in a contested cyber-electromagnetic environment. Ensuring resilience, redundancy, and defence-in-depth will therefore be essential to realising the Mission's full potential.

The following sections will expand on each component that will make up the defence system and potential cybersecurity vulnerabilities.

The Space Network

The space segment will undoubtedly serve as a crucial component of 'Mission Sudarshan Chakra'. Lessons from the Russia-Ukraine conflict highlight that space is emerging as a decisive domain in future warfare.[7] Space-based services are being increasingly employed to amplify situational awareness and transparency during conflicts, while the growing presence of commercial space service providers underscores the evolving role of private entities in shaping the dynamics of modern warfare.

Space is now a contested cyber domain with over 12,000 active satellites providing critical global services ranging from navigation to communication,and expanding the attack surface for cyber threats. India currently has 57 satellites in orbit, with the Indian Space Research Organisation expecting to triple that number in the next three years.[8] Private satellite launches are also expected to increase as India's new Space Policy and liberalised Foreign Direct Investment (FDI) rules have opened the sector to private innovation, enabling startups to design, build, and launch satellites independently.[9]

The constellation of satellites that are relevant to 'Mission Sudarshan Chakra' range from Early Warning/Radar Imaging (ISR) Satellites (RISAT series), Electronic Intelligence (Elint) and Spectrum Surveillance (eg. GISAT-1), Earth Observation (eg. Cartosat series), Defence Communication Satellites, Navigation Satellites (eg. IRNSS series) and Space Situational Awareness (eg. INSAT series).

Each satellite, its ground station, and its data links represent potential targets. The vulnerabilities that exist with earth-based networks become even more amplified with space-based networks. Studies show that roughly half of the satellite traffic is still unencrypted, meaning attackers can eavesdrop, intercept, spoof, or manipulate data and services with relative ease.[10] Ground control systems are equally vulnerable, potentially enabling attackers to manipulate satellite telemetry after compromising ground stations or mission control software, or to spoof GPS signals.[11] Legacy systems, dependence on unaudited commercial services, supply chain vulnerabilities, and attribution challenges are some of the pre-existing vulnerabilities that take on new urgency with increasing strategic competition in the space domain.

To better understand the vulnerabilities inherent in this domain, it is essential to first define what constitutes a space network. Cyberattacks on such networks extend beyond traditional computer systems; they encompass any component of the broader space ecosystem, which includes:

1. Launch segments (launch complexes, launch vehicles, payloads, R&D facilities)
2. Ground segments (terrestrial networks and other Earth-based systems like mission control and payload control stations)
3. Space segments (satellites, space stations, telescopes)
4. User segments (GPS receivers, satellite phones, satellite-internet terminals)
5. Link segments (communications links, both upward and downward).[12]

There have been no confirmed cases so far of a cyber incident directly compromising the space segments themselves. That being said, there have been numerous instances where other parts of the space network have been targeted or faced attempted intrusions. With reports of India fast-tracking its space-based surveillance programme by launching 52 dedicated surveillance satellites[13] to strengthen round-the-clock monitoring of its coastlines and land borders, it becomes equally important to secure the cyber components of these space-based systems.

Space networks face a wide range of cybersecurity threats. The Indian Computer Emergency Response Team (CERT-In) highlighted several such risks in its advisory CIAD-2025-0007, issued in February 2025. The advisory identified several threats specific to satellite communication (Satcom), including command and control interference, breaches of data integrity and confidentiality, onboard software vulnerabilities, signal jamming and spoofing, supply chain compromises, AI-driven attacks, Internet of Things (IoT) vulnerabilities, and even physical tampering.[14]

Command and control interference refers to disrupting the uplink and downlink communications between satellites and ground stations to seize control of, redirect, or disable the satellites. Such interference can disrupt critical services associated with the satellites. The risk of data breaches remains a major concern, as any interception or alteration of sensitive information transmitted between Earth and satellites, could result in inaccurate data being relayed and potentially compromise overall system security.[15]

Onboard software vulnerabilities present another significant risk, as satellites rely on complex software and hardware systems. Much like terrestrial networks, these weaknesses can be exploited by threat actors to disrupt satellite operations, inject malicious codes, or gain unauthorised access. One of the most common forms of attack involves signal jamming and spoofing, two distinct methods of disrupting satellite communications. While jamming blocks or weakens legitimate signals, spoofing sends false data to mislead systems and users that depend on satellite information. Such interference can seriously affect navigation accuracy and in extreme cases, lead to accidents.[16]

Supply chain attacks, including incidents of physical tampering, pose yet another major challenge. A breach at any point in the chain, whether through a trusted vendor or supplier, can give threat actors access to sensitive satellite data and potentially disrupt entire systems. AI can also be weaponised to attack networks, automating large-scale breaches, scanning massive data sets to look for vulnerabilities, and tailoring campaigns like phishing. It can also help adversaries design malware that is harder to detect and mitigate. IoT devices linked to satellite networks can serve as entry points for attackers seeking access to wider systems. Regular updating and securing these devices is therefore essential to reduce such risks.

Despite the threats outlined above, it is equally important to consider the rapid pace of technological change. As innovations accelerate, threat actors are evolving just as quickly. With this in mind, policymakers must anticipate and prepare for future threats, many of which may be closer than they appear. To address this, the ICARUS framework – *Imagining Cyberattacks to Anticipate Risks Unique to Space* – outlines novel cyberattack scenarios against space systems and offers probing questions to deepen and test those scenarios. The Report argues that we must move beyond generic threat categories like hacking, jamming, and spoofing signals and instead explore more imaginative, mission-specific risks and their strategic consequences.[17]

With the growing involvement of non-governmententities or private players in the space sector, these actors must integrate cybersecurity preparedness into their systems and products. At the same time, governments must understand the private sector's perspectives and challenges in building secure and resilient space infrastructure.

As a leading space power, the United States offers a valuable model for adopting best practices and addressing key challenges in space cybersecurity. For instance, in January 2025, a Report was released following sustained engagement between the White House and the US space industry leaders during the Space System Cybersecurity Executive Forum.[18] The Forum produced several critical insights that merit reflection, many of which could be relevant for India as well. One key observation from industry participants was that conventional terrestrial cyber-defence tools, such as intrusion detection systems and sensors, often lack the precision, resource efficiency, and maintenance compatibility required for deployment and integration in space missions. Regarding legacy systems, many experts argued that imposing modern cybersecurity requirements retroactively would be highly challenging. Most older space systems still rely on legacy programming languages like C and C++, which, despite their known vulnerabilities, remain deeply embedded in existing architectures.[19]

Many industry participants also view cybersecurity and space missions as largely disconnected, often perceiving cybersecurity as a constraint that hampers programme timelines and delivery. This mindset can lead companies to deprioritize security during the design and development phases. Moreover, the reliance on voluntary guidelines offers little incentive for firms to invest in even baseline cybersecurity measures for their space missions.[20]

Radars and Weapon Systems

Over the past decade, there have been multiple instances of military radar systems being hacked. One of the first widely reported cases occurred in 2007, when alleged Israeli operatives reportedly disabled Syria's radar systems, causing them to go off its operations during an air raid targeting Syrian facilities.[21] Given the central role of radar systems in detection and their wider significance under 'Mission Sudarshan Chakra', it is essential to understand how adversaries might compromise these systems. Since radar serves as a critical node within a layered air-defence architecture, disrupting it would inflict outsized operational damage and make it a particularly valuable target. In fact, cyber attacks can breach military radar networks, injecting false signals or masking real ones, forcing defensive forces to scramble unnecessarily or allowing hostile aircraft to slip into protected airspace unnoticed.[22] Risks to be considered include sensor spoofing, compromise of data nodes, denial-of-service attacks on decision-making systems, as well as the risks that come from connecting asymmetrically secure networks across the military and civilian domains.

A radar network consists of multiple radar stations linked to a central fusion centre through communication technologies. The fusion centre oversees the network's overall control and management while using data fusion algorithms to process and integrate information from all radar sites.[23] The antenna and the radar controller form the core of radar functionality, translating invisible waves into meaningful situational awareness. Although this interconnected setup enhances coordination and data sharing, it also increases system exposure. The same communication technologies that enable seamless information exchange also heighten the network's vulnerability to cyber threats.[24]

Cyber attacks against radar networks can take various forms, including Man-in-the-Middle (MITM) attacks, False Data Injection Attacks (FDIA), Distributed Denial-of-Service (DDoS) attacks, supply chain compromises, firmware or software exploitation, and malicious code implantation.[25] A MITM attack hijacks the communication link between radar sites and the fusion centre, enabling attackers to eavesdrop or tamper with transmitted data. When combined with an FDIA, attackers can modify existing tracks or create an entirely new one, undermining the fusion centre's ability to pinpoint targets accurately and leading operators to make incorrect decisions.[26]

Firmware and software weaknesses are an easy way in; for instance, unpatched bugs or default credentials left unchanged can be exploited to seize control of radar stations or the fusion centre, often because of simple human errors. Equally dangerous is the insertion of malicious codes, enabling attackers to sneak in trojans through maintenance ports or remote update channels to alter radar settings or disable critical functions. Manipulation of data consumed by peripheral systems, such as missile systems or the graphical displays operators rely on, can cause serious operational disruption because those systems depend on accurate, real-time feeds to function correctly.[27]

The layered air defence system consists of various platforms ranging from Man-Portable Air Defence systems, such as the soon-to-be-integrated VSHORAD (Very Short Range Air Defence) with a range of six kilometres as the innermost layer, to the S-400 *Sudrshan Chakra,* with a range of 400 kilometres as the outermost layer. Securing weapon systems against cyber threats is equally critical for a broader air defence architecture. Modern weapon platforms incorporate hundreds of thousands of chips, many of them highly sophisticated designs containing billions of transistors, resulting in an exceptionally complex system of systems.[28] The complexity of these architectures makes verifying component integrity extremely difficult; consequently, securing the supply chain becomes a critical requirement. Counterfeit components can be injected into real systems, raising the probability of operational failure. They also create vulnerabilities by enabling backdoors or tampered circuits to be embedded within the platform.[29] Vulnerabilities could be utilised to poison targeting and allocation algorithms, as well as missile guidance systems.

Another challenge arises from the long operational life cycles of such systems, during which the supply of spare parts becomes increasingly difficult. To ensure component availability over extended periods, mid-life upgrade programmes are undertaken, often incorporating commercial off-the-shelf (COTS) products to keep systems operational and replace components that are no longer manufactured. It is important to recognise that in modern warfare, systems are increasingly interconnected and oriented towards Network-Centric Warfare (NCW). Targeting the weakest link in this networked architecture can have catastrophic consequences, potentially rendering an entire military component incapable of operating.

History offers ample evidence that many cyber incidents have arisen from human error or system malfunction, even in the absence of any hostile activity by an adversary. In fact, such incidents are believed to have served as an impetus for developing confidence-building measures (CBMs) aimed at managing and preventing similar occurrences.[30] There are historical instances where human error triggered false alarms of missile attacks. A notable example occurred in November 1979, when a technician inadvertently inserted a training exercise tape into a computer operating the US early-warning systems at NORAD, prompting the systems to issue alerts of a massive incoming Soviet nuclear strike.[31] As 'Mission Sudarshan Chakra' moves towards integrating advanced and complex technologies, it becomes essential for authorities to invest heavily in training and developing skilled human resources to operate these systems with minimal risks of error.

AI-linked Threats

Rapid advancements in AI are demonstrating remarkable capabilities with the potential to transform multiple sectors, including the military. As AI technologies mature, their integration into military operations is increasingly regarded as a strategic imperative for States seeking to enhance decision-making and operational efficiency.[32]

AI is increasingly used to process millions of data points, enabling the automated prediction of flight paths and prioritisation of targets. For example, the US Joint All-Domain Command and Control (JADC2) architecture seeks to integrate information flows across land, air, sea, space, and cyberspace, enabling commanders to coordinate more rapidly and effectively.[33] AI lies at the core of this transformation, facilitating seamless sensor data fusion, predictive threat analyses, adaptive decision support, autonomous action, and strengthened cyber resilience. AI-enabled threat detection and tracking speed up responses to emergent threats through smart sensor fusion, anomaly detection, and cross-domain pattern recognition for automated identification of hypersonic threats and drone swarms. The military equipped with better AI enabled predictive analysis for threat prioritisation, in conjunction with adaptive interceptor allocation and AI assisted battle management systems, will have the ability to achieve faster, more accurate, and resilient responses to multi domain threats – ensuring optimised resource deployment, reduced human error, and enhanced deterrence against both conventional and hybrid attacks.

Although AI offers significant advantages, adversaries are developing novel methods to compromise such systems, revealing vulnerabilities that are still in the early stages of being understood. Some forms of attack that can disrupt AI systems include *evasion attacks,* which occur after deployment and involve manipulating inputs to alter the system's response, and *poisoning attacks,* which target the training phase by injecting corrupted or misleading data into the model.[34]

AI-enabled systems are uniquely vulnerable to cyberattacks in ways traditional military platforms are not. Their complex software architecture and data dependencies create new entry points for hackers to access or manipulate sensitive military information and disrupt operational processes.[35]

Studies of real-world security vulnerabilities in machine learning (ML) systems indicate that effective security requires a comprehensive approach encompassing software, data, and model supply chains, as well as network and storage infrastructures.[36] As AI is ultimately software, it inherits many of the traditional weaknesses found within conventional software supply chains.

As a nascent field, AI in military decision making raises unresolved ethical challenges. Reduced human oversight in rapidly evolving environments risks cascading errors within fast, automated kill chains. The ethical and doctrinal consequences of AI driven engagement decisions demand urgent and sustained attention.

Threats to Ground-based Infrastructure

The ground-based infrastructure for 'Mission Sudarshan Chakra' extends far beyond the missile-launch vehicles. It encompasses a vast ecosystem of fixed installations, data centres, and support networks that collectively form the backbone of the defensive shield. Since this infrastructure is stationary and heavily networked, it is exposed to a distinct set of cyber vulnerabilities, and often to threats that also exist in other components of the broader air defence network. For example, the server farm, or what is known as data centres – particularly the high-performance computing clusters that run AI algorithms for threat prioritisation – are vulnerable to a wide range of attacks. These include ransomware, DDoS attacks, malware intrusions, social engineering and phishing, supply chain compromises, insider threats, and zero-day exploits. Insider threat also poses a significant risk: a compromised employee with authorised physical access could directly implant malicious codes within the system.

A unique feature of 'Mission Sudarshan Chakra' is its role in protecting civilian assets such as nuclear plants and power grids. This necessitates a digital interface between military and civilian networks. This integration however, introduces significant risks. The most serious is the lateral movement: civilian networks that are internet-connected and comparatively less secure, can become an entry point for adversaries.[37] Lateral entry begins with an initial entry point into the network, which could be a malware-infected device connected to the system, stolen user credentials, an exploited vulnerability through an open port, or any similar attack vector.

Conclusion

'Mission Sudarshan Chakra' represents a transformative step in India's quest to build a resilient, technology-driven national defence architecture. However, its success will depend not only on the sophistication of its radars, satellites, weapons, and AI-enabled systems, but also on the strength of the cybersecurity measures protecting them. As the Mission integrates diverse components – from space assets and radar networks to ground-based infrastructure and civilian systems – it simultaneously expands the potential attack surface for adversaries.

The integration of thousands of sensors, platforms and weapons across land, air, sea, space, and cyber domains, demands unprecedented levels of interoperability, real-time data fusion, and AI-assisted decision-making. This sensor-rich ecosystem will generate immense volumes of time-sensitive data that must be processed securely and efficiently. Without robust data management frameworks, resilient communications, and protected C2 links, the advantages of speed and automation could quickly turn into liabilities. 'Mission Sudarshan Chakra' is therefore both strongest and most vulnerable, as a network. The very features that make it powerful—integration, velocity, AI-driven fusion—also expose it to structural risks related to over-dependence, expanded attack surfaces, and cascading failures.

Addressing these challenges will require secure-by-design engineering, rigorous testing, continuous monitoring, and specialised workforce training. In te final analysis, the cybersecurity dimension of 'Mission Sudarshan Chakra' must be treated as a core operational pillar rather than an ancillary concern. Any compromise in a single node or layer could undermine the integrity of the entire defensive shield and jeopardise the strategic objectives it is intended to serve.

NOTES

1 "Atmanirbhar Bharat: The Foundation of a Strong and Developed India", Press Information Bureau (PIB), 15 August 2025 at https://www.pib.gov.in/PressRelease Page.aspx?PRID=2156701

2 "Union Home Minister and Minister of Cooperation, Shri Amit Shah, terms Prime Minister Shri Narendra Modi's address to the nation on the 79th Independence Day as a roadmap of the past 11 years' progress, the strength of the present, and a strategy for a prosperous India", PIB, 15 August 2025 at https://www.pib.gov.in/PressReleseDetail.aspx?PRID=2156863

3 "Transformation of India's Defence and Internal Security Posture", PIB, 20 August 2025 at https://www.pib.gov.in/PressNoteDetails.aspx?ModuleId=3&NoteId=155066&id=155066

4 P.K. Roy. "Mission Sudarshan Chakra: India's Quest for a Multi-Layered Defence Shield." *Chintan – India Foundation*, 20 August 2025 at https://chintan.indiafoundation.in/articles/mission-sudarshan-chakra-indias-quest-for-a-multi-layered-defence-shield

5 "Mission Sudarshan Chakra: Army to procure AK-630 air defence guns to be deployed along Pakistan border", *The Times of India*, 4 October 2025 at https://timesofindia.indiatimes.com/india/mission-sudarshan-chakra-army-to-procure-ak-630-air-defence-guns-to-be-deployed-along-pakistan-border/articleshow/124305576.cms

6 Amrita Nayak Dutta, "Over-the-horizon Radars, Energy Weapons, Satellites to be Integrated into 'Sudarshan Chakra' Air Defence Shield", *The Indian Express*, 6 October 2025 at https://indianexpress.com/article/india/energy-weapons-satellites-radar-network-key-to-sudarshan-chakra-10289885/

7 Andrew Radin, Khrystyna Holynska, Cheyenne Tretter, Thomas Van Bibber, "Lessons from the War in Ukraine for Space:Challenges and Opportunities for Future Conflicts", RAND Report, 21 May 2025 at https://www.rand.org/pubs/research_reports/RRA2950-1.html

8 "India to Triple Its Satellites in Orbit: ISRO Chief", *The New Indian Express*, 25 November 2025 at https://www.newindianexpress.com/states/telangana/2025/Nov/25/india-to-triple-its-satellites-in-orbit-isro-chief.

9 ET Telecom, "India's Space Sector Sees Revolutionary Transformation Under PM Modi", *The Economic Times*, 27 November 2025 at https://telecom.economictimes.indiatimes.com/news/portal-in-portal/satcom/indias-space-sector-sees-revolutionary-transformation-under-pm-modi/125608255

10 Shaun Waterman, "Multi-Orbit Networks Expand the Attack Surface, But Basic Cyber Threats Remain, Experts Say",Via Satellite, 18 November 2025 at https://www.satellitetoday.com/cybersecurity/2025/11/18/multi-orbit-networks-expand-the-attack-surface-but-basic-cyber-threats-remain-experts-say/

11 Alexander Culafi, "How Outer Space Became the Next Big Attack Surface", Dark Reading, 20 August 2025 at https://www.darkreading.com/cyberattacks-data-breaches/outer-space-next-attack-surface

12 Patrick Lin, Keith Abney, Bruce DeBruhl, Kira Abercromby, Henry Danielson and Ryan Jenkins, "Outer Space Cyberattacks: Generating Novel Scenarios to Avoid Surprise", A Report of the Ethics + Emerging Sciences Group, 17 June 2024 at https://arxiv.org/pdf/2406.12041

13 "India to fast-track 52 military satellites for better surveillance at borders", *The Hindu*, 30 June 2025 at https://www.thehindu.com/sci-tech/india-to-fast-track-new-military-satellites-for-better-surveillance-at-borders/article69755996.ece

14 "CERT-In Advisory CIAD-2025-0007", Indian Computer Emergency Response Team (CERT-In), 4 February 2025 at https://www.cert-in.org.in/s2cMainServlet?pageid=PUBVLNOTES02&VLCODE=CIAD-2025-0007

15 Ibid.

16 "GPS spoofing incidents spike 400%: Does it make a plane crash? What should we know", *The Times of India*, 11 August 2024 at https://timesofindia.indiatimes.com/science/gps-spoofing-incidents-spike-400-does-it-make-a-plane-crash-what-should-we-know/articleshow/112436896.cms

17 Patrick Lin, Keith Abney, Bruce DeBruhl, Kira Abercromby, Henry Danielson and Ryan Jenkins, no. 12.

18 "Space System Cybersecurity Space Industry Perspectives", The White House, January 2025 at https://bidenwhitehouse.archives.gov/wp-content/uploads/2025/01/Space-System-Cybersecurity-Industry-Perspectives-Report.pdf

19 Ibid., p. 9.

20 Ibid, p. 10.

21 Lewis Page, "Israeli sky-hack switched off Syrian radars countrywide", *The Register*, 22 November 2007 at https://www.theregister.com/2007/11/22/israel_air_raid_syria_hack_network_vuln_intrusion/

22 "Clear skies – how anti-hacking technology can protect military radar", *Air Force Technology*, 11 August 2013 at https://www.airforce-technology.com/features/feature-clear-skies-anti-hacking-technology-protect-military-radar/?cf-view

23 R. Chen, Y. Zhang, X. Li, J. Ran, "An Analysis and Simulation of Security Risks in Radar Networks from the Perspective of Cybersecurity", *Sensors*,; 25(17), 2025, p. 5239 at https://doi.org/10.3390/s25175239

24 Ibid.

25 Ibid.

26 Ibid.

27 S. Cohen, E. Levy, A. Shaked, T. Cohen, Y. Elovici, A. Shabtai, "RadArnomaly: Protecting Radar Systems from Data Manipulation Attacks", *Sensors*, 22(11), 2022, p. 4259at https://doi.org/10.3390/s22114259

28 Robert Koch and Mario Golling, "Weapons Systems and Cyber Security – A Challenging Union", 8th International Conference on Cyber Conflict, 2016 at https://www.ccdcoe.org/uploads/2018/10/Art-12-Weapons-Systems-and-Cyber-Security-A-Challenging-Union.pdf

29 Ibid.

30 Lora Saalman, Larisa Saveleva Dovgal and Dei Su, "Mapping Cyber-Related Missile and Satellite Incidents and Confidence Building Measures", *SIPRI Insights on Peace and Security*, November 2023 at https://www.sipri.org/sites/default/files/2023-11/2023_10_cyber_mapping_incidents.pdf

31 Ibid., p.2

32 Alice Saltini, "Navigating cyber vulnerabilities in AI-enabled military systems", European Leadership Network, 19 March 2024 at https://europeanleadershipnetwork.org/commentary/navigating-cyber-vulnerabilities-in-ai-enabled-military-systems/.

33 "AI Impact Analysis on US Joint All Domain Command and Control (JADC2) Market Industry", Market and Markets at https://www.marketsandmarkets.com/ResearchInsight/ai-impact-analysis-on-us-joint-all-domain-command-and-control-jadc2-market-industry.asp.

34 "NIST Identifies Types of Cyberattacks That Manipulate Behavior of AI Systems", NIST, 4 January 2024 at https://www.nist.gov/news-events/news/2024/01/nist-identifies-types-cyberattacks-manipulate-behavior-ai-systems

35 Ibid.

36 Ibid., p. 39.

37 "What is lateral movement?", Cloudflare at https://www.cloudflare.com/learning/security/glossary/what-is-lateral-movement/

Conclusion

Aligned to ancient Indian values of blending Statecraft with military valour, 'Mission Sudarshan Chakra' embodies India's efforts to enhance its air defence and BMD capabilities through indigenous programmes and active public participation –2035 being a key milestone.

This academic study brought forth a range of perspectives on the concept, constituents and deliverables of the Mission. Whilst each author's contributions have been retained in totality, key outcomes are synthesised as follows.

The Threat Landscape

The recent decade has proliferated the threat landscape with the emergence of factors such as niche weapon technology, entry of non-State actors, geopolitical alliances and rivalries, economics and trade sanctions etc. This has reshaped modern warfare with the prominent resurgence of the aerospace domain revealing vulnerabilities for India at all three levels – strategic, operational and tactical. Immediate threats range from CUAS/ drones/loitering munitions at the lower spectrum to standoff precision-guided munitions such as bombs, cruise missiles and air-, surface- and sea-launched ballistic missiles–. In terms of emerging and evolving threats, India's adversaries are actively developing capabilities for Manned-Unmanned Teaming (MUMT) platforms, Swarm Drones/UCAVs, stealth bombers and fighters with extended standoff ranges, hypersonic missiles and ASAT weapons. Cyber warfare alongside cognitive warfare will be integrated into a unified strategy by the time we face the next conflict.

Design Principles

Insights from authors point to a 'building block approach', using the battle-proven IACCS as the foundational architecture. Enhancements in radars, weapon systems and networks can be achieved through superimposition of desired capabilities, which range from terrestrial and airborne/LEO systems to those in the space domain. The end state envisaged is a three-dimensional aerospace combat situational awareness through a modular, event-driven, multi-domain command and control system capable of managing complex, concurrent operations across strategic, operational, tactical, and sub-conventional layers.

This involves a transformational adoption of a holistic strategy that integrates Space, Cyber and Intelligence in the Air domain. Various authors emphasise that incorporation of intelligence (operational, technical, and human) is critical to strategic air battle plans and effective command and control of air operations. Similarly, space and cyber domains have transitioned from an enabling role, to becoming fundamental to strategic survival and effective deterrence.

The Current System

The IACCS architecture was conceived for pan-India networks to be integrated including BMD, civil radars and sister services. Currently, the IACCS, riding on secure networks, integrates sensors (military and civil radars), and shooters (aircraft, SAMs, AD Arty, MANPADS) into a single chain of command through respective operation rooms. Each IACCS node serves as a nerve centre for receiving tracks, creating a Recognised Air Situational Picture (RASP), identification, threat evaluation and designation of targets, to appropriate shooters for interceptions/kills. The IACCS also facilitates real-time transport of images, data and voice, amongst satellites, aircraft and ground stations. This network-centric design shares situational awareness across the Services through JADCs (*Akashteer*) and MOCs (*Trigun*) and fuses offensive and defensive operations into interdependent, synergistic air battles.

The current system is layered, with the VLRTR series of radars and BMD weapons at the outermost edge. Area defence is enabled by AWACS/

AEW&C (*Netra*), fighter aircraft (Rafale, Su30 MKI, Mig-29UPG, LCA *Tejas*), and LR/MR radars such as the THD-1955, *Arudhra*, *Rohini* and *Ashwini*. This is complemented by weapon systems of S400, MRSAM, the *Akash* Missile System, Spyder, Pechora and OSA-AK. Short-range radars such as the *Ashlesha*/*Bharini* series enable point defence along with AD Arty gun systems of the IA (L70, Schilka) and other shooters, such as the VSHORADs, QRSAM, SAMAR missile system, MANPADS (IGLA series) and CUAS systems.

Possible Architecture

It is recommended that the IACCS be upgraded to its next version, referred to as an Integrated Aerospace Command & Control System (IASC2S). A National Command Post (NCP) riding on IASC2S would serve as the core for all strategic decisions and include Command and Control for Strategic Forces, Space Assets, BMD, Extended Long-Range Missiles, Long-Range Radars (LRTRs, OTH, VHF, and VLF), Anti-satellite systems, Aerospace defence (conventional), and other strategic networks. The purpose of this layer is to launch a strategic offensive, detect cruise and ballistic missiles and provide long-lead cueing to lower layers and decision-makers. This layer offers the initial "look" at approaching threats, assesses tracks based on intent and value, and reserves high-end, scarce interceptors for the most valuable engagements. Its main role is to transform surprise into warning by detecting incoming raids or missile launches early enough to alert decision-makers. The integrated picture will be filtered both upwards and downwards, with decision flows and warnings transmitted in real time to maintain continuous engagement through all air defence layers until the threat is fully neutralised.

Upgraded IASC2S regional nodes will function at the operational level and address all conventional threats. These nodes would convert strategic warning into local denial by orchestrating a synergy of layered denial and offense-defence through multi-sensor fusion of all ground- and air-based sensors and a mix of shooters. This would be linked to the strategic layer through Aerospace C2C at the Air HQ level. The command-and-control centres below this level are provided with overarching control orders, either directly or through pre-decided procedural control. Other additional nodes necessitated at the operational level include a Surface-to-Surface Missile (SSM) Node and an Out-of-Area Contingency (OOAC) Node. During conflict situations, the SSM node (already a part of the larger C4ISR architecture) would co-ordinate launches of the Services in support of battle plans, ensuring accurate, timely and secure execution of missile strikes. This "node" is not a single entity, but a highly resilient and distributed system that interacts through the ISR grid created in IASC2S, for trajectory planning, the independent/synchronised launch of missiles, logistics coordination, battle damage assessment etc. The OOAC Node has an event-based functionality and arises out of a need for intervention and engagement, to secure India's interests or solely in aid of foreign nations, such as Operation Devi Shakti in Afghanistan and Operation Cactus in Maldives respectively. This could be developed as a modular C2C with airborne assets of AWACS and long-range fighters, complemented by rapidly deployable ground-based assets in support of envisaged operations.

Tactical layers include Low-Level CUAS, Point Defence and Deployed Forces (Army and Navy) nodes. It is envisaged that drone swarm attacks, loitering munitions and low-level fighters/other air vectors will not just limit to frontline border areas, but extend to deep penetration strikes targeting military installations, population centres and critical infrastructure, spread across the country. To counter this, a dedicated low-level integrated grid comprising low RCS detection, surveillance, electronic scanning and passive interoperable-based detectors along with shooters to counter drones, swarms, loiters, UCAVs and improvised projectiles, need to be developed. The erstwhile CRC concept may be revisited for envisaging the future structure of this node. Like the CRC nodes, these will function under the mother IASC2S network for receiving RASP and de-conflicting friendlies with requisite decentralisation, autonomy and pre-arranged modes for weapon fire. Similarly, like the TWCC/BADC concept for airbases, important assets like military installations and critical infrastructures will be covered with VSHORAD, man-portable air-defence systems (MANPADS), rapid-fire guns, counter-UAS systems, and non-kinetic measures such as electronic warfare and directed-energy weapons. This close-in weapons defence comes into effect when the defended base/assets are directly threatened, for which laid-down norms for weapon control will take effect in coordination with the mother IASC2S network.

The deployed forces of the Indian Army integrated under the *Akashteer* system can be envisaged as dynamic networks, which maintain anchor to the parent IASC2S node through existing JADCs on the northern and western borders and associated communication protocols, as they deploy and redeploy in their offensive campaigns. Tactically, this layer is frequently integrated into force manoeuvre: mobile medium/short-range launchers and vehicle-mounted radar/EO suites accompany columns and create a protective bubble. Mobility and quick reaction time are the defining features of this layer. A similar arrangement exists with the Indian Naval forces at sea, through the Trigun network across both coasts. This maintains the network's core strength– distributed sensing and synergistic application of ground fire – while adding mobility.

The system envisages a resilient and integrated network backed by ISR and cyber/intelligence networks, to create a unified RASP linked through secure wide-area communications (fibre/SATCOM/LEO/photonic links). AI-enabled applications enable rapid multi-sensor data fusion, generation of threat matrix and solutions for best-fit weapon systems providing a decisive edge for IASC2S networks to operate in increasingly dynamic, data-heavy and contested battlespaces.

Enabling Technologies

Amongst future sensors and radars for the Mission, it is envisaged that R&D focus will gather around multi-spectral, phased array, photonic, RF and quantum-enhanced radars. Equally significant is the development of passive sensors, multi-wavelength infra-red and high-sensitivity thermal detection cameras, a HAPS network, airborne ESA, space assets for undertaking ELINT, hyperspectral IMINT, high-resolution EO/SAR, C4ISR and national SSA radars/optical assets. Numbers and capabilities of satellites in GSO and LEO for IR detection in ABM role will be guided to a large extent by India's space deterrence strategy.

Amongst shooter and weapon capabilities, India is expected to expedite R&D in advanced BMD interceptors (ground- and space-based), directed-energy weapons (land/sea/air), long-range A-A missiles, layered SAM families, future long-range stealth interceptors, MUMT platforms, High-Powered Microwaves and High-Energy Lasers for the upper end of the threat spectrum. Simultaneously, development of counter-drone, drone/drone swarms, electromagnetic rail gun launched projectiles and scalable counter-UAS measures along with nets and net guns with future-guided net launchers to target swarming UAVs in coordinated attacks, will ensure gap-free spectrum coverage.

To have a space-based missile defence system there is a requirement for investing dedicated space-based systems for early detection, tracking, and potentially intercepting threats like ballistic and hypersonic missiles in space or early flight. This could offer faster reaction times than ground systems. The aim would be to design and develop the future armed interceptors to engage missiles in their vulnerable boost phase, though technical challenges and strategic concerns remain.

Present-generation missile defence systems rely on space-based assets to provide wide-area coverage through a multi-layered architecture that integrates multiple orbital regimes and specialised sensors for surveillance and early warning. Currently, space-based systems support missile defence by supplying critical weather data, secure communications, ISR inputs, and precise navigation services.

For near-future missile defence systems, achieving enhanced and persistent large-area coverage will require significantly greater investment in the space domain. A significantly larger number of space-based platforms equipped with advanced sensing, tracking, and data-fusion capabilities will need to be deployed to ensure continuous global surveillance, improved detection of emerging threats, and faster response times across all phases of the missile flight. Also, investments in ion/electric thrusters, chemical high-thrust for rapid manoeuvre, on-orbit refuelling, modular buses and servicing vehicles are essential for creating agility through propulsion and maintaining resilience in space. Development of a high-accuracy atomic clock for space use remains a key focus area.

For effective C4ISR and AI integration, the key focus areas will be high-performance distributed edge computing for real-time data fusion, master clock stamping, and protocol synchronisation for multi-domain threat tracking, quantum sensor technologies and computing algorithms for future-proof threat detection systems, alongside multicore and edge processors. Explainable AI for adaptive threat classification and predictive kinematics, secure operating systems, real-time distributed databases and adaptive packet management complement these developments. An upgraded dedicated communication network needs to be supported by quantum cryptography, indigenous waveforms, photonics, CDMA/SDR technologies, long-range links, and quantum-resilient crypto and mesh redundancy. A robust infrastructure with distributed functioning of C2 nodes and redundancy of systems is equally important, that allows operational tenacity and long-term resilience. These include EMP/NBC hardening, mesh communications, photonics and quantum-resilient cryptography, zero-trust architectures, post-quantum encryption, and multi-layered biometric operational security, including AI-driven anomaly detection, and hardened physical infrastructure.

Roadmap

For the future, a phased approach is recommended beginning with finalisation of a blueprint and task allocation, based on the area of specialisation and responsibility. Consolidation of current strengths by enhancements to IACCS architecture, rapid induction of under-development systems such as OTH radars, HPRs, the HAPS network, mountain radars, AWACS/AEW&C, Project Kusha, upgraded AFNET and CUAS weapons, must happen simultaneously with the identification of capability and capacity gaps. Additional layers for the next upgrade, including framework for NCP, LL node/SSM/OOAC node, empowering of the Defence Space Agency, a plan for integration of cyber/intelligence domain data layers, and industry scaling (gaps in sensors, shooters and networking) may be finalised in the first phase.

The second phase would see the establishment of IASC2S nodes, pitching of extended space asset capacity (ISR/TDRS) and operationalisation of refuelling prototypes. Simulation exercises to test and mature AI decision support, including integration of cyber and intelligence layers, should be completed in this phase. Complete induction of assets for enhanced pan-India coverage, operationalisation of IASC2S, including NCP and situation/event-based operational/tactical level nodes, would comprise key focus areas in the final phase. Achievement of initial manoeuvrable space constellations with refuelling, would also define the success of this phase.

Operational Risks and Mitigation Efforts

Cost and sustainability are key concerns in this long-term project. The same may be offset by modular plans, public-private financing and development of dual-use civil applications suited for the export markets. Offensive space options including ASAT technology will be guided by global geopolitical and technical developments, alongside a transparent approach to own plans. Considering that niche technology gaps will persist, prioritisation of R&D, including foreign co-development and a mixed approach (sensor diversity, non-kinetic options) is essential for areas such as hypersonic defence, quantum threats and full ASAT resilience. The system's cyber vulnerability needs careful redressal through secure-by-design engineering, rigorous testing, continuous monitoring and specialised training of personnel. It is also essential to engage both citizens and industry in the project's non-military aspects through an informed discourse and meaningful engagement, as effective Civil Defence Integration enhances citizen resilience by synchronising system response with societal awareness and preparedness. Regular activation of Early Warning Systems, creation of public shelters and practice of evacuation protocols ensures multi-agency collaboration and the fine-tuning of procedures.

Final Synthesis

Traditional concepts of deterrence and air defence have transformed to incorporate orbital warfare perspectives, supported by the cyber and cognitive domains. Hence, the Mission's credibility will depend on not only the strengths of its sensors and weapons but its ability to convert data superiority into timely, decisive action.

The guiding adage for policymakers and practitioners is to apply aerospace power through a unified strategy, consolidate the IACCS and BMD programmes, integrate the cyber, space and intelligence layers early, adapt rapidly, reinforce continuously, and indigenise at scale. If India can upscale to a robust aerospace C2 fabric by 2035, the Mission will have done more than its stated aim — just as Jayadratha faced the *Sudarshan Chakra's* wrath when invoked, this omnipresent system of systems, always in existence, will be brought to bear at any point in time and space to enforce the will of the nation.

Index